THE NEW
MAXIMARKETING

THE NEW MAXIMARKETING

Stan Rapp

Thomas L. Collins

McGraw-Hill
New York   San Francisco   Washington, D.C.   Auckland   Bogotá
Caracas   Lisbon   London   Madrid   Mexico City   Milan
Montreal   New Delhi   San Juan   Singapore
Sydney   Tokyo   Toronto

Library of Congress Cataloging-in-Publication Data

Rapp, Stan.
    The new maximarketing / Stan Rapp, Thomas L. Collins.
        p.   cm.
    Includes index.
    ISBN 0-07-052033-X
    1. Marketing. 2. Advertising. 3. Sales promotion. I. Collins,
Thomas L. II. Title.
  HF5415.R3255 1995
  658.8—dc20   95-37007
                                            CIP

McGraw-Hill

*A Division of The **McGraw·Hill** Companies*

1 2 3 4 5 6 7 8 9 0 QBP/QBP 9 0 9 8 7 6 5

ISBN 0-07-052033-X

The sponsoring editor for this book was Philip Ruppel, the editing supervisor was Jane Palmieri, and the production supervisor was Donald Schmidt. It was set in Fairfield by Don Feldman of McGraw-Hill's Professional Book Group composition unit.

Printed and bound by Quebecor-Book Press

This book is printed on recycled, acid-free paper containing a minimum of 50% recycled de-inked fiber.

For Isabel, who, rightly or wrongly,
would have been so proud of both of us.

And for Liz, who was there from the start
to cheer us on.

CONTENTS

CHAPTER SIX. MAXIMIZED ADVERTISING IMPACT: APPEALING TO THE WHOLE BRAIN TO BUILD A BRAND   143

CHAPTER SEVEN. MAXIMIZED PROMOTION RESULTS: FINDING A BETTER WAY IN THE INFORMATION AGE   169

PREFACE

The first edition of this book was written in 1986 and published in 1987. Since then, in addition to the original English-language edition distributed in the United States, Canada, Australia, New Zealand, Ireland, Britain, and other English-speaking countries, foreign-language editions have appeared in many countries around the world, including Spain, France, Germany, Sweden, Norway, Holland, Japan, Israel, and most of Latin America. Altogether there are more than a quarter of a million copies in print.

With each passing year we have expected to see the interest fade, and the book disappear from the shelves of booksellers around the world. But despite showing disturbing signs of its age in its case histories and economic statistics, the 1987 edition, like the Energizer Bunny that keeps on going in the TV commercials, just kept on selling and selling and selling and....

Frankly, it came as a pleasant surprise to us that any book claiming to present a radical new view of marketing could command such a worldwide following. The first edition was published at the dawn of a new day in marketing that knows no national boundaries. It presented a way of looking at and dealing with the impact of the new information and media technologies that are transforming business wherever consumers have freedom of choice and competition flourishes.

Now the time has come to breathe new life into the pages of *MaxiMarketing* with a total update and reworking of almost every paragraph. It is time to reflect upon and respond to the rapidly changing situation in almost every business category. It is time to rethink, refine, modify, and add to the Maxi-Marketing concepts that first charted the new direction in advertising, promotion, and marketing strategy required for the new telecomputing era.

Back in 1986, we found ourselves hard-pressed to find examples to illustrate our points. Today we are hard-pressed to choose from an abundance of riches to illustrate the process. Most of the examples we gave in the first edition represented the earliest stirrings of what became a tidal wave of change. They are now obsolete, and many exciting new marketing programs have developed in surprising ways that would have been difficult to predict at the time.

So even though the basic principles of *MaxiMarketing* have passed the test of time, it has become necessary to almost completely rewrite the earlier edition. In the course of preparing this revision, we have been forced to retrace our steps and rethink every part of the system, retesting it in our minds to verify what time has proven to be sound and what needs to be recharted.

Two of the steps in the original MaxiMarketing model—Maximized Synergy (double-duty advertising) and Maximized Distribution (adding new channels)—no longer have separate chapters. Instead we have covered these concepts as substeps in the process.

The synergistic effect of a single expenditure that fulfills multiple advertising, promotion, and marketing goals is certainly highly desirable and strongly recommended. However, it is better viewed as combining many of the functions that are basic steps in the process rather than as playing a primary role.

Maximized Distribution, as important as it is, has now become part of the conventional wisdom of marketing.

At the time that we developed the original MaxiMarketing model, an exciting trend of the 1980s was the expansion of mail-order catalog companies such as The Sharper Image, Williams-Sonoma, and Eddie Bauer into retailing, and of retailers such as Bloomingdale's and Brooks Brothers into selling direct through catalogs.

Since then this dual-track distribution trend has solidified and become commonplace in retailing, and has also become a basic component of both the hardware and software sides of the computer industry.

In addition to reducing the 9 stages of MaxiMarketing to 7, we also have renamed some of the steps in order to sharpen their focus.

The process of constantly reviewing and reexamining our own hypotheses has brought us to a simplified and updated definition of the MaxiMarketing concept. We see it today as the way to *maximize sales and profits by means of selective interaction and involvement with identified prospects and customers.*

What follows is some of what we wrote about the irreversible march toward greater accountability and addressability in the preface to the original edition, 10 years ago. We are satisfied today that almost everything we said then remains valid. In fact, it is surprising to us to find how contemporary what we wrote at the time still sounds:

> The computer revolution that has profoundly changed production and communication is destined to change marketing just as profoundly. The common wastefulness of the mass advertising of the past is giving way to the newly affordable ability to locate and communicate directly with a company's best prospects and customers. And this newfound ability can be equally rewarding to a manufacturer, a retailer, a service company, or a catalog merchant. Product sales in stores can now be supported with the precise accountability once reserved for mail-order advertising.
>
> This new kind of marketing goes under many names. Database marketing, relationship marketing, integrated marketing—these are just a few. But we have observed that none of these labels fully described or captured what is happening or, more important, what we believe is coming.
>
> For in addition to the computer, other changes—technological, social, political, and economic—are sweeping through the marketplace and demanding a review of every component of the traditional advertising, promotion, and marketing process.
>
> The eighties will be remembered in marketing history as the decade of transition. Every established norm in advertising

and promotion is being transformed by the new economy and the new technology. We are living through the shift from selling virtually everyone the same thing a generation ago, to fulfilling the individual needs and tastes of better-educated consumers by supplying them with customized products and services. The shift from "get a sale *now* at any cost" to building and managing customer databases that track the lifetime value of your relationship with each customer. The shift from crudely accountable "creativity" in advertising to the scientific accountability of each advertising expenditure. The shift from reliance on a company's familiar single channel of distribution to a multichannel mode which breaks rules as it breaks down walls.

Of all these changes, surely the most revolutionary is the ability to store in the computer information about your prime prospects and customers and, in effect, create a database that becomes your private marketplace. As the cost of accumulating and accessing the data drops, the ability to talk directly to your prospects and customers—and to build one-to-one relationships with them—will continue to grow. A rising tide of technological change has brought this golden moment of opportunity.

The fifties and sixties were the heyday of mass marketing. There was one kind of Coca-Cola soft drink for the thirsty. One kind of Clairol hair dye for hair coloring. One kind of Holiday Inn for the traveler. The seventies became a decade of segmentation and line extension. It was followed in the early eighties by intensified niche marketing that sliced markets into smaller and smaller groups of consumers— each group with particular needs and wants to satisfy.

By the mid-eighties, Robitussin was offering four kinds of medicine for four kinds of coughs. If you wanted to color your hair, Bristol-Myers offered eight kinds of Clairol in a choice of lotion, mousse, gel, foam, or shampoo. Even travel establishments like Holiday Inn and Hilton offered a choice of deluxe or budget accommodations.

The trend is as clear as the name on your checkbook. From mass marketing to segmented marketing to niche marketing to tomorrow's world of one-to-one marketing—the transformation will be complete by the end of the eighties.

When the bright sun of a new day fully illuminates the marketing scene in the early 1990s, the once-familiar terrain of 1980 will be as foreign to the new marketers as the 1960 scene seems to us today.

In this new land, you will know the name and address of the end user of your product—regardless of where or how the purchase is made. Your advertising will be linked directly to measurable sales. You will hunt down individual users of competing brands and lure them away with a dazzling array of value-added services.

We believe the time has come for every company that advertises its products or services (or should) to review its advertising and promotion strategic planning in light of these new developments.

And the name we have given to this new direction in strategic thinking is MaxiMarketing. We hope that when the present generation of Young Turks in companies large and small meets in hallways, they will use the *new* password to corporate and individual success: "MaxiMarketing!"

More than that, we hope that what this book describes and advocates will not just be whispered in the hallways but openly discussed in conference rooms and boardrooms, whether under the name we have chosen or another. We believe that is what will happen—indeed, *is* happening already—in the smart companies.

Of course, what this new way of thinking is called is not important. What *is* important is that almost every business, whatever its size and whatever products or services it sells, can benefit from the principles of MaxiMarketing. Not all these principles are new. Some are as much as 100 years old but call for a new look and a new application. Others are emerging from the conditions and capabilities of the new era we are entering.

MaxiMarketing is not a textbook or how-to book. It is a "think" book that aims not to solve your advertising and marketing problems but to stimulate you to think about them in a new way so that you can solve them yourself.

This book will *not* give you a magic formula for marketing success. It *will* tell you how other marketers are building new structures as they observe the old order crumbling. In it we point out ways to make your advertising, promotion, and distribution more effective every step of the way.

We hope you will find many of the specific case histories and ideas relevant to your own strategic thinking, but we designed the book to be broad enought to be useful and stimulating to *all* companies engaged in marketing to consumers—large and small companies; manufacturers and retailers of hard goods, soft goods, and packaged goods; companies selling services and products; single-product companies and diversified companies; direct and indirect marketers; and promoters of both high-ticket and low-ticket sales.

The case histories and references provided to illustrate the themes of the book often will not come from your own industry situation. If you find that some part of the book does not apply directly to your current problems, we hope you will go through it with us anyway in order to comprehend the entire process. Besides, you may surprise yourself with sudden insights and innovative lateral thinking while reading material you had considered irrelevant to your situation.

We have, by and large, confined ourselves to examples of the marketing of consumer goods and services, although much of the thinking certainly applies to business-to-business selling. The recent surge of breakthrough developments in business-to-business marketing is a very large subject that could take an entire book to cover fully.

Our book is part description, part advocacy. In it we point out efficient and wasteful current practices, and we offer a number of specific antidotes to the ills of current obsolete practice.

Now we believe the time has come for all companies to break out of the box of past assumptions. Time to push ahead into a brave new world of virtually unlimited options. Time to master the new computer capabilities and take direct control of your future. Time to move in a new strategic direction and reap the rich rewards of MaxiMarketing.

Shortly after the preceding thoughts were published, both of the authors decided to leave the agency business and devote themselves entirely to speaking, writing, consulting, and observing the shift from mass marketing to individualized marketing in countries on every continent. We had found that just keeping up with the dizzying rate of change, making sense of it all, and being spokespersons for the MaxiMarketing strategic point of view was becoming a full-time job.

The worldwide network of agencies we founded has continued to grow, and Rapp Collins Worldwide now consists of 29 offices with total annual billing of over $1 billion. It is satisfying to see the agency we launched so many years ago, now among the 25 leading agency networks in the world.

A number of marketers following the MaxiMarketing approach (though not necessarily directly derived from what we have written) have chalked up truly remarkable records of accomplishment. You will find some of their stories in our other books, *The Great Marketing Turnaround* and *Beyond MaxiMarketing: Success Secrets of the MaxiMarketing Winners*. And you will find many of their accomplishments updated in this book as well, with new information never presented by us before.

Tracking down and analyzing the details involved in an attempted survey and analysis of virtually the entire marketing scene is more than enough work for two people. In preparing this revised edition we were enormously aided by—and are deeply indebted to—our editorial associate, Wallis E. Wood. Wallis performed Herculean tasks of research, and he assisted us with skill, understanding, and unquenchable good nature. All authors should be so fortunate as to have such a stalwart resource to draw upon.

Jane Palmieri at McGraw-Hill provided outstanding support, understanding, and professional skill when the time came to turn our words into type and produce a finished book on schedule.

No matter what country you are living and working in as you read this book, it may occur to you that you have your own story of MaxiMarketing accomplishment to tell, or know of someone else who does. We are able to cite so many achievements by companies in North and South America, Europe, South Africa, and the Pacific Rim simply because we have been privileged to converse with so many participants in our seminars on every continent and with our consulting clients in the United States, Europe, and South America.

So we would like to hear from you, to stay in touch on a continuing basis with the growing band of innovative MaxiMarketers throughout the world. We now publish an up-to-the-minute newsletter, *MaxiMarketing Insights*. With an international distribution soon to reach 30 or more countries. Both the newsletter in print and its electronic presence in the Internet offer a truly unique and universal view of the new marketing as it evolves. Send us information that we can use in our newsletter, and we will be pleased to credit you as the source.

You can write to us at: The MaxiMarketing Center, Suite 31J, 200 East 33rd Street, New York, NY 10016, or send E-mail on the Internet to ThomasC200@aol.com or MaxiStan@aol.com. If you would like to know more about how you can become a subscriber, turn to page 321.

We would also be pleased to receive your comments about this book, whether favorable or not. We constantly learn and grow from the feedback we get from our readers.

And now—on with the show!

Stan Rapp
Thomas L. Collins

For a special offer from the authors, turn to page 321.

PROBLEMS AND CHALLENGES IN TODAY'S MARKETPLACE

THE BIG PICTURE

*Remember what Gertrude Stein said about Oakland,
California? "There is no there there."*

*Today, older marketers may well be wondering whatever
happened to the market that was once "there." The mass market
has splintered into a fragmented, "demassified" market. The
traditional picture of the American family with husband, wife,
and 2.4 children has virtually disappeared. Mom isn't home
watching soap operas—she's managing the marketing
department at the soap company. Dad's cruising the supermarket
aisles, doing the family shopping. When the kids aren't in
school—or day care—they're watching their own cable television
networks, reading their own magazines, playing video games, or
surfing in cyberspace. And almost 15 million of America's 67
million families are functioning with a single parent.*

*The three television networks, which have attracted the
largest audiences in world history, have lost much of the power
they held a generation ago. Fox has joined CBS, NBC, and
ABC as one of the national networks reaching 95 percent of all
television homes, while new cable channels continue to arrive
on the scene.*

*But people remain hooked on video. Spending for TV
advertising in the 1995–1996 season surged to a record high.
The movie industry makes more money from movies watched at
home—without commercials—than from those shown in
theaters. And merger madness is reshaping the powerhouses of
the media and entertainment world.*

*The market "out there" may really be an elusive and a
constantly shifting web of allegiances, but the market "in here"
never looked more real. Smart marketers nowadays know who
their end users are—by name, address, telephone number,
family income, lifestyle, brand preferences, personal tastes, and
buying behavior. Through that knowledge they not only serve
their customers according to their individual needs and
interests, they also are learning how to keep them coming back
for more and how to cultivate long-lasting relationships.*

There is a new there there.

Can anyone reading this book doubt that the marketplace
has changed, and that there is a need to rethink every
aspect of marketing in response?

At one time or another you may have read about the problems and challenges we will be describing. However, you will
find (as we have) that when these phenomena are reviewed in
the aggregate, the cumulative impact is overwhelming. So no
matter how much you may already have responded to one or
more of these changes, hang on to your hat as we take you on a
guided tour of the new marketplace. Only when the panorama
of change is viewed in all its multifaceted sweep can one appre-
ciate the urgent need for a new approach to the marketplace.
And the changes we see happening in the United States also
apply in varying degrees almost everywhere else in the world.

"DEMASSIFICATION" OF THE MARKET

Alvin Toffler coined the word *demassification* in his book *The
Third Wave*, 15 years ago. Toffler described how and why the

mass society created by the industrial revolution is splintering more and more into a "demassified society."

"The mass market has split," he warned then, "into ever-multiplying, ever-changing sets of mini-markets that demand a continually expanding range of options, models, types, sizes, colors, and customizations."[1]

Ten years later, in *PowerShift*, Toffler noted that this process had, if anything, accelerated. He describes the "super-symbolic economy":

> This is not, as some belatedly insist, a sign of "de-industrial-ization," "hollowing out," or economic decay, but a leap toward a revolutionary new system of production. This new system takes us a giant step beyond mass production toward increasing customization, beyond mass marketing and distri-bution toward niches and micromarketing, beyond the monolithic corporation to new forms of organization.[2]

As we move through the years leading up to the twenty-first century, the trend toward customization and micromar-keting continues to intensify. There are over 200 breakfast-cereal brands competing for supermarket shelf space in America, and over 300 car models to choose from. In Holland there are 200 cigarette brands to choose from, and in Argentina over 100 perfumes. In 1972, Philips manufactured 100 different color television models; today it produces 500. Bridgestone Cycle Company in Japan is promoting the "Radak Tailor-Made" bike—essentially a different model for each indi-vidual customer, or thousands of models. Washington Shoe offers semi-customized women's shoes—32 designs for each size, the size depending on the individual customer's feet that a computer in the shoe store measures.[3]

When Coca-Cola bowed to public protest and brought back the old Coke as Coca-Cola Classic while keeping the new Coke, it added yet another segment to the already finely segmented soft-drink market. Today there is Coke, Coke Classic, Cherry Coke, Diet Cherry Coke, Diet Coke, Caffeine-free Coke, Caffeine-free Coke Classic, and Caffeine-free Diet Coke, each available in 12-ounce can, 1-liter bottle, or 2-liter bottle. To compete with "New Age" fruit drinks like Snapple, Coke introduced an 8-juice Fruitopia line with names like The Grape Beyond and Lemonade Love & Hope. And the proliferation of product choices among yogurts boggles the mind. Where once there was just plain *yogurt*, now there is regular and low-fat, fruit and no-fruit, solid, creamy, or liquid.

No longer is there simply a Marriott Hotel chain, as there was in 1980. Now you get to choose from a Courtyard (moderate prices), a Fairfield Inn (economy prices), or a Residence Inn (suites, moderate prices), as well as a Marriott Hotel, Marriott Suite (full-service), or Marriott Resort.

And why not? "The more products you can go to market with, the more constituencies you can attract," says Jesse Meyers, publisher of *Beverage Digest*.[4]

But to reverse the old Chinese proverb, opportunities are problems in disguise. After a different product has been created for each of the many constituencies in the marketplace, is it possible to sell them all—and to keep them sold—by means of the same old shotgun approach to marketing that worked so well in the past? Experts tell us that it takes a minimum of $10 million of brand advertising in American mass media to effect any change at all in share of mind and share of market. Obviously, niche marketers must develop new, better-targeted, more efficient ways of reaching and converting the prospects in their special markets.

THE CHANGING AMERICAN HOUSEHOLD

A generation ago the marketing target was the typical American family of husband, wife, and 2.4 children. The 1990 census shattered that image. It revealed that only 7 percent of the 82 million households surveyed fit that description. America in the 1990s looks like this:

- Almost 55 percent of all households have only one or two members.

- The number of singles living alone increased 31 percent from 1980 to 1992, and now represents a full quarter of all households.
- The birth rate per 1000 American women fell from 87.9 children in 1970 to 70.9 children in 1990, while the number of immigrants admitted rose from over 500,000 in 1980 to over 1,500,000 in 1990.

The character of the population is changing. According to the latest U.S. Bureau of the Census figures, the percentage share of white Americans decreased 6 percent between 1980 and 1990; the percentage share of the black population increased 13 percent (to about 12 percent of the total population); the percentage share of the Hispanic population increased 53 percent (to 9 percent of the total), and the percentage share of the Asian or Pacific Islander population increased 108 percent (to almost 3 percent of the total).

It certainly isn't news that women are working outside the home. Today they represent more than 45 percent of the total labor force, which means, among other things, that there are a lot of working moms out there. The Census estimated that in 1992, 54 percent of all women in the labor force aged 18 to 44 had given birth to a child during the previous year, a percentage figure that had risen one point in each of the previous 10 years.

Toffler has pointed out that a new kind of family is growing by leaps and bounds, the "aggregate family." Two divorced people with children remarry, bringing the children of both marriages into the new, expanded family.

The "new old" people are also becoming more and more important to marketers. They are healthy, vigorous, and solvent. The 26 percent of the population over the age of 50 controls more than half of the nation's financial assets and half of its spending power—with $130 billion in discretionary income.

And so on and on and on. We can't say to what extent these demographic changes will continue to be reflected by the next census. But periodically we are hit by startling new numbers that dramatize the accelerating rate of change in our society.

Communicating with and selling to these moving, changing households calls for radically new marketing strategies and models.

THE DECLINE OF BRAND LOYALTY

Once upon a time, when the world was a simpler and more homogeneous place, consumers swore by, and were doggedly loyal to, their Pepsodent toothpaste, Bayer aspirin, Arrow shirts, Florsheim shoes, Swanson TV dinners, 7 Crown whiskey, Texaco gasoline, and Chevrolet automobiles.

A generation ago, a 1975 survey revealed that 4000 male and female heads of household, 74 percent of the women and 80 percent of the men, agreed with the statement: "I try to stick with well-known brand names."

By 1984, after a decade of product proliferation, increased imports, inflation, recession, and couponing, agreement with the same statement had dropped to 58 percent of women and 52 percent of men.

And the trend continues. According to Roper Starch Worldwide, the percentage of consumers who, when they enter a store, know what brand they are going to choose from 13 packaged-goods categories dropped from 56 percent in 1988 to 48 percent in 1993.

The erosion of advertised-brand dominance in America is reaching new depths. In the late 1970s and early 1980s, low-priced, no-name generic products in plain wrappers began to appear on supermarket shelves. At first they weren't considered a significant threat to advertised brands, and it seemed as if generic products and house brands might eventually fade away. They didn't. The share of supermarket shoppers' dollars spent on store brands rose from 12.5 percent in the late 1980s to almost 20 percent by the mid-nineties. *Brandweek* reported the prediction of no fewer than three securities analysts that this share would rise to 30 to 45 percent of the market within the next brand-name decade. Nor was the decline in brand dominance only an American phenomenon. *Business Week* reported that in Europe, private-label goods may now "account for as much as 32 percent of supermarket sales volume in Britain, and 24 percent in France."[5]

Retail store managers, of course, couldn't be happier. Profit margins usually are 4 percent higher on store brands than on established brand names. As a result, among headache remedies, for example, the number-two brand after Tylenol was "private label." It was the number-one brand among cold and flu remedies (Vicks Nyquil was #2) and "private label" was first among adult multiple vitamins (Centrum was #2).[6]

Although Wal-Mart is Procter & Gamble's biggest customer for Tide, the chain recently introduced Ultra Clean, "a concentrated powder packaged in a box that's the same size and shape as Tide's most popular package—but priced far lower."[7] Retailers of course have long offered private labels; what's new is that stores are now marketing them as top-quality rather than bargain-basement alternatives, with names like President's Choice, America's Choice, Master Choice gaining their own loyal customers.

In packaged-goods promotion, as cents-off coupons have proliferated like the progeny of sex-starved rabbits, the consumer is constantly tempted to jump from brand to brand. Many consumers are no longer loyal to any one brand but will switch to whatever cola, paper towel, raisin bran, bath soap, toilet tissue, pasta, or frozen orange juice is the cheapest—or to say the same thing another way, the one for which they have a coupon on the day they are shopping.

As we will detail later, frantic promotion efforts staged just to maintain market share can actually end up producing the opposite effect—and we will show you what you can do to find and retain loyal customers in a marketing world drowning in over-promotion and burning up in fierce price competition.

NEW WAYS TO SHOP AND PAY

Projections show that by the end of this century, the world will have almost 700 million telephone lines operating, all of them interconnected and almost all accessible by direct-dial.

Of course, the presence of a phone in virtually every American home is hardly front-page news. Nor is the rise of the credit card, toll-free calling, and overnight delivery services. But the fact that there is now a reliable phone in so many homes in Kuala Lumpur, Manila, Santiago, and Buenos Aires *is* news. And quite often now, the state of telecommunications technology in emerging markets leapfrogs the standard in America and Europe.

When the authors were in Buenos Aires late in 1992, the wait for a telephone line seemed endless, and our calls to New York sounded as if we were in an echo chamber. On returning two years later, we found a totally new, state-of-the-art fiber-optic system installed by France Telecom. Our calls back to the United States were crystal-clear, with sound quality better than that we get when phoning within Manhattan.

The toll-free telephone; the fax machine; the credit card; and now, on-line shopping services readily available through computer modem—all these have revolutionized how people shop and pay around the world.

From its humble beginnings in the 1950s, credit card usage has now soared to such a height that the cards are now used in more than 25 million transactions a day, adding up to over $441 billion in annual sales. The mind boggles at the almost 2 billion cards (the average American spender carries *11*) believed to be in use in the United States alone today.[8]

The leaders of the credit card industry, MasterCard and Visa, were shaken in 1990 by the introduction of the AT&T Universal Card, with its dramatic "no-fee-for-life" charter membership offer, and by the growth of the Discover card, to over 40 million cardholders. Co-branding is another major development transforming the rules of the credit card marketing game. A few examples are Citibank with American Airlines; Chase with British Airways; Citibank with Ford; and the GM MasterCard, with 5 percent of every purchase being credited toward the purchase price of a Chevy, Cadillac, or any other GM car or truck.

The incredible spread of credit card usage has built a broad base of creditworthy customers and has made possible extraordinary ease of ordering via toll-free telephone numbers. These developments, along with the rapid rise of reliable, overnight, low-cost delivery services in America, have turned mail-order catalogs into an awesome marketing force. By the mid-nineties there were over 10,000 retail and business-to-business catalog titles; a total of almost 13 billion copies a year were being mailed, with 1994's estimated sales pegged at over $57.4 billion, according to the Direct Marketing Association.

Catalog marketers are constantly innovating with new technologies, to augment their offerings. Use your fax/phone to call a toll-free number in the MacWarehouse catalog of Macintosh computer products, touch-tone the code number of the product you'd like to know more about, and you immediately get back a fax-on-demand—a detailed product-information sheet.

Meanwhile, hundreds of thousands of people are watching the home-shopping networks—QVC and Home Shopping Network—where product presentation is a form of entertainment. Nordstrom and J.C. Penney are collaborating with US West to bring viewing shoppers a service that provides them with an opportunity to browse through retail offerings and buy merchandise using a television remote control.[9]

Super stores dot the American landscape, some of them so vast that they distribute maps to guide shoppers to different departments. Staples; Home Depot; Bed, Bath and Beyond; Super Stop & Shop; Toys 'R' Us; Barnes and Noble; super stores in every category have drastically changed the American retailing landscapes.

And while on-line shopping by means of the home computer is still in its infancy, merchants on CompuServe, Prodigy, and America Online are selling everything from books and CDs to shirts and sunglasses. Because these subscription services already have the customer's name, address, and credit card number on file, ordering an item is simply a matter of a few keystrokes. Within just a few months of setting up shop in cyberspace, 1-800-FLOWERS was getting 10 percent of its direct-order business from the on-line services.

With so much happening to provide so many different ways to shop, marketers willing to look beyond the old "tried-and-true" outlets and selling methods have an overabundance of new challenges and opportunities.

THE BOOM IN DATABASE MARKETING

Not all the profound changes in the marketplace create problems, of course. Some provide extraordinary new opportunities.

One such development is database marketing, into which companies large and small have leaped (or been pushed). A great many consumer marketing companies, and almost all business-to-business marketers, now maintain some form of detailed prospect and customer profile using geographic, demographic, and psychographic characteristics, and purchase history. Marketers can tailor special products, services, and offers to selected segments of the database to increase both market share and customer satisfaction and loyalty. As Michael Shrage wrote in *Adweek* as far back as the mid-eighties, in a word of warning to complacent ad agencies:

> If a company has a database replete with the phone numbers and addresses of key customers, it can target potential customers with a higher level of confidence than it could by merely spraying a few spot-television ads in key markets around the country. Thus, a blend of computer and telecommunications networks can become a strategic asset for service companies seeking to position themselves in their markets. And, by extension, the absence of such a capability can cripple an otherwise strong marketing effort....
>
> In order to survive beyond the immediate future, advertising agencies will need to accommodate themselves to the fact that their clients rely increasingly on computers to store, index, and analyze more and more information about their customers. The agencies are going to find themselves deluged with information and analyses about target markets, and they will have to integrate this material into their advertising plans. "Know thy client" will mean "Know thy client's database."[10]

As the cost of accessing data has fallen, marketers have embraced what once seemed to be a costly process that would be forever out of reach.

When the first edition of this book was published in 1986, Kraft General Foods did not retain information related to the names and behavior of consumers purchasing their 40 different brands or responding to their numerous promotions. Today, as Kraft Foods (the General has been retired), the company maintains and augments a relational marketing database containing individualized information on 30 million households.

In her keynote address to the Direct Marketing Association in 1992, Lorraine C. Scarpa, who was then senior vice president of marketing services, spoke about what had led Kraft to embrace database marketing: "By applying our new model to this database, we plan to identify heavy using households and project their current value to the company."

Why risk real money on direct marketing when tried-and-true mass marketing is putting bucks on the bottom line? Why, indeed? Because direct marketing works; it represents the wave of the future.

The following year, in a *Brandweek* interview, Scarpa added:

> We want to go further. We think we can use modeling techniques to identify what KGF products these households should be buying and then we can customize marketing plans that will be significantly more impactful on their shopping.[11]

The decade of the nineties is the decade of the massive consumer marketing database. General Motors reportedly has 14 million GM credit card holders being contacted, questioned, tabulated, tracked, and romanced each month when the credit card statement is delivered. Marriott has over 5 million members in its Honored Guest database; Waldenbooks Preferred Reader Program has over 4 million members; MCI keeps tabs on 12 million Friends & Family long-distance callers; there are 34 million-plus travelers in frequent-flyer-club databases; and millions upon millions more are in the relational databases of hotels, department stores, financial service companies, HMOs, and all the rest.

Getting customers is still important, but information-driven strategies for *keeping them* have become vitally important to marketers everywhere in the world. The first step in the process of retaining customer loyalty is to go out and learn everything worthwhile you can about the individual. Keeping track of the customer's personal characteristics, preferences, and purchases in a relational marketing database, and pushing a customer-focused marketing strategy, together represent the single most significant development of modern-day marketing.

THE RISE OF THE SERVICE ECONOMY

Over a 10-year period, the growth of lawn-care services wiped out 40 percent of all retail lawn-care product sales. Service occupations now account for more than 75 percent of the U.S. national income, employing 4 out of 10 Americans who have jobs. Manufacturing employment continues to decline, while employment in the service economy has risen from 28 million in 1980 to over 40 million today.

A service, whether it offers to invest your money, insure your life, change your oil, maintain your washing machine, or protect your business, cannot be packaged and shelved. It requires a different kind of marketing from that usually adopted by a product manufacturer. Service involves personal contact with the customer, which naturally leads to the accumulation, storage, and analysis of information in a prospect and customer database.

Great opportunities exist for threatened product manufacturers to find innovative ways to wrap a service around the product, as Buitoni pasta has done in the United Kingdom with their Casa Buitoni Club and as Harley-Davidson has done in marketing heavyweight motorcycles through the Harley Owners Group. As a Harley Owners Group (HOG) member, the owner receives emergency pickup service, Harley rental service around the world, insurance coverage, theft protection, a magazine subscription, touring handbooks, tuition reimbursement for taking safety lessons, and a chance to socialize at local Harley-Davidson get-togethers and group rides. And you thought Harley-Davidson just sold motorcycles!

THE FLOWERING OF THE INFORMATION SOCIETY

Closely related to the development of the service economy is the rise of the information society. As Toffler points out:

> The advanced economy could not run for thirty seconds without computers, and the new complexities of production, the integration of many diverse (and constantly changing) technologies, the demassification of markets, continue to increase, by vast leaps, the amount and quality of information needed to make the system produce wealth. Furthermore, we are barely at the beginning of this "informationalization" process.[12]

Almost daily, it becomes easier for individual consumers to learn more about products, services, and companies. Dreaming about that new car? Check out the *Consumer Reports* rating on CompuServe. Want to know about basal cell carcinoma? Check out the Health and Medicine menu on the Internet. Want to see what announcements have been made by public companies in the last 24 hours? Call PR Newswire's toll-free number, for a fax listing all the companies that have released news; call again, for a fax of the exact release in which you're interested.

According to the Electronic Industries Association, manufacturers shipped over a million consumer fax machines in 1994, and almost 10 million home computers. There is a growing number of on-line service subscribers in the United States—America Online doubled to 2 million in a year—and the number of networks and home sites connected to the Internet continues to zoom upward.

And remember, somebody out there still knows how to read. Since the first baby boomers sat transfixed before the first television set, the book-publishing industry has multiplied by a factor of 10. Indeed, the consumer book market in the

United States is an almost $15 billion industry. Book industry studies indicate that reading is an increasingly popular activity, particularly as an alternative to television with some 65 percent of U.S. households buying at least one book a year.

A better-informed, better-educated consumer is ready to challenge the marketer at every turn and to become an active participant in getting exactly what is wanted when it is wanted.

THE PROLIFERATION OF NEW PRODUCTS

Seeking to beat their competitors to the punch, companies have been swamping the market with new products and line extensions backed by king-size advertising budgets, couponing, premiums, and sweepstakes. True, the pace has dropped somewhat; according to *New Product News,* marketers introduced 17,571 products in 1993, up less than 5 percent from the 16,790 they introduced in 1992. During the previous 10 years, however, the growth rate averaged over 14 percent a year.

Most of these products, of course, are line extensions. According to Marketing Intelligence Service Ltd., line extensions accounted for nearly 75 percent of all new-product introductions in 1994 compared with 63 percent a few years earlier. It's an inexpensive way to build brand volume, say some marketing executives. "We try to get facial tissue in every room of the home," James Bernd, executive vice president of Kimberly-Clark, told *The Wall Street Journal.* To achieve this result, Kimberly-Clark now offers 20 varieties of Kleenex facial tissues, including lotion-impregnated tissues, boxes of tissues decorated with nursery-rhyme drawings for children's rooms, and tissues two-thirds larger than regular Kleenex in a "man-sized" box.[13]

Here are more examples of the pace of product proliferation. In 1985, manufacturers were offering 42 toothbrushes and 96 different brands of toothpaste; in 1994 they offered 88 kinds of toothbrushes and 152 kinds of toothpaste. The number of products carried in supermarkets has doubled in the past 10 years.

All this translates into a dazzling and mystifying number of choices for the consumer. C. Manly Molpus, president-CEO of the Grocery Manufacturers of America, recently pointed out that grocery manufacturers offer for sale 644,782 bar-coded items. Stuart Elliott, advertising columnist for *The New York Times,* commented:

> There is no such word as *overchoiced,* but perhaps there ought to be, for there is a widespread belief among consumers pressed for money and time, as well as among retailers overwhelmed by overcrowded shelves, that products are proliferating beyond necessity, practicality, and perhaps, rationality.[14]

Elliott then quoted David Olson, vice president and group research director at the Leo Burnett Company, who has said: "Retailers are starting to eliminate what they see as wasteful duplication." Club Foods Stores, a Midwestern supermarket chain, has started to "limit the number of products in the cereal aisle."

It seems that retailers aren't the only ones who are beginning to resist the proliferation of new products. While there are no exact industry figures for them to draw upon, many marketers believe that something like 80 to 95 percent of *all* new products—line extensions, new packaged goods, new consumer durables, new financial services, new television shows and movies, new books, new *everything*—fail to show a satisfactory return on their investment.

Peter Rogers, executive vice president of Nabisco Brands, sums up the mood of exasperation in this way: "We would have done much better had we just taken our new-product dollars to the bank and put them in an ordinary passbook savings account." According to Rogers the company's new-product development did excite the sales force and maintain the consumer's interest, but "they have failed to increase tonnage or market share, and have not enhanced the value and position of existing brands."[15] There is little reason to believe the situation will change very much, so long as the current practices continue to pervade.

The cost of introducing a new product continues to soar. It is estimated that at least $50 million is needed to establish a national brand in a major category. Still, manufacturers believe that they must keep at it, for they are caught in a vicious circle. To maintain and increase their share of market in a category, they must pour out new products...but the flood of new products tends to shorten product life spans...which sets up a further demand for more new products.

The answer is to break the cycle by custom-designing special products for special audiences, and to open new channels of communication and distribution for them. We'll be telling you more about this promising new direction in Chapter 9, Maximized Customer Cultivation.

MULTIPLICATION OF DISTRIBUTION CHANNELS

Back when Sears dominated the retailing industry, General Motors dominated the automobile industry, and Radio Shack was a major catalog marketer, most companies distributed to the consumer through one of three more-or-less watertight channels: retailing, sales agents, or direct mail. This conscious and voluntary dependence upon a singular distribution channel was one of the first principles of marketing.

But just as floodwaters spread out any way they can, so the torrents of new products and services in the demassified society refuse to be confined to a single channel. The mindset that insists on only one method of distribution has given way to a new open-mindedness toward and appreciation of the rewards of multiple distribution. This shift in attitude grows out of a rediscovery of the fact that distribution is not merely a *consequence* but also a *component* of marketing. The question is not "How do we distribute?" but "How *else* can we distribute?"

Changing households and lifestyles have stimulated new thinking about distribution. How do you sell door-to-door, when in 7 homes out of 10 no one is around during the day, and in 10 out of 10, people are afraid to open their doors at night? How do you demonstrate a $600 exercise machine in a store, when the sales clerks are too busy or too untrained to do so? How do you catch up with an affluent career couple, when both partners are working long hours during the week and then dashing off to their country home on the weekend?

To come up with answers to these questions, companies have come up with new forms and combinations of distribution methods:

- NordicTrack has added retail stores, and displays in shopping malls, to its mail-order distribution system.

- Dial-A-Mattress (their motto: "Call 1-800-MATTRES— Leave off the last 'S' for savings") has built a $65 million business by selling bedding by phone and now on-line with CompuServe.

- The personal computer industry has added one distribution channel after another, from value-added resellers to specialty retailers (CompUSA, Computerland) to office-supply superstores (Staples, Office Max, Office Depot) to mass merchandisers (Circuit City, Best Buy) to department stores to direct sales.

- Eddie Bauer, which began its mail-order operations in 1946 and which still runs a thriving catalog business, now has almost 300 retail and outlet stores in 39 states and three Canadian provinces, and has begun to open larger (33,000 square feet) Premier stores.

- 800-FLOWERS has gone from selling $200 million worth of fresh flowers ordered by phone and shipped by other retailers to opening its own retail stores and now selling through America Online and CompuServe.

THE PROBLEM OF ADVERTISING CLUTTER

Ever since the majority of U.S. households sprouted a bumper crop of "couch potatoes," network television has been the driving force behind the marketing of a host of products. The power of television to reach and influence the mass market remains awesome. Indeed, its power has been so great that Edwin L. Artzt, chairman and chief executive officer of Procter & Gamble, fears for his company's future if network TV viewing goes away. "We simply must preserve our ability to use television as our principal advertising medium," he told the annual meeting of the American Association of Advertising Agencies in 1994, because "Procter & Gamble in a given year has to sell 50 million tubes of Crest and 400 million boxes of Tide—and to do that we have to reach our consumers over and over throughout the year."

In the past, marketing planners have found that, other things being equal, a given "weight" in gross rating points translates directly into a predictable share of market. In the real world, those "other things"—such as the effectiveness of the commercial, or the aggressiveness of the competition, or the ability to obtain distribution—seldom are equal.

Over the past 20 years, charges for network television commercials have gone up much faster than the rate of inflation, while the audience for programs has fallen from just over 90 percent in 1978 to somewhere just above 60 percent today (the latter figure reflects a leveling-off in recent years). The viewing audience for commercials has shrunk even faster than the viewing audience for the programming. The reasons? They sound like the name of a Martian advertising agency: Zip, Zap, Surf & Tug.

The *clutter* of commercial messages that bombard the average household (some estimate the total to be 50,000 a year) is causing many viewers to avoid commercials in every way they can. Some record the show so they can watch at a more convenient time and *zip* past the commercials during playback. Some *surf* the channels, using the remote to switch from program to program or to catch a snippet of news, weather, or music video at the first sign of a commercial break.

The *tug* coming from other attractions on the tube (as well as from other pastimes such as socializing, attending sports events, working out, and participating in community affairs—not to mention working two jobs or longer hours) means that people are spending less time watching the Big Three network shows. The TV menu now includes not only a new network, Fox, but also a profusion of cable network choices including CNN, HBO, Comedy Central, A&E, Nickelodeon, MTV, the Disney Channel, and ESPN. And of course video games, movies on videocassette, pay-per-view, on-line chat groups, and surfing the Internet all compete for the viewer's time.

Before he retired as P&G's chairman–CEO in mid-1995, Ed Artzt said this:

> From where we stand today, we can't be sure that ad-supported TV programming will have a future in the world being created—a world of video-on-demand, pay-per-view, and subscription television. Within the next few years—surely before the end of the decade—consumers will be choosing among hundreds of shows and pay-per-view movies. They'll have dozens of home shopping channels. They'll play hours of interactive video games. And for many of these—maybe most—no advertising at all.

Mr. Artzt's solution is to put advertisers back into the programming business, just as they were back in the early years of both radio and television. Indeed, "P&G's show *Ma Perkins* started the soap opera era, so-named for its sponsor and melodramatic content." We find it difficult to believe, however, that packaged-goods manufacturers will be any better at developing programs that attract mass audiences than the specialists in the business today, people whose only business is to create shows that will appeal to the broadest possible market.

Of course, attracting a mass audience isn't a challenge that appeals to every marketer. Indeed as far as some companies are concerned, the trend toward media fragmentation is just fine with them. They don't *want* mass audiences, they want a specific target. And as television channels and Internet links continue to sprout like dandelions in the springtime, those companies are finding it easier and easier to reach more of those prospects and consumers whom they do want.

For the advertiser, the issue isn't network television versus everything else (spot TV, cable TV, magazines, newspapers, radio, outdoor, direct mail, and the new interactive electronic media). The real issue is—as it always has been—how do you connect most effectively and affordably with your target market? And if you have been dependent on the power of television advertising, where do you now turn to gain share-of-mind and share-of-market?

If you are concerned about the high cost of reaching an ever-shrinking mass market or have never been able to afford the astronomical cost of such advertising (and you suspect that a 30-second spot a couple of times a month wouldn't move the needle for you), perhaps the new information-driven MaxiMarketing model described in this book can provide you with a positive alternative.

THE NEW PLAYING FIELD

Taken individually, any single change we have touched on can profoundly affect the success or failure of a business in reaching its marketing objectives. Taken collectively, these new circumstances represent nothing less than a new playing field requiring a new set of ground rules for business management.

The revolutionary turnaround from mass marketing to individualized marketing, which we first wrote about in our 1990 book *The Great Marketing Turnaround,* is now virtually complete. Many of the trends we identified then—from steam-rollering the market to filling each niche, from advertising monologue to consumer dialogue, from bombarding the marketplace to building relationships, from passive consumers to involved participants—are no longer radical concepts. Increasingly, they are accepted as the marketing imperatives of the new information economy.

It's the morning after the revolution. Everything is in place for forging a radically new type of relationship between buyer and seller. We are moving from living in an industrial society to living in an information society where more and more digitized information is produced and exchanged to meet the different needs of different people. At such a time, all the marketing assumptions that once worked so well must be reexamined.

Those who fail to do so risk falling behind competitors who are already pioneering new approaches to capture the high ground of today's unfamiliar terrain. New information and media technologies make it possible to single out the most likely prospects, provide accountability for each advertising expenditure, and link advertising and promotion response to a dynamic database used to maximize your share of the customer's lifetime value. Today's smartest marketers go beyond merely finding prospects and making the sale to building caring relationships in daring new ways. Within the MaxiMarketing framework, as you will see in the following chapters, innovative solutions to the problems and challenges of marketing in an information society are readily available.

THE BOTTOM LINE

The marketplace is changing dramatically, whether you like it or not. Demographic and lifestyle changes, and radically new communication technologies, have delivered a body blow to mass-marketing practices and the conventional approach to brand loyalty. Ours is the ultimate multi-option society, and the consumer is undisputed king. Throughout the world, the U.S. economy is watched and studied as the world's largest. In varying degrees, every economy with a relatively free market already faces or will soon face the very same challenges that we do. Many of the examples in this book are drawn from outside the U.S. marketplace. MaxiMarketing is not just an American phenomenon. It is a worldwide phenomenon and the lessons illustrated have international application.

Thanks to the development of proprietary and public databases, marketers now can reach out to their own customers and to competitors' customers with special products, services, and offers customized to individual preferences and behavioral characteristics.

The toll-free telephone call; the 6 to 10 credit cards per household; scanner data from computer terminals; the pinpointing by direct mail of individual lifestyles and psychographics; the surge in formation of frequent-buyer and customer-recognition clubs; the rise of interactive communication home shopping, TV, and the Internet—all these are reshaping how shopping is done and how sales are made.

There are new considerations on every side: the service economy; the information society (and superhighway); the flood of line extensions and new products; the new distribution options; the changing demographics of society; the turnaround from mass marketing to one-to-one customer relationships.

The good news is that there are now proven or highly promising new ways to meet these challenges—bold innovations by companies and organizations fully able to understand that living in a new age demands new thinking and new pathways to success. We're going to explore these with you, and illustrate them for you at each stage of the MaxiMarketing process.

THE ESSENCE OF THE MAXIMARKETING SOLUTION

THE BIG PICTURE

The drastically changed marketplace sketched out in the previous chapter demands of us a basic shift in thinking about product development, advertising, promotion, research, and all the other steps in the selling process.

Demassification has transformed yesterday's monolithic consumer market into smaller and smaller fragments. Data stored and analyzed on the computer, use of the credit card, the toll-free call, and the merging of telephone, computer, and television technologies have all drastically changed the very nature of communication and the sales transaction. Integrating a relational customer database into the marketing process offers an opportunity to get closer to your customers, to keep them longer, and to gain incremental profits once the sale has been made.

Just when absolutely nothing seems to be what one would expect, a new, tangible reality has begun to emerge, a reality in which giving priority to interaction with individual prospects and customers has already gone a long way toward replacing the mass-market mentality of the past. This new reality of business life is replete with new opportunities. You can make your advertising and sales promotion more accountable than ever before. You and your information-driven marketing strategy can talk to each customer in response to his or her personal needs and wants. You can decide which customers to keep because they contribute to the bulk of your profits and which to leave over for your competitors because you lose money on every sales transaction. You can replace the discontinuity of the old marketing—in which each step in the selling process went its own way—with an organic continuum. You can make your advertising do double-duty by inviting a response from your best prospects while increasing overall marketplace awareness of your product or service.

All of this is made possible by a new way of thinking about the selling process. We call it MaxiMarketing. This chapter will give you an overview of the MaxiMarketing concept—and a model for staying ahead of the competition in an age of constant and bewildering change. Then the following chapters will examine each MaxiMarketing step in detail.

MaxiMarketing is the emerging, dominant selling process of the information economy. It is much more than just "integrated marketing" or multi-media marketing or "database marketing" or "relationship marketing" or "one-to-one marketing" or any other single aspect of the new marketing. It is a unified answer to doing business in what Toffler has described as the emerging Third Wave of civilization. You can follow the MaxiMarketing path whether you are the marketer of a product or a service, the manufacturer or the retailer; whether your product is sold in stores, by direct media, or by a personal sales rep; whether you are a small-business entrepreneur or a big-business tycoon; whether you sell in America, Europe, Japan, or one of the fast-emerging markets of the Pacific Rim or Latin America. What we are both examining and advocating is a shift in thinking about the way goods and services are sold. It is the new direction in advertising, promotion, and marketing strategy that increases the likelihood of success at a time when advanced telecomputing technology is changing the pace of the business landscape throughout the world.

If you are a decision maker with marketing or management responsibilities, you certainly have been aware of the sweeping changes outlined in the previous chapter, even if you have never stopped to consider them all at the same time. Undoubtedly your company already has responded to or been directly affected by what is happening in various ways.

Perhaps a special committee of your top people has sat around the conference room table and concluded: "It's a very different world out there and change is a constant. How should our company be behaving differently? What vision or mission statement would serve us best now? We know what business we are in now, but what business should we be in tomorrow?"

And if a full realization of the shift from a mass-marketing to a customized-marketing economy is still lacking at the top in your company, maybe you have been thinking, "How can I take action at my level anyway?"

In the decade since *MaxiMarketing* was first published, you have seen some big, impressive corporations slip backward or fall apart. If there have been shortfalls in your own results, you certainly are concerned about the warning signals of what might follow. On the other hand, if your product, division, or company has been experiencing growth and profit increases, you know that this is no time for overconfidence. So it's likely that you and your company *are* changing and experimenting and reaching for new answers.

Very likely members of your top management team, or you on your own if you are running a small business, are applying to your day-to-day operations some of the late-twentieth-century management concepts of Total Quality Management (TQM), Reengineering the Corporation, Core Competency, and the Value Discipline of Treacy and Wiersema. At least as important, however, is a systematic review and questioning of all the assumptions in your *marketing* thinking.

As Professor Phillip Kotler has said: "It is time to reengineer your marketing from A to Z." It is time to make TRC (your Total Relationship Commitment) as much a part of the company's mission statement as TQM. It is time to give as much attention to constant improvement in marketing practices as to constant improvement in the manufacturing, service, and distribution processes.

It took years to drag department stores, kicking and screaming, into the age of MasterCard, Visa, and American Express. General Foods was slow to recognize the potential represented by the development of frozen foods and later the trend toward natural foods. The Sears "big book," once a mainstay of catalog marketing, is gone because management failed to respond fast enough to a demassified market demanding specialty catalogs. And, while MCI was gaining 6 share points in the long-distance phone category, it took AT&T 3 years to come up with an effective counter to MCI's Friends & Family program.

So it's understandable if you have a nagging feeling in the pit of your stomach that your company may not be doing enough to keep up with a changing world.

We became convinced in the early eighties that coping with the great socioeconomic changes of our time calls for a more personal form of marketing. As Professor Theodore Levitt expressed it in *The Marketing Imagination:* "The future will be a future of more and more intensified relationships, especially in industrial marketing, but also increasingly even in frequently purchased consumer goods."[1]

Already many major service industries—banking, retailing, insurance, travel, telecommunications—have totally transformed how they interact with their customers. Vast databanks control a constant stream of communications that maximize sales and contacts with their best customers by mail, phone, fax, on-line bulletin boards, and most recently the World Wide Web. The direct-relationship marketing revolution that began with the first frequent-flyer program introduced by American Airlines in 1981, then moved from one service category to another in the eighties, is now transforming the marketing of everything from a bottle of ketchup to personal computers and luxury automobiles.

But we have observed a wide variation in the business responses to this avalanche of change. Some companies have performed brilliantly. Some have made halfhearted commitments to meet the challenge of forming a value-added personal relationship with end users of their products and services, then quickly turned their attention elsewhere. And some are still living in the past.

Today most companies are doing at least some things right, but many are not yet fitting those right things into a unified, holistic strategy, and they are still missing some important pieces.

In our work that led to the first edition of *MaxiMarketing*, we saw many smart, successful companies dabbling in a curious, awkward mixture of tried-and-true practices from the past industrial era and some of the new practices made possible by the early stirring of the Information Age. We decided then that a model was needed that would show what was emerging from this curious mixture. The result was our 9-step—now 7-step—MaxiMarketing process.*

Now, 10 years later, we can observe the MaxiMarketing process at work in the companies we call the "MaxiMarketing winners."

It isn't a matter of the old order being entirely swept away by the new. There continues to be "gold in the old." Rather, new experiences and new technologies are transforming what has gone before and making possible what never has been before.

Whether your company is large or small, a brand advertiser, a retailer completing transactions face-to-face, or a catalog house selling by mail or phone, you require a frame of reference for reviewing and reengineering all of your marketing. A MaxiMarketing step-by-step review can help you to see which parts of your advertising and sales promotion strategy are taking new developments into account, and where gaping holes and cracks are allowing opportunities for additional sales and profits to slip away.

---

*In the original model, there were nine steps. In the current version we have eliminated the Maximized Synergy and Maximized Distribution steps as not having sufficiently wide applicability in the MaxiMarketing model to justify a separate chapter. Aspects of each of these subject areas will be touched upon in other parts of this book.

We began to develop the MaxiMarketing model by reviewing and diagramming how things were done in the past in the
four traditional selling modes. The result was the four dia-
grams you see in Figs. 1 through 4.

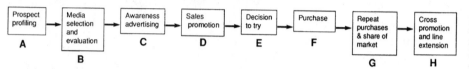

FIGURE 1.   Brand Marketers.

Brand merchandising usually begins with PROSPECT PROFILING (A), employing
market research to learn as much about the prospect as possible. Then quanti-
tative and qualitative yardsticks are applied to MEDIA SELECTION AND EVALUATION
(B).

AWARENESS ADVERTISING (C) is created to carve out the product's image and
positioning in the marketplace and to condition prospects to want or prefer it.
Sometimes SALES PROMOTION (D) is used to activate the prospect—to turn vague
buying intention into measurable action.

Sometimes, but less often, additional consumer contact is interposed
between the awareness advertising or sales promotion and the sale. At the
request of the prospect, more information (E) is provided in an effort to convert mild interest into buying intention and SALE (F). Repetition of this
process over time results in growth of SHARE OF MARKET (G) or "consumer
brand franchise."

This share of market is a corporate asset, albeit a tenuous one, that creates
the possibility of CROSS-PROMOTION AND LINE EXTENSION (H). A company with a line
of successful products can use one of them for cross-promotion to another,
through on-pack, in-pack, or joint promotion. The built-up popularity of the
brand name can sometimes (but not always, alas!) rub off onto the introduction of new products with the same brand name.

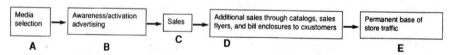

FIGURE 2.   Retailers.

The retailer, selling merchandise of either general or special interest, advertises to just about everybody in the market area and uses various guides for MEDIA
SELECTION (A) from the available local choices.

Retail advertising may promote some AWARENESS (B) of a favorable image of
the store or the products it advertises (sometimes through co-op advertising
supplied and partially paid for by manufacturers) but most retail advertising is
ACTIVATION ADVERTISING (B), such as bargain sales or promotional offers, to turn
the customer's interest into immediate store traffic and SALES (C).

The sales may result in building a customer database, usually limited to
charge-account transactions, though sometimes a store will ask cash cus-

tomers if they would like to be added to the store's mailing list in order to receive special offers. This database may be used to promote ADDITIONAL SALES THROUGH STORE CATALOGS, SALES FLYERS, AND BILL ENCLOSURES (D) sent to customers targeted by past behavior.

Constant repetition of store advertising and promotion directly to customers over time raises the level of PERMANENT STORE TRAFFIC (E).

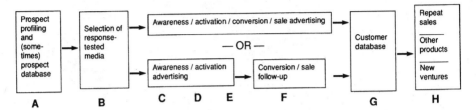

FIGURE 3.   Direct-Order Merchants

Direct-order selling, by mail, phone, fax, and on-line services, is essentially nonstore retailing, whether by the originator of a product or service or by a direct-order merchant engaged in buying from manufacturers and selling to end users. Catalog marketing (also referred to as classic direct marketing) can be used for selling to the consumer and for business-to-business selling.

It starts with detailed PROSPECT PROFILING (A). This is based sometimes on classic market research, but more often on analysis of past direct-response results and customer buying behavior in relation to the same or similar products. Increasingly, direct-order selling may begin with the construction of a DATABASE OF PROSPECTS (A) identified not only by name and address but also by a number of other known and useful characteristics, often including past buying behavior.

SELECTION OF MEDIA (B) is guided not so much by advertising cost per thousand readers, viewers, or listeners, although that is a factor, as it is by testing and comparing the advertising cost per *response* to inquiry advertising. Even in a start-up, when the product category has no response media experience for guidance, the response history of various media used for other direct-sold products provides a guide to selecting media for the test schedule.

Traditional "mail-order advertising" usually focused on making the sale without regard to the effect of the advertising on the public image of the company or the product. Today the largest and most successful direct marketers know the importance not only of making the first sale but also of beginning a profitable continuing relationship. These marketers are therefore very interested in fostering favorable public awareness of the company or product image created by their direct-response advertising. Some of the largest direct marketers, such as Land's End, do brand-image advertising that also calls for a response.

A direct-response advertisement by a direct-order merchant aimed primarily at acquiring "hot" prospects may seek to get respondents either to place an order immediately or to ask for more information.

The process then is completed with follow-up communication devoted to CONVERSION (E) and SALE (F).

Completion of the sale adds to the CUSTOMER DATABASE (G). This database can be used to stimulate REPEAT SALES of the same product, the sale of OTHER PRODUCTS that may be selected or customized to fit the customer's individual interests, or the launching of NEW VENTURES, sometimes with almost push-button ease.

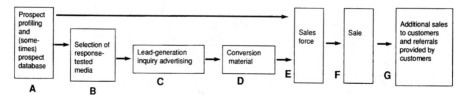

FIGURE 4.   Personal Selling Organizations.

Personal selling to consumers and to businesses has traditionally taken one of two routes.

The first route is often called "cold canvass." After the target market of PROSPECTS (A) has been defined, the SALES FORCE (E) solicits sales by phone call or personal visit to "cold" prospects who have not been "warmed up" by any previous interaction with the company. Often little or no awareness advertising paves the way for the sales representative's call.

The second route is "lead conversion." It too begins by identifying the universe of PROSPECTS (A). To reach into this universe, ADVERTISING MEDIA (B) are selected and ADVERTISING (C) is designed to presell prospects and usually to get them to request more information. The resulting inquiries and calculation of the advertising cost per inquiry makes it possible to compare the efficiency of different media and different advertising appeals and select the most productive. (The unfortunate truth, however, is that far too often the advertising prepared to produce inquiries for a sales force does not take full advantage of this important capability.)

The advertising usually combines two aims, the building of favorable AWARENESS and the achievement of ACTIVATION in the form of requests for more information. The inquirer may receive CONVERSION MATERIAL (D) prior to the call by the SALES REPRESENTATIVE (E), who seeks to make the SALE (F). This sale may be followed up with ADDITIONAL SALES TO CUSTOMERS and to REFERRALS (G), names of friends and relatives offered by the customer. These additional sales may be made either by the sales agent or through direct communications from the company.

WASTE AND INEFFICIENCY ARE RAMPANT

In business as in medicine, we live in an age of specialization. As organizations get bigger, skills and tasks become more specialized, and this specialization has its weaknesses as well as its strengths. Specialists can become so focused on their narrow view of the problem and generalists so focused on one or two points of leverage that millions of advertising and promotion dollars can leak through the cracks in the floorboard and the opportunity for millions of dollars in sales can be lost.

The newfound ability to customize advertising and promotion right down to one small segment, or even to just one individual consumer or business target—and the ability to single out prospects having the same characteristics as your best customers—can add an unprecedented degree of cost-effectiveness to the marketing process.

What is needed is a fresh view of this process, one that allows the many seemingly unrelated advances in advertising and marketing efficiency to be assembled into a meaningful pattern. This makes it possible to combat the waste and inefficiency built into the mass-media advertising that fails to call for a response and the undifferentiated promotion of a conventional marketing campaign—without discarding what still works from the past.

THE THREE COMMON DENOMINATORS OF THE SELLING PROCESS

To develop such a master model, we first reduced all the steps in the previously diagrammed ways of doing business (Figs. 1–4) to the simplest terms possible—their three common denominators (see Fig. 5):

1. *All* marketing must reach out to satisfy the needs and wants of prospects, whether clumsily or skillfully.

2. *All* marketing must lead to a sale—converting the prospect's interest into buying intention and actual purchase.

3. And *almost all* marketing, after the first sale, should seek to develop an ongoing relationship with the customer in a way that results in additional purchases or continued loyalty.

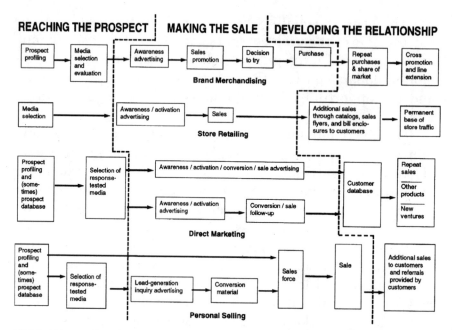

FIGURE 5.   The Three Common Denominators of the Marketing Process.

THE MAXIMARKETING PROCESS

Building upon these common denominators, we found that it was possible to construct the new *MaxiMarketing* model (see Fig. 6). In this 7-step progression, the recent breakthroughs that we have observed in advertising and marketing (plus our own refinements and additions) have been fitted into a sequence that you can easily follow to maximize your own company's opportunities to benefit from what works best today.

1.   MAXIMIZED TARGET SELECTION

The ideal selling process begins with the traditional step of learning as much as you possibly can about your prospect. But with computer-memory capability doubling every 18 months, it can now include, whenever and wherever desirable, selecting just the right individuals to target and finding them in—or adding them to—a prospect database. This database ideally contains not only the names and addresses of likely prospects

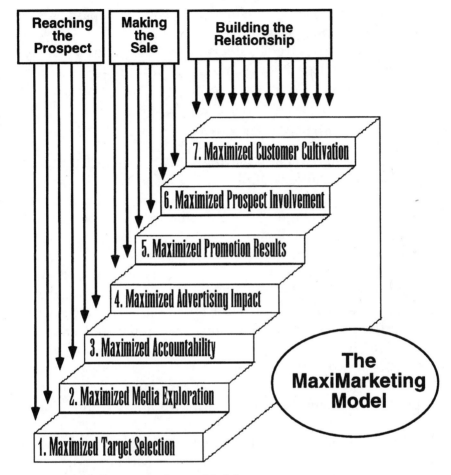

FIGURE 6.   The MaxiMarketing Model.

but also a wide range of important information about each prospect. It could be a public database that happens to contain or yield the information you need; a private database you have constructed out of the responses to your advertising, sales promotion, and customer referral requests; or a composite of both.

The most cost-efficient object of your advertising and promotion expenditures is the individual who needs or wants your product or service and is ready and able to buy it. Singling that person out of the mass consumer market, at the least possible cost, is more easily accomplished with each passing year of the Information Age.

With the new target selectivity at our command, *less becomes more* and a New Marketing Math predicts the outcome of every move before it is made.

2.   MAXIMIZED MEDIA EXPLORATION

In pursuit of your rapidly moving, ever-changing target, you will want to examine carefully—and to explore as far as your budget permits—the dazzling, almost bewildering array of new media options that are either available now or soon will be throughout the world.

But you will want to keep this exploration under control. The media tested should be held fully accountable and made to justify the expenditure—whenever feasible, by means of keyed, tabulated responses to advertising that invites a reply. Testing the effectiveness of various communication channels is surprisingly easy when you use the tools perfected by earlier generations of direct marketers for recording, adding up, and comparing the number of responses per dollar of expenditure from each magazine or newspaper insertion, each direct mailing, and each television commercial.

The panorama of media options has vastly broadened in the past decade, to include on-line information services; the Internet; CD-ROMs; videocassettes; fax-on-demand; television infomercials; selective binding and imaging in magazines; and many other opportunities both in the new interactive media and in new ways to use traditional media. The common denominator shared by all of these alternatives is the opportunity not only to communicate in exciting new ways but to generate a response, and in a number of the new media to carry on a conversation in real time as well. The consumer is no longer a passive target but rather an active partner in today's brave new world of two-way marketing communications.

The implications of this development for rethinking the proper role of advertising and all marketing communications are enormous.

3. MAXIMIZED ACCOUNTABILITY

The proliferation of media choices and the escalation of media costs have increased the need for truly accountable advertising expenditure.

Until recently, the conventional wisdom of mainstream advertising decreed that media must be evaluated by advertising cost per impression, and advertising copy by audience opinions based on less-than-perfect copy-research practices.

All advertising, whether by image-building brand advertisers or by direct marketers, must be fully accountable. The search for a research method that will reliably indicate advertising effectiveness is as old as advertising itself. But even among the practitioners themselves fundamental doubts remain about the value of any such methods.

What is surprising is that a remarkably effective alternative to today's imperfect copy-research methods does exist. It makes possible exact comparisons of advertising alternatives. Not just the old campaign versus the new, but comparisons of a number of possible new campaign approaches and of various ways of presenting different elements in the advertising tested one against the other. It is inexpensive. It takes place in the real world rather than in a simulated environment. And over and over again it has been proved to work reliably.

In the MaxiMarketing model advertising becomes truly accountable.

Management's ability to reengineer the steps in the manufacturing process soon will be matched by similar activity at every stage of the marketing process.

4. MAXIMIZED ADVERTISING IMPACT

Stimulation of favorable awareness is common to all advertising, even the response advertising used by direct-order merchants, since most prospects will buy your product or service only after they have first developed a favorable view of it.

The MaxiMarketing approach addresses the need to maximize the impact of awareness advertising, by giving more careful attention to the duality of human thought processes. It makes it clear that the number of responses the advertising generates is often a far better index of its value than what "creative people" say that it is.

The new level of sophistication in advertising often will appeal equally to the left and the right brain—that is, to both the rational and the nonrational side of our nature. The highest creative challenge will be to appeal to the *whole* brain of the prospect. The problem with a surprising amount of the awareness advertising generated today is that it suffers from a high degree of misguided creativity. In terms of its effectiveness, it is costly "no-brain advertising."

Advertising impact is often achieved without spending a dime on advertising. Publicity, event marketing, sponsorship of sports and theatrical entertainment or social and charitable causes, and so on can often work as well, and sometimes more cost-effectively. Advertising has experienced the least change in the past 20 years and will change the most in the next 10 years.

5. MAXIMIZED PROMOTION RESULTS

Sales promotion is a broad umbrella under which we group anything designed to get the favorably inclined consumer to act "right now" instead of "someday."

In the United States, sales promotion is a $300 billion piece of the marketing pie. Yet much of today's sales promotion merely cuts into profit margins by paying a premium for sales to existing loyal customers, while failing to hold the new customers it attracts.

The continued dependence of packaged-goods marketers on the mass-media distribution of cents-off couponing in Sunday newspapers is one of the more inefficient holdovers from the mass-marketing era. Until now, what has been missing is a way to monitor and measure the true cost-effectiveness of each new sales promotion fad before the copycat adoption of the idea gets out of control and everyone in a category begins to practice the new prevailing wisdom.

The new development that may finally bring accountability to sales promotion is the art and science of "datamotion."

Rather than blindly offer the same promotional incentive to everyone in a market segment, we can now use the data in our database to move each individual prospect with a differentiated promotional offer.

Kraft, with its proprietary database of 30 million households, can use its storehouse of data about prospects and customers to target the right person for the right promotion at the right time—and in the right way. Similarly, airlines and hotels can hunt and pick from their airline or hotel databases the best prospects for each promotional offer to frequent buyers.

Welcome to the new age of "datamotion"—a whole new way to move the prospect to making a purchase, using different strokes for different folks.

6.   MAXIMIZED PROSPECT INVOLVEMENT

Too often, advertising leaves the prospect dangling, with no idea of what to do next, where to buy, or how to obtain more information. It fails to build a bridge between the prospect and the sale. At the very least, the ideal advertising and marketing process should reach out and involve the prospect.

We call this *bridging*. It is the key to focusing more advertising effort and dollars on the most desirable, most interested prospects.

Rather than spend, say, 50 or 60 cents out of each dollar in the marketing budget on advertising to a broadly defined target (generally that means on television, as far as most national advertisers are concerned), and less than 1 percent to send something to those individuals who happen to write or call for more information, MaxiMarketing tells you to use the advertising budget to get a response from the strongest prospects and then spend as much as necessary to turn those prospects into customers and loyal friends.

Electronic advances in communication such as the fax machine, voice mail, CD-ROMs, on-line bulletin boards, e-mail, and Internet homesites vastly increase the number of sales tools that will be available for "bridging" in the years ahead.

We predict a dramatic shift of dollars into the "bridging" budget as marketing grows more interactive with each passing year. A growing number of companies have put someone in charge of caring for the customer. But who is putting someone in charge of caring for the prospect?

7. Maximized Customer Cultivation

All of the steps in the MaxiMarketing process outlined can result, if well planned and effectively executed, in a significant increase in sales and profits. But MaxiMarketing doesn't end with the first sale to a new customer. What happens *after* that sale can be as important as what led up to it.

This emphasis on what happens after the sale was still a fairly new idea when we discussed it in the first edition of *MaxiMarketing* a decade ago. Today, it is gaining increasingly widespread acceptance. Once you start to compile the names and addresses of buyers, warranty card returners, rebate applicants, coupon redeemers, frequency marketing program members, charge account and credit card users, and so on—and add other identifiable characteristics to each customer's name and address in your growing marketing database—you possess a powerful new instrument for cultivating customers and keeping them away from the competition.

In effect, you now have your own private advertising medium that you can use for repeat sales. You can begin to apply the "new marketing math" by making every sale lead to two, three, or four additional sales that you weren't realizing before. You can begin to make sharing a relationship with customers as important as share-of-mind and share-of-market. You can

- Increase customer lifetime value
- Impact the chance for success of line extensions and new products
- Cross-promote different products in your line
- Shut out competitors by bonding with your customers

- Turn your own customers into your best sales representatives
- Customize sales promotion incentives based on past behavior

The mastery of database marketing capabilities naturally leads to the implementation of relationship marketing strategies. In the first edition of *MaxiMarketing* we identified various relationship marketing models you can use to maximize sales and profits. In Chapter 10 of this edition we revisit the relationship models and show how a number of innovative MaxiMarketing winners are making these pathways to success pay off and how the smartest marketers now combine several different strategic models into powerful customer-bonding programs.

Keep in mind, the fundamental truth underlying all marketing success, as pointed out by Peter Drucker in the January 1995 issue of the *Harvard Business Review,* is: "The only profit center is the customer...." Nothing is more important than cultivating the right customer relationship.

HOW THE MAXIMARKETING STEPS ALL WORK TOGETHER

An intriguing and significant aspect of the *New MaxiMarketing* approach is how the various parts fit together and work together. The common thread is a measurable response from (or interaction with) each individually identified target to whom you want to sell or have already sold.

- *Responses* can tell you if your advertising is correctly targeted, and measure its effectiveness.
- *Responses* can provide an index to the comparative efficiency of different media, different product positionings, different benefits, different copy approaches, different offers.
- *Responses* can identify by name and address your most interested prospects, so that you can lead them across the "bridge" from the advertisement to the sale.

- *Responses* can build and constantly update an in-house prospect/customer database.
- *Responses* to ongoing promotions to your database enable you to develop predictive modeling formulas that lead to ever-improving results from future contacts.

Response is such a key part of improving performance in the new interactive environment that the term *responsive advertising* should begin to get the kind of attention bestowed in the past on so-called creative advertising.

We object not to "creativity" but to the overuse of the term and the pursuit of the goal of being creative to the point of absurdity. In the advertising establishment, the term *creative advertising* is bandied about almost entirely without reference to the sales effectiveness of the advertising under discussion. Too often, what is being lauded as "creative" is nothing more than whatever advertising fad or ad-agency style happens to be in vogue at the moment.

Let us say it again, loud and clear, today's marketing imperative demands responsive advertising. It must

- First and foremost, be measured against the marketing objective
- Whenever practical, seek a response to a meaningful offer that leads to a subsequent relationship between the advertiser and targeted prospects and customers
- Always be held accountable for the measured results achieved
- As far as possible, determine cost effectiveness by weighing expense against measured performance
- Always support the positioning of the brand while at the same time reaching out and getting as close as possible to the real needs of real prospects

On this new playing field, genuine creativity in the pursuit of appropriate interaction with the prospect or customer will always be as welcome as it is beneficial. Creativity "for art's sake," or for the sake of ego satisfaction or superficial enter-tainment value—still all too common today—is a mindless lux-ury that your company and your product simply cannot afford.

THE SELF-EXAMINATION PROCESS

As we put a spotlight on each step in the MaxiMarketing process in the following chapters, some of the details may strike you as not being sufficiently related to your immediate problems.

For instance, if you are a retailer, the discussion of sam-pling may not seem relevant to your situation. Or if you're in a business that markets to other businesses, the consumer mar-keting examples we provide may seem to be too unrelated to your own marketing problems.

Maybe so—but don't be too sure! Whenever the example or the subject applies to a different category than the one you're in, try to force-fit that experience into your own situa-tion anyway. Some of the most productive breakthroughs in marketing occur when smart people adapt to their own situa-tion what is happening in an unrelated area.

Keep in mind that MaxiMarketing is essentially a *self-exam-ination* process—an opportunity to look at each step that can influence *your* business success. Our purpose is to stimulate you to ask yourself over and over again, "What can I learn from what is happening here? Is there something—or something *more*—that we could be doing about this? If so, what is it?"

Then, we hope, *you* will become a master MaxiMarketer and participate in leading *your* company into the twenty-first century as one of the new breed of cutting-edge Maxi-Marketing winners.

THE BOTTOM LINE

MaxiMarketing does not mean giving up what your company is already doing. It means examining every step of your selling process, from visualizing and finding your prospect to what you do after the sale is made in order to maximize profits. It gives you the chance to add powerful new capabilities to what you already do very well by "reengineering your marketing from A to Z."

MaxiMarketing places you in a direct, interactive, and customized relationship with both prospects and customers. The responses you get from likely prospects, and the relationship you create with the end users of your product or service, make it possible for you to monitor the effectiveness of your marketing practices in real time.

With MaxiMarketing, you experience the difference between merely making a sale and making friends with a customer you can count on for repeat sales and a mutually rewarding relationship. By focusing on the 7 steps of the MaxiMarketing model, you will be positioned to think creatively about enhancing brand equity, boosting sales revenue, and increasing the loyalty of your customers.

MaxiMarketing is a holistic strategy for maximizing sales and profits by selective interaction and involvement with identified prospects and customers. It is the marketing process that takes maximum advantage of the new media and the new electronic information and communication technologies of the information economy. How do you make it happen? Read on!

MAXIMIZED TARGET SELECTION

FINDING YOUR BEST PROSPECTS AND CUSTOMERS

THE BIG PICTURE

Targeted marketing is considered an absolute essential for success in today's demassified marketplace, but seldom is it clearly defined. Our working definition here is that target marketing *is the art and science of identifying, locating, and contacting individuals and groups who are prime prospects for whatever you are selling or for whatever message you want to deliver.*

The various targeting strategies can be seen as going in five basic directions. Three are old wine in new bottles, and two derive their power from the magic elixir of modern-day database marketing.

Maximized targeting is the essential first step in the MaxiMarketing process. In today's marketplace, if you don't know who your true prospects are and where to find and contact them one at a time—or if you fail to go after them as individuals in a cost-effective way—you will lose ground to competitors who do.

The highest form of the art of target selectivity is the ability to target and win over your competitor's best customers.

Whether the advertiser or the advertising creator realizes it (and sometimes they don't), all advertising communication begins with what you know about the prospect. Since all promotion of goods and services presents an answer to someone's need or desire somewhere, the advertiser is always talking to an individual within the total population.

For as long as there has been advertising there has been targeting, whether conscious or unconscious. Copywriters may think they are merely writing *about* the product's benefits, but unavoidably they are also writing *to* some particular person or persons who will be more interested than other people.

In the days of mass-appeal products and mass advertising, this was a matter of less concern to the biggest advertisers. "Everybody" was more or less interested in drinking Coca-Cola or Pepsi-Cola and in brushing their teeth with Pepsodent or Ipana or one of the other heavily advertised brands.

But the astounding rate of product proliferation in today's marketplace means *prospect* proliferation as well. The more different kinds of prospects there are, the more waste is built into messages that continue to talk to "everybody" (even though a certain amount of waste may be necessary in order to reach genuine prospects).

So today's corporate managers are looking for ways to avoid spending so much of their money on nonprospects in order to reach the true prospect. Segmentation and specialization of print media and the electronic media make the process of identifying, locating, and engaging the attention of prime prospects more cost-efficient with each passing year. And even more important is the explosion in availability of both public and proprietary databases that can pinpoint just about any one of America's 250 million-plus citizens by individual characteristics.

We see essentially five ways of finding and talking to your best prospects:

1. *Fishing*—hooking prospects
2. *Mining*—digging for prospects
3. *Panning*—sifting out the best prospects
4. *Building*—in-house databasing
5. *Spelunking*—probing market niches

Numbers 1 and 2 have been around for a long time, but are taking on added importance. Numbers 3 and 4 are a powerful Information Age marketing force that is having a profound effect on marketing strategy. Number 5 is a traditional form of marketing now being given a new lease on life.

If, as some claim, all marketing is becoming niche marketing (the only real issue being the size of the niche), it is useful to keep in mind that a given product may fit more than one niche. Your overnight delivery service, originally designed to take packages from one business to another, may just as successfully take packages from a catalog retailer to its customers. Your credit card, originally designed to pay the travel and entertainment expenses of businesspeople, can be marketed to consumers who travel frequently. Available addressable sources of information make it relatively easy and inexpensive to locate, explore, and reach these new market niches.

As we work our way through these five basic modes of prospecting, try to imagine your own company's prospects as the target of the strategy and to see what ideas emerge for you.

1. FISHING FOR PROSPECTS

Fishing for prospects is as old as advertising itself. It goes back at least a century, to the time when a maker of, let's say, a soothing stomach potion, would go fishing in newspapers for potential users by means of a two-inch ad topped by a single word in bold black letters: "ULCERS?" Fishing involves luring an individual out of the sea of people and hooking him or her with a message that is highly meaningful only to that prospect. It is very much like hearing your name being paged amid the cacophony of a busy airport.

FISHING WITH WORDS

Out of necessity, advertising headlines for mail-order ads have always excelled at defining and attracting prime prospects. A classic example still runs in many women's magazines, advertising a home-study course in writing: "We're looking for people to write children's books." (This obviously is derived from the wildly successful ad run for years by the Famous Artist School: "We're looking for people who like to draw.") The prospect is that one person out of—how many?—who has always thought that she could write for children and who is therefore a prime prospect for a home-study course in the subject.

Failure to visualize the prime prospects whom the advertising is attempting to reach, and to *call out* to them as they turn the page, is the single greatest and most wasteful fault in print advertising today. (Chapter 6 discusses this issue in greater depth.)

The clever, punning headline that conceals the advantage or benefit that the ad is meant to offer will attract people who enjoy cleverness and puns, including some real prospects. They may be snared by a curiosity-provoking headline such as "Sprunch It! Here's Big News from the Lab" or "It is what it was...and more" or "Nine out of ten Americans don't get it every day." But many other, busier prospects will hurry on past, unaware that something of interest to them is hidden in these ads for a styling hair spray, a new car, and a better diet.

Advertisers caught in the squeeze between rising media costs and dwindling audiences can no longer afford to let so many fish get away after they have briefly admired the clever but ineffective lures cast into the water.

FISHING FOR USERS OF COMPETITIVE PRODUCTS

In a mature market where there is little room to expand, advertisers who want to grow are forced to try to steal customers away from their competitors.

One fiendish way of fishing for competitors' customers is to offer a reward to a prospect who sends in proof of purchase of your *competitor's* product!

L'Oréal, for instance, once ran an ad offering a free sample of its semipermanent hair color lotion that said: "Loving Care users: L'Oréal wants you to change the way you color your gray hair. For free." The reply coupon offered a free sample in exchange for a panel from Loving Care hair coloring *only.*

("Front panels from any other hair color or L'Oréal brands cannot be accepted.")

Catalina Marketing Services has built a $100 million business by enabling packaged-goods manufacturers to target consumers of competitive products at the supermarket checkout. When the clerk scans the customer's Folger's coffee or Progresso soup purchase, a thermal printer automatically spits out a discount coupon for Maxwell House or Campbell's that the customer can use the next time he or she goes to the store. By the end of March 1994 the network was in 7400 stores and was reaching over 90 million shoppers a week.

Still another way to target users of a competitive brand is to run a side-by-side comparison chart naming the competitors and showing where they fall short. The fast-growing Oxford Health Plan in New York has used the comparison chart strategy to take members away from other HMOs by the thousands.

FISHING WITH LIVE BAIT

Most exciting of all, you can go fishing with words *and* pictures that attract prospects, ask for a response, and follow up with the development of a continuing relationship.

Take the example of Nestlé's Buitoni Pasta in the United Kingdom.

Out of a huge worldwide pool of pasta consumers, Buitoni is fishing out only those with a special fondness for the Italian culture, and teaching them to think of *authentic* Buitoni Italian Pasta when they think of pasta.

The Buitoni brand traces its history back to Mama Giulia Buitoni of the tiny Tuscan village of Sansepolcro, where the company got its start in 1827. A few years ago Peter Brabeck, Nestlé's chief marketing strategist and general manager of the food business worldwide, discovered that the Buitoni family villa was still standing. Nestlé acquired it and had it restored and rebuilt to serve as the brand's world headquarters, Casa Buitoni.

The restored building houses the company's first research center ever to focus on a single brand, and includes a public relations unit, kitchens, and sleeping accommodations for 20 people. Casa Buitoni immediately became part of the new Buitoni packaging, which bears an oval "seal of quality" with a picture of the building and the words "Dalla Casa Buitoni, 1827."

With the restoration of Casa Buitoni, Duncan MacCallum, the marketing manager of the Nestlé Food Division in the United Kingdom, launched an ad campaign built around the Casa Buitoni connection. Each of a series of full-page ads in women's and cooking magazines repositioned the Buitoni brand for authentic lovers of the Italian lifestyle. A panel in the ads and in the new television commercials invited people to call for a free 20-page recipe booklet.

Nestlé collected the names of 200,000 respondents who had requested the recipe booklet in a state-of-the-art relational database. In short order they converted 80,000 booklet requesters into members of The Casa Buitoni Club, the heart of the marketing strategy.

Club members receive a magazine filled with features about the mystique of Italian music, food, art, history, and travel at its best. Nestlé plans to offer club members an opportunity to win trips to The Casa Buitoni villa in Tuscany for cooking lessons and participation in product development.

By using the right advertising offer (the line bait) to attract the right prospect and then beginning a relationship with individuals in the target market, Nestlé has shown you how far fishing for the right prospect can be taken to start the process of building a loyal following.

FISHING WITH THE HELP OF FRIENDS

Your good customers can help you to find prospects. People in a circle of friends and relations tend to have similar socioeconomic backgrounds and tastes. So someone recommended by your customer is very likely to be an excellent prospect also.

Perhaps the most dramatic example in recent times of using customers to target prospects was MCI's Friends &

Family program. It was used to go fishing for AT&T customers with the help of MCI's own loyal long-distance callers.

MCI customers were invited to form a "Calling Circle" by giving MCI the names and phone numbers of up to 12 people (later increased to 20) they called the most. Then calls to and from any of those names who were or who became MCI customers would enjoy a 20 percent discount. At the time AT&T had 67 percent of the long-distance market, so two out of three names in each MCI subscriber's Calling Circle were likely to be AT&T customers.

MCI's customers not only provided referrals, which anyone in personal selling will tell you are priceless sales leads, but were motivated and encouraged to call these referrals themselves and urge them to join the fun. Thanks to an extraordinarily sophisticated computer program, MCI could send customers a monthly Calling Circle Status Report on each friend or family member in their Calling Circle.

First, it listed the new members of a person's circle who had also signed up. ("You could be saving 20 percent. Why not give them a call?")

And just as important, it listed the names and numbers of that person's "nominees" who had not yet been converted to MCI. "To save 20 percent on calls to each of the nominees below, help us encourage them to join MCI and our circle. They can join quickly and easily by calling the toll-free number."

Did it work? In the next three years MCI gained seven share points, which adds up to billions and billions of dollars in added revenue. MCI estimates that at least 5 million members switched from AT&T as a result of the Friends & Family program, before AT&T finally responded with their own discount-phoning reward program.

Going "fishing" for prospects is the simplest and most obvious way to practice the art of target selectivity. What is surprising is how few marketers do the obvious. So get out your fishing lures and think how you might start catching the big ones—your competitors' best customers—beginning next week.

2. MINING A RICH VEIN OF PROSPECTS

Mining is the art and science of digging wherever there is a rich vein of prospects. Everything else being equal, you are going to do better selling yachts in *Yachting World* magazine than in *The New York Times,* personal computers in *PC World* than in *Business Week,* and skis in *Skiing* than in *Sports Illustrated.* Once mass advertisers had abandoned the great general-interest magazines—*Life, Look, Collier's,* and *The Saturday Evening Post*—for television, which offered even larger audiences for lower costs per thousand, those magazines were doomed. Since then, special-interest magazines have multiplied like a lush cash crop in the rich soil of the demassified market—everything from *Working Mother* to *New Woman,* from *Skateboarder* to *Snowboarding,* from *Eating Well* to *Beer: The Magazine of Beer Techniques.*

But what if you are selling toothpaste or floor cleaner? There is no *Toothpaste World* or *Floor-Cleaning Digest.* And even if there were, the circulation would be microscopically small compared to the entire market, and within it would be advertising by all of your competitors. Therefore, many brand advertisers who want or need more precise and efficient targeting than can be achieved through mass media or even specialized publications and cable channels are increasingly communicating with a rich vein of prospects found in a "public database" where you can single out your individual target.

THE RISE OF THE PUBLIC DATABASE

A public database has already done most of the hard work for you. Some of them identify by name and address just about every household in their database that uses your product category but does not use your brand, or has exactly the hobbies or equipment or lifestyle that your product or service targets. Talk about a rich vein of prospects! You can't get a richer concentration than 100 percent. You can coupon them, sample them, send them private advertising, and not waste a single cent.

Furthermore, your competitors often don't have a clear idea of what you're mailing. Your private message is largely hidden from view, so it's difficult to neutralize your effort by means of a deliberate counter-promotion.

Note that there are two kinds of databases, *transactional* and *compiled*. A transactional database is built on—what else?—transactions. A customer or prospect has subscribed to a magazine, bought a product through the mail, sent in an inquiry, made a donation. A compiled database contains names and information taken from public records—car registrations, marriage licenses, birth certificates, telephone books, and the like—and sometimes also from answers to questionnaires. Generally, marketers consider a transactional database more desirable, because by the very act of responding to an offer, people in the database have shown that they are likely to respond again. What a large public database company offers is its own *compiled* database.

Public database companies in North America and Europe have taken two general approaches to building their databases. In geodemographic segmentation—the route taken by PRIZM (Claritas), Cluster Plus (Donnelley Marketing Information Services), and Acorn (C.A.C.I., Inc.), and others—the lifestyle data is linked to zip codes and at times all the way down to block groups of 400 households. Jonathan Robbin, a founder of Claritas, has said: "Geography is destiny. I can predict what you eat, drink, drive—even think." The idea is that these companies can help you to identify the best geographical areas in which to concentrate your marketing efforts—in other words, the best vein of prospects to mine. Take one zip-code cluster as an example: "Young Influentials" drink fresh-brewed coffee, jog, travel abroad, eat yogurt, and vote Republican.

The other general approach has been to compile databases from public records combined with warranty cards and questionnaires that people return. Wherever you are in the world, there are or will soon be (if you are in an emerging market) the equivalent of the major database companies in the United States. So let's take a closer look at what America has to offer.

CHOOSING PROSPECTS BY LIFESTYLE

The Lifestyle Selector, a subsidiary of National Demographics & Lifestyles (NDL), processes the warranty cards of dozens of major manufacturers, cards that include demographic and lifestyle questions as well as customized-product or company-related questions. This compiler asks about size of family, occupation, income, education, credit cards, home ownership, interests, and activities. It now possesses such information about more than 27 million respondents in the United States, and is one of the most widely used public databases in the United States.

While thus building a proprietary database for each manufacturer that signs up with NDL to process their warranty cards, NDL also exercises its right to make consumer information available to any company that wants to rent the combined list of all NDL data gathered for their clients.

Thus, for a golf resort they were able to find high-income prospects over the age of 65 who play golf, travel, and own recreational vehicles.

THE METROMAIL MEGA-UNIVERSE

Metromail, a subsidiary of R.R. Donnelley & Sons Company, offers a number of database options. The largest, the National Consumer Data Base, contains information on over 140 million individuals and 90 million households. Metromail compiles it from thousands of public and proprietary sources and updates the record 65 times a year. Their BehaviorBase comprises over 25 million households and contains individual household information obtained from consumer surveys that people voluntarily complete. In addition to standard demographic information, BehaviorBase offers category and brand usage—for food products, health and beauty aids, household products, and pharmaceuticals—and lifestyle information—hobbies and interests, occupation, mail-order purchases, and disposable-income indicators.

You can also go looking for a rich vein of prospects in one of Metromail's proprietary specialty lists such as National

Family Index (over 18 million families with children by age and sex—updated weekly); and Young Family Index (virtually all new births every week).

Recently, Metromail and Fair, Isaac announced the introduction of DNA—Distinct Neighborhood Analysis—a new data-segmentation system that combines geographic segmentation with consumer purchase information. DNA Demographic and DNA Lifestyle use individual household data, combined with relevant geodemographic data, to assign households with similar characteristics to one of 104 cells. These share similar demographic, direct-mail-response, and lifestyle patterns. This approach provides advanced segmentation capabilities for "mining" at the household level.

GO WALTZING WITH CAROL WRIGHT

Of course Donnelley also markets the grandmother of all direct-mail co-op programs, the *Carol Wright* mailing, which traces its roots back to 1922. Today Carol Wright targets 30 million households ten times a year, with an additional 14 million households (age 50-plus) twice a year. The names are selected from the Donnelley DQI^2 database, which has marketing intelligence on approximately 87 million households. The program offers geographic selectivity (182 designated marketing areas), category exclusivity, and demographic selectivity for any advertiser that wishes to place a "buck slip" (a printed slip of paper) in the Carol Wright mailing envelope. By combining the offers of many advertisers in a co-op mailing envelope, Carol Wright offsets the high cost of solo mailings.

For example, "Select Segments" are the ones Donnelley picks for you. These could include Children Under 12, Health Conscious Households, Mail Responsive Households, Teens, or whatever. A company can create its own "Custom Segments" based on marketing information contained in the Carol Wright database, including household composition, income, and category/product usage. Finally, with "Targetmatch" your company can compare your database to Carol Wright's to find a profile match with Carol Wright consumers. Then, using Donnelley's proprietary information, you can identify other households with similar profiles to select for a targeted offer.

OPENING UP A NEW MINE SHAFT

If Carol Wright is one of the oldest public databases, *The Address Express* is one of the newest. It is the largest collection of pre-mover names in America. The information is developed from a computerized address-correction program offered as a service to consumers who are moving. Jay Feinberg, vice president of sales, told us that the consumer who moves needs to notify on average 47 mailers: magazines, catalog companies, frequent-flyer programs, and the like. The Address Express does it for them.

"Consumers who have used this program have had a 97.5 percent satisfaction level," says Feinberg, who adds that companies use the program for both retention and acquisition. A kit goes out 30 days before the anticipated move, and may include offers from a bank, a van line, a long-distance carrier, a homeowner's insurance company, etc. By mid-1994, The Address Express was obtaining 50,000 to 60,000 names a month, and they expected to hit 100,000 a month by 1995.

AXCIOM PUTS IT ALL TOGETHER

Axciom Corporation houses over 100 public and private databases, and offers marketers a number of services. It has proprietary merge/purge software that compares every element in a name and address so it can identify and purge more true duplicates than conventional matching systems. AddressAbility, another proprietary software system, reduces the number of inaccurate or incomplete addresses in a list. Its List Order Fulfillment System gives clients on-line access to Axciom's network. Finally, InfoBase List Enhancement enables a list user to supplement information already stored in the user's database. Using InfoBase, marketers can better identify prospects, because they can easily access information such as exact ages, detailed lifestyle characteristics, and telephone numbers.

BUSINESS MARKETERS GO "MINING" TOO

We have been talking about marketing to consumers, but of course there are also public databases available for business-to-business marketers as well. Dun & Bradstreet has over 10 million company and 11 million executive names in its computers, and it offers a variety of segmentation tools that marketers can use. To name only a few: Dun's Market Analysis Profile (examines business potential in new and existing markets); Dun's Market Optimizer (finds prospects that most closely resemble a firm's best customers); Dun's Response Modeling (improves direct response and ROI); and Dun's Credit Screening (locates companies with good payment patterns).

Whatever you sell, whether to a consumer end user or to another business, a public database represents a rich vein of prospects, one that you may be able to mine profitably with your precisely targeted direct-mail offers.

AN IMPRESSIVE EXAMPLE OF NO-WASTE ADVERTISING

Here's an example of the potential benefit of mining a public database, drawn from a leading pharmaceutical company that broke new ground.

In a pioneering effort, Menly and James tested four ways to reach the target audience for Ecotrin, an aspirin product specifically for people who suffer from arthritis. The goal was to get target prospects to try Ecotrin medication and then to remain loyal.

The control was a coupon ad in freestanding inserts in Sunday newspapers—a common route for reaching a target audience with a promotional offer. Three direct-mail packages were tested against the newspaper insert. They were mailed to a list of arthritis sufferers culled from a public database.

Certain details of this case history were not made public, but we can assume that the packages were mailed to arthritis sufferers who were not currently using Ecotrin medication, since the purpose of the campaign was to get new customers. The three direct-mail offers and the response rates were as follows:

1. Free sample enclosed, plus coupon good for 50 cents off the price of a full-size package—over 50 percent redemption.
2. $1 rebate coupon enclosed—over 50 percent redemption.
3. Send for a free sample—75 percent response.

A startling result of these offers was that the advertising cost per redemption of the direct mail with the $1 coupon was as low as that obtained from the freestanding insert (fsi)—and that was the cost *before* the waste in the fsi ad due to misredemption is figured in. The result debunked the notion that direct mail to a public database is necessarily a more costly medium for distributing coupons or a rebate offer. It demonstrated that although the cost of *distributing* an offer by targeted direct mail might be 50 or 100 times higher than the cost of an fsi ad, its *efficiency* was at least as great and probably much greater.

The other shocker was the 75 percent response to the offer of a sample. Although direct-mail response generally varies widely by list and by offer, the response to a direct-mail package is commonly expected to be no more than a few percentage points. The 75 percent response to the Ecotrin medication sample offer showed that when you introduce database-driven targeting to the equation, your results may zoom far beyond what is considered the norm.

The "New Math" of Database-Driven Direct Mail

To mass marketers accustomed to thinking in terms of reaching and influencing millions of television households or magazine readers, prospects and nonprospects alike, the traditionally small percentages of direct-mail response may not seem worth the bother. But if you can obtain the names of prospects who are known to use your competitor's brand or who have a matching consumer profile, and if you understand the "New Math" of database marketing, wonderful things can happen. Mining a vein of carefully selected prospects in a public or proprietary database is one of the key elements of the new marketing.

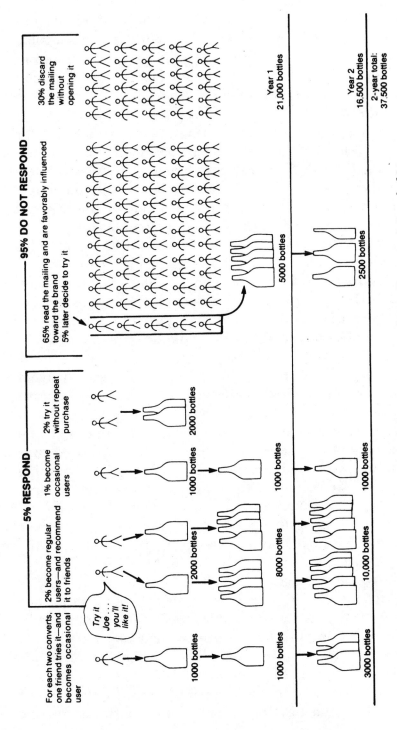

FIGURE 7. A Possible Outcome of Mailing to 100,000 Known Users of Your Competitor's Brand of Liquor.

Figure 7 is a visual forecast, one that was diagrammed in the first edition of *MaxiMarketing* to demonstrate the possible results of a mailing plan promoting an expensive brand of liquor. Let us assume, we said, that the brand sells for around $20 a bottle. Through a public database the advertiser has secured the names of 100,000 consumers who drink one (or both) of the two leading competing brands, which sell for about $12 a bottle. The advertiser prepares a mailing packaging inviting these drinkers to try his brand and taste the difference, and encloses an $8 gift certificate to make up the difference in price between the competitors' brands and his own.

The diagram depicts our working assumption that 5 percent of the recipients of the mailing would accept the offer and use the certificate. (This is a conservative assumption—remember that the Menly and James mailing saw the enclosure of a $1 coupon produce a response 10 times as great—over 50 percent redemption. We chose a much more conservative estimate here because a bottle of premium liquor is a more costly and considered purchase.)

If you limit the math in calculating payout to the 5 percent response, or a sale of 5000 bottles to 100,000 names, it doesn't sound like much. But as Fig. 7 shows, much more than that is involved. At the extreme right we indicate the 95 percent who did not respond. Of these, we assume that 30,000 tossed away the mailing without bothering to open it. The remaining 65,000 we assume opened the envelope and glanced through the mailing. These recipients did not redeem the certificate, but we are assuming that 5000 of them—just 1 out of every 20—received a favorable impression of the brand from the mailing and eventually purchased one bottle as a result of exposure to the message.

Of the 5000 mailing recipients who did respond, our hypothetical forecast predicts that 2000 will use the certificate to try the brand, then return to their old brand; 1000 respondents will be sufficiently pleased by their trial to buy one more bottle; and 2000 respondents—just 2 percent—will become converted enthusiasts. Each of these converts in our example will then buy four more bottles of the advertised brand. Furthermore, because of their enthusiasm, word-of-mouth advertising will influence one friend to try the brand as well.

That's what could happen just in the first year. In the second year, the enthusiastic converts each buy five more bottles. The friends they persuade to try the brand each buy three more bottles. The semi-enthusiasts each buy one more bottle. And half of the favorably impressed nonrespondents who had purchased a bottle each now buy an additional one.

So we end up with a projected grand total of 37,500 bottles sold in the first two years as a direct result of the mailing to 100,000 liquor consumers—quite a different picture from the 5000 bottles sold that might superficially be taken to be the total sales return.

Four factors in the hypothetical liquor mailing outlined in the first edition of *MaxiMarketing* set it apart from routine promotional solo direct mail, and should make it far more cost-effective:

1. There is zero waste circulation. We are mailing only to prime prospects—known users of competing brands.

2. In addition to the gift certificate, the mailing contains a four-page letter with potent, persuasive brand advertising. So it influences the buying attitude of many nonrespondents as well as respondents.

3. The total sales effect of the mailing on respondents, friends, and nonrespondents over a two-year period is estimated and factored in. (Post-research could pin down the exact numbers.)

4. Names and addresses of respondents are captured by redemption of a rebate certificate with the recipient's UPC identification number encoded for later analysis.

A Crowning Achievement: The Theoretical Becomes Actual

How hypothetical has the example just given turned out to be? Less and less so with each passing year. Richard Shaw, vice president of marketing communications at The House of Seagram, has shared with us the data from his database-driven conquest-marketing campaign in the real world, and it bears a remarkable resemblance to the hypothetical case we presented a decade ago.

Shaw's marketing team decided to launch a carefully researched campaign aimed at winning over for Crown Royal, Seagram's most important profit-maker, 3500 competitive-brand users. The firm sent three different mailings to the same 150,000 names over a five-month period, all designed to tempt competitive-brand users to try Crown Royal. (Names were selected from Seagram's proprietary database of 10 million users of alcoholic beverages. With its advanced profiling techniques, Seagram could identify the users of competing Canadian whiskies and the Jack Daniels brand.)

The first mailing enclosed a little booklet telling a whimsical, tongue-in-cheek fairy tale, and offered a pair of Crown Royal on-the-rocks glasses as a premium with proof-of-purchase. The second mailing used a playing-cards theme, and offered two sets of Crown Royal playing cards. The third was a self-mailer with a sweepstakes offering a chance to win a stay at your own "castle" in the Bahamas, Acapulco, or Bermuda, as well as a pair of free highball glasses.

Using pre- and post-research, Seagram measured not only the number who responded but the "slippage"—Seagram's name for the recipients who did not respond to the mailing offer but who were directly influenced to make a purchase by the mailing. They found that for every person who redeemed the offer, two additional people bought the product as a result of the mailing (twice as many as we had guessed in our hypothetical example).

Response rates were only the beginning of the result analysis, however. Management wanted to know what a new customer is worth. Now they do. The final conversion rate (the percentage of triers who became repeat buyers) was 54 percent, and the actual number of bottles sold per person was incorporated in the breakeven analysis.

As our model had predicted, the direct-mail campaign also did wonders to increase brand awareness among the 150,000 prospects who received the mailing and did not respond. House of Seagram researchers found that unaided brand awareness among nonredeemers went up from 14 to 23 percent—quite an improvement, for a series of just three mailings. Among these consumers, the program reinforced Crown Royal's favorable brand image in the areas of quality, prestige, "giftability," and impressive packaging.

Also as expected, the impact on friends of respondents was an important factor in the campaign's overall success. Later mailings sent to referral names generated response at three or four times the norm. The campaign's goal was to win over 3500 competitive-brand users and to earn back the entire investment in the mailing within two years. When all the numbers were added up for the test campaign, Seagram found that it had attracted *more* than 3500 new customers and that the breakeven point had been reached in 2.3 years. The hypothetical "New Math" of our earlier example was confirmed on every level by the House of Seagram Crown Royal test mailing.

But the real-life example didn't end there. Using predictive modeling so as to refine their database target selection, Seagram was able to reduce the payback time in future campaigns to *less than nine months!*

You Can Teach an Old Mailing List New Tricks

There is another kind of public database that is hardly new but that shouldn't be overlooked: the mailing list. List brokers around the world, in both the developed and the developing markets, have thousands of lists for rent, containing the names both of people compiled from public records and of people who have responded either to a commercial offer or to a nonprofit appeal. If the price of your product or the lifetime value of a customer is high enough to justify direct mail's high cost per thousand, somewhere out there are lists of people you can mail to who closely match your target profile. Often the efficiency of this approach can be increased by selecting, when available, the most recent respondents—or just those in certain neighborhoods, or just a particular set of demographics, and so on.

More and more, list brokers are offering more than just names. They are becoming marketers of functional databases. For instance, *Worldatabase* offers over 11 million consumer and 13 million direct-response business-buyer names. This latter list includes more than 6 million businesspeople who have fully functional offices in their homes. A marketer may segment this list by home office versus home-based business, by gender, by occupation, SIC code, computer hardware and software purchased, estimated income, age range, credit card usage, vehicle type, or any combination of these factors.

As their functional databases come to resemble the public databases more and more, list brokers often are able to take your profile of existing buyers and to extract only the names on the lists offered that match the profile.

Spiegel, L.L. Bean, Lands' End, and other catalog marketers maintain and offer transactional databases of their customers. They can select names for mailings in as many as 50 different ways—by state, city, or zip code; by purchase frequency, purchase size, or purchase date; by merchandise category, size, or color; and by any combination of these factors. Add demographic and lifestyle data to these names, and the marketer knows whether professional women earning more than $35,000 in the northeast are better prospects for cashmere sweaters than the same women in the northwest.

Many brand advertisers and agencies have been slow to realize the potential for dramatic sales increases inherent in public databases and increasingly sophisticated mailing-list targeting. This is changing, of course—but there are still too many marketing directors, ad managers, and their counterparts at the advertising agencies who would prefer to expend their energies on the highly visible (and, for the agencies, highly profitable) world of television and print media advertising, where reputations rise and fall on the "creativity" of the latest campaign.

If you work in an advertising agency, just think what you could be doing to steal the march on your agency's competition—and your client's competition—by focusing your agency's creativity on the task of talking directly to your best prospects, and using the wealth of information now readily available to allow your private advertising to break new ground and new sales records. (Agencies specializing in direct-response advertising are doing this already—and are thriving. In 1995, the three leading direct-marketing advertising agency networks in the world—Ogilvy and Mather Direct, Rapp Collins Worldwide, and Wunderman Cato Johnson—each billed close to or more than a billion dollars a year worldwide.)

Digging for prospects wherever you have identified a rich vein may be the most cost-effective solution to building your business that you will ever find. So pick up a pickaxe and a shovel, decide where you want to start digging, and get to it before your competition lays a claim to the same stake.

3. PANNING FOR PURE-GOLD PROSPECTS

The third way to target prospects profitably is through *panning*. This approach involves sifting promising names through ever-finer screens until only nuggets of pure gold remain in your pan.

Remember our example of the Seagram Crown Royal mailing? We told you that after mining the vein of competitive-brand users in their database, they were able to generate a payback on their promotional campaign within about two years. And that over the next few years, results were improved to the point where the complete cost of the promotion to convert users of competitive Canadian whiskies and Jack Daniels had been cut to a payback in less than a year.

Seagram was able to constantly improve their results in each campaign by "panning" their database and ending up with increasingly responsive prospects for each new mailing campaign. Through the use of predictive modeling after the first mailing, the Seagram database was classified into 20 groups arranged from the greatest likelihood of response the next time around down to the least likely. "The focus of the analysis was to target the highest-scoring cells, groups one to four," says Richard Shaw. "Representatives of groups five to twenty were included in subsequent mailings, in modest quantity, in order to validate the performance of the model."

With the predictive model in hand, Seagram was able to select 150,000 precisely targeted prospects for the second round of testing. The same three packages, with minor revisions, were used in the second campaign a year later, and the goal was to double the response rate of about 3.5 percent achieved the first time.

The second series of mailings to the top four cells pulled an astonishing 8 percent response, actually slightly better than *double* the previous result and just about what the predictive model had forecast. When Seagram factored in the two-to-one "slippage" ratio previously established, the percentage of converts (respondents converted into steady customers) produced by the mailing soared to almost 25. The mailing to the names that predictive modeling had "panned out" surpassed by a comfortable margin the response level necessary to pay out in two years. When the Crown Royal conquest-marketing direct-mail program was further extended and refined in a third round of testing, it achieved the astonishing nine-month payback rate mentioned earlier.

PREDICTIVE MODELING TAKES THE GUESSWORK OUT OF THE NEW INDIVIDUALIZED MARKETING

Predictive modeling becomes a more powerful marketing tool with each passing year. For example, retailers can now take the first steps down this road by means of software that tracks in-store purchases of identified customers in the same way that a catalog merchant tracks the history of a mail-order customer.

The program enables the retailer to compile detailed information on a customer's buying frequency, total dollar purchases, type of merchandise, and preference indicators by taste, price levels, and size ranges. By adding census data, the retailers can then determine (1) where their best and worst customers live; (2) what census characteristics they have; and (3) which types of census tract are therefore most and least likely to respond to certain mailed offers. By tracking response to promotions over time, the retailer can use regression analysis to model who should get what offer for what type of merchandise, how often to mail to each individual, and much more.

Blockbuster Entertainment Corp. used its database of 40 million customers to select just those families with children that they wanted to reach in January and February of 1994. The company wanted kids to rent video-game cartridges for the game player they had received in the preceding Christmas season. To that end, Blockbuster sent a targeted direct-mail promotion that obtained a phenomenal 30 percent redemption rate. Robert L. Carberry, Blockbuster's vice president of technology, pointed out that the firm was able to create a promotion to meet existing user preferences by using database modeling to determine which titles and product features appealed to which youngsters. Moreover, the experience taught Blockbuster a great deal about packaging, video-game preferences, and how to perfect target mailings.[1]

How many pure-gold prospects are out there, just waiting for you? Master the art of predictive modeling and with each new mailing campaign you will be panning more and more pure gold.

4. BUILDING YOUR OWN DATABASE OF PRIME PROSPECTS

The ultimate in sophisticated database prospecting is to construct and constantly improve your own proprietary in-house prospect database.

Blockbuster's mainframe computer stores information from more than 2 billion videocassette rental and sale transactions and grows by 1 million customer transactions a day. The computer contains each customer's name, address, credit card number, spending patterns, and video rental tastes.

As you add bits of information to each file, you learn more and more about who your prime prospects for future marketing are, what they are like, and where they reside. Out of this comprehensive relational database you can build a subgroup of prospects for any specific marketing objective.

Tourism Canada, a branch of the Canadian government's Department of Regional Industrial Expansion, offers an outstanding example of in-house database building. To attract American tourists, the Department had been sending mailings to prospects in the United States, principally to people who hunt, fish, or engage in other outdoor activities. They decided, however, that they weren't realizing the program's full potential, and therefore they brought in an experienced professional, Aimee Britten, to help.

One of Britten's first moves was to confer with the Department's agency, Business Services Inc., and ask how the program could be expanded to attain better results. Might there be a sizable market of people out there who were *not* active outdoors? What about tourists who wanted to visit Canada for the sake of its cities, history, and culture? Were most trips self-planned, or arranged through a travel agent? By what mode of transportation were tourists traveling?

To begin to answer these questions, Tourism Canada restructured one of their mailings to prequalified prospects so as to include a detailed reply coupon and questionnaire. It asked respondents for their age, occupation, travel frequency, travel interests, and so on.

The information provided by the replies was entered in the database, along with the keyed source of the advertising that generated the response. The database was updated regularly, allowing Tourism Canada to customize their mailings and ads to appropriate market segments.

No longer did families that plan their own trips receive mailings telling them to contact their travel agent. Nor did a 60-year-old librarian who was interested in visiting Montreal's museums receive brochures about fishing and resorts. The source code identified exactly which mailing piece, list, publication, or ad produced the best results from specific target groups.

Nonetheless, results aren't truly results until a prospect has become a customer. An ingenious feature of the campaign tracked actual visits to Canada by respondents in the database. A prepaid business-reply card was enclosed with each fulfillment package. Returning the card made the respondent eligible for a premium or a prize, but to qualify *the card had to be mailed in Canada.* This told the department not only which and how many of the inquirers had actually visited Canada, but also (from the postmark) at least one specific place that they had visited.

THE SMALLEST BUSINESS CAN PLAY THE GAME

Even the corner service station can build its own database and thereby bring in more customers. *Servistat* is a software program for automobile service stations that, among other things, tracks when a car requires certain services such as a tune-up and or lube/oil/filter check. Every week or every month the station owner can send out postcards to every customer whose car had a tune-up three months ago, five months ago, or seven months ago. The cards are personalized: "It is now time to have your 1987 Cadillac with plate number AB 123 CD tuned up. The last time it was tuned, it had 89,873 miles on it. Tuning your car will save you gasoline." Or whatever else the operator wants to say in personalizing the message.

Database-driven relationships have other benefits as well, says Harry Stern, Servistat's president:

> Now somebody comes in and says, "Gee, you did my brakes three months ago and they're not working right." The technician can go to the computer and respond, "We did the brakes two years ago, and it's time you should redo them."

Prior to the introduction of this kind of database, service-shop operators were thumbing through records; often they couldn't find the record, so—to keep the customer happy—they did work that wasn't really necessary.

ANTICIPATING THE PROSPECT'S NEXT MOVE

Murphy Realty/Better Homes & Gardens of Bergen County, New Jersey, once developed what may well be the last word in a prospect database: a database of *future* home-buying prospects.

To build it, Murphy sent out a mailing to 75,000 Bergen County households, offering information on Murphy's services. It included a questionnaire with such questions as, "What type of home are you presently living in? How long do you intend to stay in your present home? What factors make a move unlikely within five years? What factors would influence you to move? If you do plan to move in the future, what type of home will you be looking for?" Signing the questionnaire was optional. Within three weeks of the mailing, Murphy had received a 4 percent response, and half of these were signed with the names and addresses of respondents.

Murphy was now in a position to accelerate the buying decision (and to get to the prospect long before the competition!). If an appropriate property came on the market, Murphy could approach a likely prospect and say, in effect, "Look, I know you said you weren't planning to buy a new house until a year or two from now, but since I have something that is right up your alley, I thought you might like to consider it." (Plus, undoubtedly: "And don't worry about selling your present house. We can take care of that for you too.")

If you aren't already building a proprietary database of your own, and gathering into it all the specific prospect and customer information you can use, you may be missing the opportunity of a lifetime. The more you know about each individual you do business with, the more you can do to fatten your bottom line.

5. SPELUNKING FOR PROSPECTS

Spelunking is the exploration of caves. A cave is a really deep niche, right? Ergo, "Spelunking for prospects" is our name for *niche prospecting*. There are essentially two kinds of niche prospect marketing:

1. Finding or developing a niche for your product

2. Finding how to dominate an existing niche

A campaign for *Searle's Metamucil* affords a fascinating early example of finding a new niche while not endangering or confusing the existing market. It is also an outstanding example of MaxiMarketing, incorporating as it does many of the steps in the MaxiMarketing process. Among other things Searle demonstrated an intelligent use of targeted couponing, in striking contrast to the wasteful mass-couponing we see so often and will discuss in a later chapter.

Metamucil laxative was popular with laxative buyers at the time of the campaign—largely elderly and lower-income people with poor dietary habits who have a problem with "regularity." But there was a different niche market, if it could be reached and persuaded, of people who did *not* necessarily have a health problem. On the contrary, they were health- and fitness-conscious people who were passionate about dieting, jogging, and working out.

Many of these folks were already predisposed to use a "fiber supplement" as part of a fitness program. If Searle could position Metamucil as a fiber supplement, an integral part of an everyday fitness program, a whole new market could be opened up. But it might be at the expense of the traditional market, if the positioning were done in media to which Metamucil's usual customers were exposed.

To resolve this dilemma, Searle turned to "private advertising" and database-driven marketing. They targeted three niche markets:

1. *Dieters,* to whom the appeal would be "feel fuller, eat less, and get the fiber your dieting body needs."

2. *Laxative users,* selected from a public database as more upscale and urban than the typical Metamucil user and known to use a competing product.

3. *Young urban professionals,* who didn't habitually use a laxative but were aware that their bodies need fiber and that they might not necessarily be treating their bodies right. If this niche could be persuaded to make Metamucil a daily

habit, like taking a multivitamin, the sales potential could be huge.

The economics of the program allowed about $3 for the acquisition of a customer. Searle defined a customer as a person who would buy two boxes of Metamucil Instant Mix at retail within a year.

The company sent a test mailing—in the form of a self-mailer—targeted to a random selection of each of the three niche groups. The post-paid reply card offered free samples, a "calendar of coupons" (40 cents off, each month for a year), and a booklet of health tips.

The overall response rate was more than 15 percent. Thus the advertising cost per inquiry was only a little more than $1. If just one out of three of the respondents became customers, the program would be a success. And the likelihood of conversion was probably much better than that, since the respondents would already have demonstrated a keen interest in the product simply by responding to the offer.

How would Searle know which respondents actually became customers? To each respondent's name and address it assigned a serial number, which was printed on the back of each of the 12 monthly coupons. As these coupons trickled through the retail channel and coupon clearinghouse, the serial numbers were noted and recorded.

Searle tracked not only the macro results but also the names and addresses of triers, buyers, and multiunit buyers from the ongoing program. An analysis of the micro results revealed to Searle the potential and actual behavior of each niche market in the test.

The Burger King Kids Club, another example of spelunking, has been one of the few bright spots in that company's marketing efforts. Throughout the 1980s and early 1990s, Burger King was notorious for one misguided advertising campaign after another: the much-ridiculed "Herb the Nerd" was followed by "Sometimes you got to break the rules." When that message confused customers and angered franchisees, Burger King dropped it after 18 months. The number-two fast-food marketer then fired the agency and held what *The Wall Street Journal* described as "the most torturous advertising account review in recent memory." The next agency didn't do any better.

But while Burger King was stumbling from one TV advertising disaster to another, the Kids Club it launched in 1990 has *tripled*. Different age groups get their own customized publications: the three- to five-year-olds' magazine is called *Small Fries*; five- to seven-year-olds get *Great Shakes*; and eight- to ten-year-olds receive *Have It Your Own Way*.

The kids get involved in solving mysteries and puzzles. There are fun products they can pick up at Burger King at pint-sized prices. There are offers from Disney and other Kids Club partners. And as you might expect, every issue offers cents-off coupons for burgers and fries.

At last report the Burger King Kids Club had four million members. At one point, kids were signing up at the rate of 100,000 per month. One out of every ten children in America was getting a Kids Club magazine four times a year, with direct results at the point of sale. The Burger King Kids Club has been a spectacular spelunking success!

Is there an undiscovered niche out there, just waiting to accommodate itself to your product or service? Or an empty niche for which you could create a brand-new product or service? Why not get out your explorer's headlamp and go spelunking, to locate a "cave" full of valuable prospects?

THE BOTTOM LINE

In order to start reaping the rewards of MaxiMarketing, you must find out who and where your best prospects are, and what are the most efficient ways of reaching them. A market research firm can help you to develop a profile of your best prospects. A geodemographic mapping firm can help you to locate concentrations of them. The actions of your prospects and customers can help you to do both, through the kinds of appeals to which they respond and from the information they provide you with on questionnaires they fill out and return.

Most important of all will be how you take advantage of the power of the computer to store and analyze everything you learn throughout the targeting process. You can invite your likely prospects to identify themselves by responding to targeted appeals and offers in the available media, enabling you to add names and information to your in-house database. And you can go straight to your best prospects by selecting them either from a publicly compiled or a transactional database. You can practice the art and science of predictive modeling. And you can make a narrow niche market a target for profitable exploration.

By following any one or more of the five MaxiMarketing prospecting models we have laid out for you in this chapter, you can take the first step toward minimizing the waste of your advertising dollars and maximizing the effect of your individualized and personalized marketing strategies.

MAXIMIZED MEDIA EXPLORATION

THE NEW EMBARRASSMENT OF RICHES

THE BIG PICTURE

Along with the proliferation of products and services in the past decade has come an extraordinary proliferation of media options. There are totally new forms of media, new developments in traditional media, and new uses for media. Increasingly, the new opportunities are tools for targeting a segmented or niche market (and most recently, for reaching out to a single individual) rather than for blanketing the mass market. As we review these new media possibilities, ask yourself, "Is there something here for my company?" Exploring one or two new directions could breathe new life into longstanding media-buying habits.

Nobody would want to use or even test all of the options in this chapter, but you do need to be aware of the wide range of media choices out there if you are to make the most intelligent and cost-effective selections. And because there are so many choices nowadays, the need for greater accountability and a practical method of measuring comparative cost-effectiveness is greater than ever.

This means that as much of your advertising as is practical should call for the measurement of responses from each media buy, so that you can calculate the advertising cost-per-response and compare this with the results from other buys.

73

We will focus entirely on current media developments in the United States. But keep in mind, if you are reading this in Kuala Lumpur, Buenos Aires, Bombay, or Cape Town, that it is probably only a matter of time before most of these options and many others become available to you.

*T*he *Winegrowers of California* test-marketed a new television campaign in the northeast region of America shortly before the first edition of *MaxiMarketing* was published.

The two 30-second spots featured Julia Child giving suggestions on the proper wines to serve at lunch or dinner. The spots included a toll-free number that consumers could call to receive free, non-brand-specific wine tips. Inclusion of the number would also "provide a gauge on how the ads are being received," according to the management supervisor of the advertiser's agency.[1]

This was one of the earliest uses of television as a direct-response medium in prime time, and as predicted in *MaxiMarketing*, it was followed over the next decade by campaigns from Procter & Gamble, MCI, General Motors, and other mass marketers demonstrating the power of television as a response medium.

From our point of view, this early test was a pointer indicating the direction that media would take with each passing year of the Information Age. The Winegrowers of California TV campaign provided a method of measuring real-world consumer reaction to the message and to the medium being used. And although we don't know if a database of respondents was created at the time, the potential benefit of such a database is obvious today.

If they had compiled a sizable database of interested consumers generated by the campaign, the Winegrowers could have gone to their member vintners and said: "Let's do a co-op mailing to these people since they are prime prospects, people concerned enough about the correct choice of wine to make a phone call for more information." Each member could have prepared its own leaflet on its brands, and the Winegrowers association could then have inserted the leaflets into its co-op mailing envelope and mailed them at very low cost-per-prospect. The co-op mailings could have included offers and rebates for specific brands, which would have provided a basis for tracking sales and, ultimately, the cost-per-sale generated by the TV commercial.

Hardly a week now passes without another media innovation, proposed or proclaimed, making news. How about The Good Health Channel, which planned to put television screens, and pet-oriented programming and commercials, into veterinarian waiting rooms? Or Food Court Entertainment, which planned to put television sets and "Café USA," "half-hour programs of entertainment, fashion news, and locally tailored commercials," in—where else?—shopping mall food courts.[2] And now, the opening up to advertising messages of the World Wide Web on the Internet. The advertiser wandering through this vast ocean of media possibilities without some down-to-earth method of evaluating sales effectiveness can be like a ship plowing through dark waters without a compass.

Furthermore, our captain (that's you) must somehow steer between the Scylla of timidity and the Charybdis of foolhardiness. If you are too timid, your competitors may race on ahead of you. If you are too bold, you may fritter away your precious advertising resources on the latest media novelties and end up having nothing to show for them.

FINDING YOUR WAY THROUGH THE MAZE OF POSSIBILITIES

We cannot hope to provide you with an in-depth examination of all the available media opportunities out there. No sooner could we claim to possess such a guide than the next innovation would present itself. What we *would* like to do here is to open your eyes to some of the more intriguing recent developments, and to stimulate you to consider which media opportunities might apply to the product, service, or business that you wish to promote.

No doubt you will find that some of the possibilities mentioned are too "far out" for what you are selling. But if you uncover just *one* exciting new opportunity to pursue, then taking a moment to review all of them will have proved to be well worth your while. Gaining familiarity with what is available out there will arm you with the right questions to ask the next time a so-called "media expert" attempts to sell you on staying with the tried-and-true, familiar choices. And if you are located in a country where some of these options are not available, you will be alerted to what may be coming your way next.

We urge you to apply, whenever and wherever you experiment with these new media options, some strict test of accountability. Without such accountability, in the form of tracking measurable sales or responses, you may never know whether you have spent your money wisely.

Maximizing media in the MaxiMarketing process means being on the alert for every opportunity to better target the best *individual* prospects you have profiled. There is no longer any excuse for wasteful hit-or-miss buying of established media in the conventional way, or for passing up an opportunity to test totally new media that offer pinpoint targeting and interactive technology.

We will start our review with those new opportunities that use familiar media, then briefly survey some of the emerging new forms that have varying degrees of promise.

WHAT'S NEW IN NEWSPAPER ADVERTISING

In America, newspapers have perhaps the greatest need to change in response to a changing media environment. Over the past 10 years the industry has suffered from consolidation, declining readership, and eroding national ad sales. At the start of the 1980s over 150 U.S. cities supported two or more competing weekday newspapers; by the mid-nineties, only 63 had two or more.[3]

According to Simmons Market Research Bureau, the *percentage* of adult Americans who read a daily newspaper has declined quite steadily over the last 10 years, from 66 percent of the population in 1982 to 61.7 percent in 1993. The *absolute* number of readers (the total was over 114 million in 1993) has risen because the population has increased, and more people than ever are reading Sunday/weekend papers—69 percent of the adult population in 1993.

Despite this relative decline, however, from a Maxi-Marketing point of view it is worth noting that a drop in "reach" is not necessarily a decline in advertising *efficiency.* In making a media buy, the cost per-page per-thousand and—even more important, if the advertising calls for a response—*the advertising cost per inquiry* is more important than the size of the circulation. For a product or service whose advertising calls for lots of information and persuasion, newspapers still are a major contender for that advertising. And they are still unrivaled as the medium of choice for local retail advertising.

The percentage of national advertising placed in newspapers has been trending downward—it accounted for less than 5 percent of all the national media purchased in 1993. Part of the problem is that it is cumbersome for an advertiser to buy in many newspaper markets at once. "An advertiser contemplating a national campaign involving a hundred or so newspapers can rarely deal with a single source to buy space in all the desired newspapers," says a spokesman for the Newspaper Association of America.

Moreover, even when the advertiser has bought space in a number of papers, the rate quoted is usually the aggregate of the national rates for each paper (or group) in the buy. Such an aggregation may make no allowance for the size of the total buy. National advertisers have long complained that individual paper's national ad rates are higher than their local display rates. "When individual national rates are aggregated without discount for the size of the buy, the resulting rate may seem to advertisers to be still more objectionable," says the NAA. Further, there is usually no single person to whom the advertiser can turn to try to negotiate a better rate. The wonder is that newspapers carry *any* national advertising!

To address these issues, the NAA asked the Department of Justice for permission to form a national newspaper network, a plan that the department approved at the end of 1993. Now there is a National Newspaper Network (NNN) to sell space to national advertisers. The goal is to offer advertisers space in many papers at a single competitive price, to be determined by the NNN joint venture. At long last, national advertisers can buy space in newspapers in much the same way that they buy television time, negotiating a price that is competitive with other media.

PUTTING YOUR MONEY WHERE IT PAYS

New ground was broken when America's national newspaper, *USA Today,* offered to measure advertising results and to tie ad rates to them. One office-products marketer, for example, agreed to make *USA Today* part of its next ad buy if its test ad generated an agreed-upon number of sales leads via a toll-free telephone number. If results fell below the goal, the advertiser had to pay only a percentage of the full rate.[4] This is similar to the deals some magazines have quietly been offering for years to direct-order advertisers, in which the advertiser pays only so much per response.

If you are buying space in a local newspaper in the United States, or if you are a newspaper advertiser in Latin America, Europe, or Japan, see what you can do to get your local paper to follow *USA Today*'s example.

The Newspaper Association of America's senior vice president and chief marketing officer, Ray Gaulke, supports the concept: "The area of measurement, or *proving it,* is the next place advertising is going to go." Gaulke adds that new technology makes it easier and more cost-effective to design programs that use scanner data to track resulting action at the point-of-sales or from calls to 800- or 900-numbers. Carolyn Vesper, *USA Today* senior vice president of advertising, says: "If the media think their products are appropriate for a call-to-action ad, they ought to be willing to stand behind it." A sentiment with which we are in total agreement.

NEWSPAPER ADVERTISING WITHOUT PAPER AND INK

Many newspaper publishers seem to feel that their future lies less in paper and ink than in the microchips paving the information superhighway. As *Advertising Age* has reported, newspapers are going on-line: selling electronic classifieds, and experimenting with electronic display ads. "There is a tremendous amount of hype out there now...and a bit of a frenzy," said Roger Fidler, director of Knight-Ridder Information Design Laboratory. "Many things being done today are purely from a defensive standpoint. Many feel they've got to do *something*."[5]

The *Atlanta Journal-Constitution*, for example, has gone on the Prodigy on-line service, offering news and classified ads drawn from the printed paper. As a hint of what may be coming, display advertising takes up a part of each screen display, and Rich's department store has been testing the waters with its ads. "We wanted to learn about different ways to communicate with our customers," said Don Van Suilichem, senior vice president and director of marketing for Rich's/Goldsmith's Department Stores. "We don't know where it's going to go, but we think we have to be in there and learn at the beginning of it." Tracking the orders will tell Rich's how well the ads are doing. Recent Clinique ads included telephone numbers so that viewers could order directly from the store.

San Francisco advertising agency Hal Riney & Partners, Inc., is forecasting that classified ads will go electronic. At a recent conference the agency said:

> Newspapers and television are likely to merge services, creating a classified advertising revolution. Electronic classified will soon connect buyers and sellers. In fact, in Orlando, Florida, Time Warner and the *Orlando Sentinel* are planning a classified channel. A customer shopping for a used car, for example, could double-click-on the ad and a screen would provide photos and additional information.[6]

Clearly, everyone still has a lot to learn. "Advertising in an electronic environment is not merely a display ad posted on a computer screen. That's not very engaging," says Don Brazeal, editor-publisher of *The Washington Post's* Digital Ink subsidiary. "Customers have to be constantly in control of what they are looking at, and it has to be inviting, useful, and time-saving." Brazeal seems to be saying that it has to be less like "advertising" and more like "information." It sounds like a MaxiMarketing mindset to us.

TELEVISION ADVERTISING IN AN INFORMATION ECONOMY

The decade from 1985 to 1995 has been—to be kind—a time of "turmoil" for the NBC, CBS, and ABC television networks. Their share of total American television viewers declined almost steadily during the decade, even as the number of commercials rose. TV advertising clutter got a big boost in August of 1985, when CBS officially endorsed the new 15-second spot by saying that it would accept a 15-second buy as a stand-alone ad, not just as half of a 30-second buy. Less than 5 years later, 15-second spots were accounting for almost 38 percent of all network commercials.

The cost of both commercial time and advertising production continues to rise, and commercial clutter seems to get even worse each passing year. In 1993, according to the Television Bureau of Advertising, 713 advertisers promoted 3177 brands on network television and 2070 advertisers promoted 11,111 brands on spot TV.

Yet despite a shrinking audience and a rising crescendo of commercials, network television still has a lot of life left in it. And to everyone's surprise the demand for TV time climbed to new heights in the mid-1990s. The networks are hardly on the verge of extinction, even as television evolves into a 500-channel universe. As *The Wall Street Journal* has pointed out, it will take years and megabillion-dollar investments to install the hardware—computers, cable, and telephones—required to fully create the information superhighway, and broadcast television will still be the best place for advertisers to reach a mass audience for some time to come.[7]

The clout of network TV remains awesome. The four television networks booked $10.3 billion worth of advertising in 1992. A year later, CBS and ABC scored record profits. And when NBC introduced a new hospital-drama series, *ER*, within weeks it was attracting an audience of 27 million people— 32 percent of all households watching TV on Thursday night.

Hal Riney & Partners has suggested that in the future the standard 15- and 30-second commercial units will be less common:

> Companies will find that long messages will have a larger role in the telactive age. For example, Saturn [a Riney client] recently aired a twenty-two-minute film on national cable and local television stations. Five-minute spots are likely to become the prevalent long-form commercial unit in the future.

Television remains a powerhouse because virtually every household in America owns a TV set (the penetration is over 98 percent) and the typical household spends over seven hours a day watching.

As Bob Nance, the vice president of marketing services for Pearle Vision, the national eyeware retail chain, said not long ago: "With the nature of our market being just about everyone in the United States, network TV is attractive."[8] Along with the new opportunities to deal with prospects and customers one-on-one, the power to build a brand using the mass media, if you can afford it, remains a constant.

Television Advertising Goes Direct

One of the most spectacular success stories of using television as a direct-response medium has come out of Brazil. In 1979, Dr. Edson de Godoy Bueno and his associates launched Amil Assistencia Medica International, or AMIL, a health provider offering both medical insurance and hospital care. Two years after they began, their largest competitor was still 140 times bigger and AMIL was struggling. Dr. Bueno knew that perception often becomes reality, that how people perceive a company can be as important as how big the firm really is. To be taken seriously, AMIL had to be perceived as a major player in the health-care field. But what could they do, with so little capital and such a tiny market share?

AMIL drew upon the MaxiMarketing way of looking at media. It combined the power of direct response with the image-building strength of brand-awareness commercials. AMIL may well have been the first advertiser anywhere in the world to establish a dominant presence with direct-response TV advertising in prime-time programming.

They poured advertising dollars into commercials that always included the phone number so as to generate a steady flow of leads for the sales force. It was the kind of double-duty advertising that makes every dollar work twice as hard. In addition they found a way to turn their phone number into one of the best-remembered numbers in Brazil.

Because Brazilian phones don't have letters on the buttons or the dial, it isn't possible to substitute an easily remembered word or phrase such as "Dial 1-800-COLLECT" for MCI's collect-call service. But since *mil* means "thousand" in Portuguese, the company obtained a phone number for Rio de Janeiro and later for São Paulo ending with 1000. "Call AMIL, 221-1000" is a message you can't escape or forget in Brazil.

In 1982, Amil was producing annual operating revenue of over $5 million. In 1990 it shot up to $165 million, and by 1997 they expect to hit a billion dollars in annual revenue.

GET READY, GET SET, IT'S TIME TO GO INTERACTIVE

As if to hint that television advertising may be moving in an exciting new direction from a MaxiMarketing perspective, NBC used interactive promotions to promote its 1994 fall season. With "NBC and McDonald's Go Interactive," the two companies "aired" the first multimedia television "commercial" available from an on-line computer service. It was a

McDonald's spot adapted to run in QuickTime video on America Online. "Interactive media is something that all of America is talking about, so we decided to do some fun, interactive things to generate awareness for our new shows," said Alan Cohen, a senior vice president of marketing at NBC.[9]

The promotion included on-line "board game" trivia contests about McDonald's and NBC's new shows, back-to-school safety tips, an electronic mail service that enabled computer users to communicate directly with McDonald's, a click-and-win sweepstakes that offered a variety of premiums tied to NBC and McDonald's, including $10,000 in computer equipment, a special *Saturday Night Live* CD-ROM, NBC screensavers, and McDonald's gift certificates.

"Interactive" is the hot new thing in television. KICU-TV, an independent station in San Jose, California, began to build an extensive database of viewers in February 1993. Its 24-hour telephone information line offers continually updated recordings about news, weather, sports, business, flight information, station programming, contests, community events, entertainment, and more. KICU sends out regular mailings promoting advertiser's products to the more than 400,000 members on its database. It doesn't sell the names to anyone, but offers its advertisers a chance to use the list, with the station printing and sending redeemable coupons to potential customers. David Wolfe, KICU's director of promotion and marketing, says, "It's target marketing. That is the future. It *offers accountability* and generates results."[10] (Emphasis added.)

KICU's experience may be an isolated phenomenon, or it may be an early glimpse of a low-tech road to interactivity for the television medium. Smart advertisers will seek out the TV stations that promise not just to put a commercial on the tube, but to provide a direct route to viewers as well.

THE ONE-TWO PUNCH MAXIMARKETERS LOVE

What we have seen again and again, in looking at the history of media, is that the new often merely *supplements* the old rather than replacing it. The sheer power of one-way visual communication for television commercials will continue to impress. For instance, in just 15 seconds the four-wheel-drive Jeep commercial creates a lasting image of its incredible agility by showing it easily climbing up a steep incline of boulders. Repeat that image often enough, and the world understands what it is a Jeep can do better than almost any other car. But for MaxiMarketers there is a second dimension of TV spot and network advertising that is waiting to be fully exploited.

We have long touted the effectiveness of "direct mass marketing"—i.e., combining television advertising's emotional impact with the power of a direct-response follow-up, and thus providing the ultimate one-two punch.

You can see "direct mass marketing" at work in the Lebenthal & Co., Inc., success story.

Jim Lebenthal, who heads the municipal bond broker Lebenthal & Co., Inc., one of the most innovative firms in the field, has provided an outstanding demonstration of the power of this one-two punch through his selling of bonds with a spot-TV advertising budget:

> There was a myth when I started that bonds were an investment for the wealthy, stodgy, or conservative. There is an enduring image of the well-endowed spinster sitting in the parlor, clipping coupons with a pair of gilded scissors. None of the stereotypes are true, of course. Municipal bonds are for everyone. Real bonds are for real people. My problem was to get that across to people who want to invest, but are afraid of bonds.[11]

Lebenthal knows that he is in the direct-response business. Although the spots he runs in local markets are designed primarily to build awareness, they include a phone number to call for more information.

> I am using the most powerful medium, television, to plant an impression about owning bonds that I hope will make a real impression on the viewer when they read my ads in the newspaper or listen to me on the radio. Television breaks the resistance to bonds, which are a mystery to most people. In the bond business, inquiries are our lifeblood. Conventional

wisdom is that it costs $100 per inquiry. Television, especial-
ly when paired off with radio and print, is expensive. But my
advertising program brings me inquiries at $30 an inquiry.
It's because my "spots" on TV make bonds "friendly." My ads
say—that is, me saying, since I am the focus in the ads—
"Aren't bonds wonderful?"

I regard advertising as a form of poetry, in that images are
meant to make you see something or hear something for the
very first time. Advertising mainlines an incontrovertible
truth that reaffirms present set values.

What Lebenthal has demonstrated so well, multinational
advertisers are starting to use on satellite television programming. Already CNN in its European broadcasts may show 15
different phone numbers to call for each country-specific contact. Most of this advertising is for direct-order marketing, but
there is no reason why it can't work for brand-building promotions and service company advertising as well. The willingness
of the consumer today to pick up the phone in response to a
TV offer is far greater than many advertisers realize. Direct-
response television is really the forerunner of interactive television, only it happens to be here *now* and you can take advantage of it *today* anywhere in the world.

CABLE TELEVISION IN A
500-CHANNEL WORLD

If network television has had a difficult decade, cable television has enjoyed constant growth in household penetration,
advertising revenue, and time spent watching.

According to Cabletelevision Advertising Bureau figures,
cable penetration of all television homes rose from 49 percent
in the mid-eighties to almost 66 percent by 1993. Total cable
television advertising revenue in America zoomed from $965
million to over $4.5 billion. And people who subscribe to
cable are watching more of it. In 1988, viewers watched less
than two hours of basic cable a day; now they watch almost
three.

Still, cable TV program audiences remain minuscule by network television standards, because the cable audience is divided up among so many different channels. "If you took all twenty of the biggest cable channels and combined their ratings," says David F. Poltrack, senior vice president for research at CBS, "you'd only get to 48th place among the network shows."[12] Most ad-supported cable networks don't meet Nielsen Media Research reporting standards. Because viewing is spread over so many channels, any one channel will have less than a 1 share (i.e., fewer than 1 percent of all TV sets in use watch the channel), an audience of less than one million homes, and on average less than 0.1 percent of the cable subscribers will watch daily. Of course that's irrelevant for companies that advertise heavily on cable television. They aren't looking for (or can't afford) mass audiences.

THE MARRIAGE OF DIRECT RESPONSE AND CABLE TV

Perhaps the major (and growing) appeal of cable, in an age of niche marketing, is its ability to offer special programs for special interests, in much the same way as special magazines appeal to special interests, providing clearly defined audiences for direct-response appeals. Tune in daytime or nighttime to any cable channel, and you will find that a large number of the commercials are carrying a toll-free 800-number and a "call now" offer. Yes, the usual direct-marketing offers are there, but also a surprising number of mainstream advertisers.

The J. Walter Thompson ad agency has tracked responses over the years and has found that the more targeted the programming in which the agency can place spots, the more efficient they become: they generate more responses (another example of the value of the *yardstick* you are provided with when you call for—and measure—responses). With that in mind, the agency created 60-second commercials for American Hawaii Cruises that ran only on cable, and 30-second spots that ran on broadcast TV. They worked with The Weather Channel to vary the spot endings locally, directing 800-number responses to regional travel agents.

"We think the future for advertising, if you can describe it in one word, would be *relational*," says William Airy, president of Vision Group, TeleCommunications Inc.'s subsidiary responsible for marketing, sales, and advertising for new cable networks. *"Advertisers will begin to build relationships, almost one-on-one, with customers."*[13] This sounds very much like what we were saying 10 years ago, even though at that time we didn't foresee the approaching world of 500 television channels, not to mention what such a proliferation of channels would mean in terms of targeting and interaction.

One example of just *how* targeted cable programming can get is *Living with Diabetes*, a half-hour weekly newsmagazine running on CNBC on Sunday afternoons. While there are other health-care shows on TV, most of them are intended for professionals. "Our show is the *patient* show," says Pat Gallagher, a diabetic who is the program's producer, writer, and host. "It's patient empowerment, selling education, and support." What a great place this would be for makers of diabetes drugs and other health-care providers to place their direct-response commercials.

THE TV HOME-SHOPPING BONANZA

In a sense, TV home shopping on cable is its own, entirely new medium. According to its annual report in 1993, QVC logged over 53 million calls, shipped 34 million packages, sold $1.2 billion worth of merchandise, and increased net sales by 14 percent. TV home-shopping sales on all channels now top $2 billion a year.

What's the appeal of shopping via the television screen? "I bought a lot of crystal from them, because they explain how crystal is made," Loa Booth, a 78-year-old home shopper from Murray, Utah, told a reporter. People shop the HSN and QVC channels "because they perceive that the prices are lower, the service is prompter, the sales help is friendlier, and the product information is better. And it's good companionship."[14]

The annual revenue per one-time QVC customer has risen from $43 in 1989 to $50 in 1993, while the annual revenue per repeat customer has shot up from $380 to $531 in the same period. And clearly, if an item connects with viewers, the advertiser can strike it big.

Stan Herman manufactures chenille robes. During his debut on QVC in October 1993, Herman sold 9689 robes in less than 12 minutes. By the end of the day he had sold 22,312 for $661,000.[15]

As Alan Gerson, Home Shopping Network's executive vice president of marketing, has pointed out, this represents a new way for marketers to test consumer products. He suggests that giving HSN viewers the first crack at a new product gives the manufacturer the benefit of a national test for as little as $100,000. "We can help them figure out the pricing, the packaging, the messaging," says Gerson.[16]

Department stores are watching these developments closely, and a few are even testing the waters. Recently Burdine's, the Miami-based chain, produced an hour-long TV home-shopping program devoted to fashion and beauty that it promoted heavily through newspaper TV listings, a VCR-Plus* number, and radio and TV spots. It also mailed a four-page program to its top customers that listed all the outfits in the fashion show, along with prices. According to a store spokesperson, the show and the vehicles used to promote it cost little more than producing the traditional spring catalog.[17]

Other television advertisers could profit (but probably won't) from studying the powerful communication techniques developed by home-shopping shows and determining which of these techniques could be borrowed or adapted for their own purposes.

TARGET MARKETING VIA RADIO

Radio, long seen as television's poor little kid brother, has been booming in the United States.

---

*As most devoted TV couch potatoes know by now, VCR Plus is a special remote-control device that makes it possible for even the most inept VCR owners to record a time-distant program simply by punching in the published code numbers of the program.

In the first half of 1994, combined local and national spot revenue was up 11 percent over the previous year, according to the Radio Advertising Bureau. Furthermore, radio is expected to grow at an annual compound rate of 7.1 percent over the next five years, "fastest of all the measured media" according to the *Communications Industry Forecast* released in July 1994 by the investment banking firm of Veronis, Suhler & Associates. That 7.1 percent represents a doubling of radio-listening growth, and it will result in radio revenues reaching over $13 billion by 1998. The *Forecast* noted that radio's share of advertising revenue rose to over 11 percent of the total in 1993, despite double-digit increases in cable ad growth and the burst of new advertising options available.

What's going on? A couple of things.

The craze for talk-radio programs like that of the controversial talk-show king Rush Limbaugh, for one, and a new focus on cost efficiency and niche marketing, for another.

Back when FM radio gobbled up many music listeners, many AM stations became mere appendages of the more profitable FM outlets, coasting on marginal profits gleaned from advertising directed to a tiny fraction of the population. Satellite communications, however, have now made it possible for individual stations, unable to afford the high cost of producing their own talk shows, to pick and choose from a range of syndicated programs. For instance, Limbaugh was able to launch his daily three-hour show nationally in 1988, from WABC in New York. By 1990 it was reaching over 100 stations, and in 1994 it ran on 648 stations, reaching 20 million people who heard him at least once a week. The days of mass-market reach on radio have returned!

HITTING THE BULL'S-EYE ON RADIO

Gary R. Fries, president of the Radio Advertising Bureau (RAB), attributes much of radio's revenue growth to the new pursuit of cost efficiency and niche-marketing capability. "Two years ago, advertisers wanted to make sure they put money into reaching the target market," he said at the end of 1993.

"Now they want to hit the bull's-eye and put it down the throat of the potential audience."[18]

Gerry Boehme, senior vice president and research director at Katz Radio Group, believes that radio is booming because during the last recession the industry sold the medium as the cheaper, quicker, and more effective way of reaching target audiences. "Many nationally known advertisers have used radio either exclusively or as their primary promotional tool," he says, citing Motel 6, Snapple, Vermont Teddy Bears, and Hooked on Phonics. He adds:

> The visibility and documented success of these companies led other clients to view radio's potential in a new light. These campaigns worked because all the elements were in place: the right product, a good creative message, and enough reach and frequency to make the plan work.

Tom Moon, the managing editor of *Radio Business Report*, told *The New York Times*:

> Radio is taking some business from other media largely because radio broadcasters have become a good deal more sophisticated in how they market their stations. There's less emphasis today on selling by raw audience numbers and more on saying, "Here's a profile of your consumers, and here's how that matches the profile of our listeners."[19]

As Rebecca Pirto pointed out in *American Demographics*:

> In some ways, radio listeners act more like magazine subscribers than television viewers. They tend to listen habitually, at predictable times, to stations with narrowly targeted formats. They are loyal, identifiable, and cheaper to reach than are TV audiences.[20]

The Vermont Teddy Bear Company of Shelburne, Vermont, used only direct mail until 1990, when it began to advertise on national radio. Barbara Haase, sales and marketing director, says that 800-number sales now account for 90 percent of the company's business, and its catalog mailing list includes more than 500,000 names. The company spends 95 percent of its ad budget on national radio, with most ads being placed on major talk shows, including Howard Stern.

As an indication of how a talk-show host can help an advertiser, Stern—unprompted—debated at length whether he should get his wife a Bear-Gram, a message-bearing bear dressed in one of 150 different outfits. Rebecca Pirto:

> Callers offered various lewd opinions about which outfit Stern should buy; the teddy bears got extra minutes of air time and free testimonials. "The great thing about talk is that the format's looser," Haase says. "On Top 40 [music programs], you get 60 seconds. Then they're on to the next song."[21]

The rise of cellular phones in cars means that a commuter stuck in traffic can order a teddy bear, flowers, or theater tickets within moments after hearing a commercial, a trend that can only continue to grow.

Radio, like cable TV, has fulfilled its promise of providing a well-stocked river in which MaxiMarketers can go fishing for new customers while bonding with existing customers.

MAGAZINES FIGHT BACK

Ten years ago we asked rhetorically: *Can magazines survive the video onslaught?* The answer is that they have done so—and then some. Movies didn't kill stage plays. Free music on radio didn't kill recordings. Free drama on television didn't kill Hollywood movies. And television did not—and will not—kill listening to the radio or reading magazines, newspapers, and books. Every time a communication medium comes under attack, it transforms itself in order to survive. And this is what has happened to magazine publishing.

There are literally several hundred new magazines introduced every year. Magazine circulation continues to grow, both in absolute terms and as a percentage of the U.S. adult population, according to the Magazine Publisher's Association. While magazine ad pages and revenues fell during the 1991-93 recession, they came bouncing back when business picked up.

With possibly three exceptions (*Reader's Digest, Modern Maturity,* and *TV Guide*), the era of the great mass-market magazines—*Life, Look, Colliers, The Saturday Evening Post*—is long gone. Even the mass-market women's magazines—*McCall's, Ladies Home Journal, Family Circle,* and *Woman's Day*—have cut their circulation guarantees as they have become less of a mass and more of a special-interest medium. *McCall's* went from a circulation of 6.2 million in 1985 (its high point) to 4.6 million nine years later; *Family Circle* went from 8 to 5 million in a decade; and *Woman's Day* went from 6.8 million in 1993 to 4.5 million just one year later.

Today there are special magazines for every imaginable interest. New publications announced just in the month of October 1994 included *Remember,* filled with "the people and news we can't forget"; *Fabio's Healthy Bodies Magazine,* "a fitness magazine for people not into fitness"; *Saveur,* which "combines travel with a focus on authentic cuisine from around the world"; *Cinescape,* devoted to movies and TV programming for the male-youth market; *Evolving Woman,* edited for women who are working to enhance their inner-growth process; and *Sisters in Style,* for African-American women "too old for *Right Now!* but too young for *Essence.*"

If you use a special-interest magazine as an advertising medium, you may pay a higher cost per page per thousand *readers* compared to a larger, more general-interest magazine such as a newsweekly, but often you pay a far lower cost per thousand *prospects.*

Some magazines target relatively confined market areas, such as a single region (*Southern Living, Sunset*), a state (*South Carolina Farmer*), or a city (*New York, Chicago, Los Angeles*). And many broad-based magazines offer city segments of their total circulation. It's possible to run a full-page black-and-white ad in the Cleveland edition of *TV Guide* for $490, whereas a comparable ad in the national edition would run you $107,600. This is an opportunity many advertisers overlook (or ignore, because such buys are complex and, on a cost-per-thousand basis, expensive). For direct-response advertisers this is a secret weapon—especially *TV Guide.* You can do A-B split tests in a number of different regional editions at modest cost, then roll out the winning ad in the national edition. *Time* offers a choice of 11 regional, 50 state, and 50 city editions.

TRANSFORMING THE MAGAZINE MEDIUM THROUGH SELECTIVE INTERACTION WITH PROSPECTS

Selective binding, which harnesses the computer to the printing press to produce individually targeted magazines, is a technology whose time may finally be coming. It is growing in popularity, and it could offer you a high road to putting the right ad in front of the right person. It is a MaxiMarketer's media buying dream come true.

Currently *Farm Journal, Time, Money, Sports Illustrated, Travel & Leisure, The Atlantic Monthly, Child,* and *American Baby* are among the magazines that can analyze their subscriber databases so as to pick out individuals that are attractive to advertisers and assemble an issue that includes articles and ads targeted to each subscriber and delivered only to the subscribers the advertiser wants to reach. For example, selective binding allowed Cadillac to reach specific audiences within the same magazine database through separate messages; ads published in those copies delivered to young, affluent car buyers promoted the Allante model, and ads in copies sent to mature car buyers promoted the Fleetwood model.[22]

Farm Journal gives us some idea of where selective binding may go. The agricultural magazine offers a choice of 7 national and 8 regional editions, 26 state editions, 8 crop-market editions, 5 special editions for larger producers, and 405 combinations of demographic factors such as crops, acreage, livestock, and degree of business involvement. R.R. Donnelley & Sons' patented computerized selective-binding system automatically assembles a collection of articles, ads, and inserts for each subscriber, depending on the reader's agricultural specialty and other details found in the magazine's database.

The system prints and puts together more than 700,000 issues every month, and one month the printer assembled

8896 different versions of the same issue (counting the various combinations of advertising and editorial material, and renewal messages to readers whose subscriptions were expiring). This means that Mobay Chemical could reach most of America's wheat farmers but exclude those in Florida, Alabama, Georgia, and the Carolinas. Sperry New Holland has used the system to target only the largest dairy, hay, and beef producers and ignore soybean and hog producers.[23]

On the consumer side, only 25 percent of *Travel & Leisure*'s subscribers received a 28-page section on European travel bound into their March 1993 issue. The magazine used the American Express database and predictive modeling to identify those subscribers most likely to travel to Europe and stay at a luxury hotel, and only those subscribers found the special section in their copies of the publication. By eliminating the waste of running the section in copies going to those not interested, the relatively small cost-premium of selective binding was easily affordable. Selective binding enables magazines to offer the targeting power of direct mail at a fifth or a tenth of its cost.

Just as a magazine can bind in a special section, it can also bind in a card that includes such customized data as the subscriber's name and address, preapproved finance limits from General Motors Assurance Corp. for a Blazer purchase, and a printed list of three or four dealerships that are within, let's say, 15 miles of the subscriber's home.

GM ran such a card insert in *Time, People,* and *Sports Illustrated* in the fall of 1994. Combining the subscriber lists of all three publications, GM went looking for the characteristics of those readers who currently drive Blazers, Explorers, or Grand Cherokees. Those subscribers who matched this composite profile were targeted as those with a high probability of buying a sports utility vehicle as their next auto purchase, and were selected to receive the special customized insert card with the preapproved financing.

"We've done this before in bits and pieces, but never anything this integrated between media and direct marketing," one GM executive told *Inside Media,* and a magazine executive added, "it's a very crowded field with auto launches this fall, and GM wants to make sure it can do something to stand out of the pack."[24] Could one possibly ask for a better example of the MaxiMarketing process of *selective interaction* at work?

Chrysler ran a similar effort for its new Cirrus. It matched car registration information from R.L. Polk & Co. with subscription lists from four Time Warner publications—*Time, Sports Illustrated, Money,* and *Life*—and identified subscribers who own Honda Accords, Toyota Camrys, and Nissan Altimas that are less than four years old. Those subscribers received in their copies an eight-page insert with detailed product information about the Cirrus. The clear goal was to lure young families away from their Japanese imports, and while in the past auto marketers have aimed magazine ads at specific zip codes, the Chrysler campaign is the first to have "this degree of specificity" says a Time Warner spokesperson.[25]

REACHING THE TARGET AUDIENCE WITH A CUSTOM MAGAZINE

In addition to targeting individual readers of a publication through selective binding, another important trend among magazine publishers is custom publishing. Magazines like *Colors* from Benetton; *Elements* from Timberland; *Masters Choice* from A&P; *Target the Family* from Target Stores; *Sony Style* from Sony; *Know How* by General Motors; *Tell,* a teen magazine from the NBC television network; *Your Body & Your Health* from Jenny Craig; *Beauty* from Mary Kay Cosmetics; and *Sun* from Ray-Ban (Bausch & Lomb) represent a break with the past. These company magazines are published by the same people who produce traditional magazines, and some of them welcome advertising from other, noncompeting companies.

David Whalen, the vice president of marketing at Bausch & Lomb's eyeware division, says that Ray-Bans' purpose in publishing its own magazine is to go beyond the limits of traditional advertising and bring readers several messages about the sunglasses. It is part of the firm's plan to get people to buy and wear at least one and maybe more than one pair of Ray-Bans. "We want readers to say, 'Wow! This magazine has demonstrated to me that sunglasses should be an integral part of my attire. I should go buy a pair of Ray-Bans,'" says Whalen.[26]

THE NEW POWER OF DIRECT MAIL

If you were to ask uninformed people, "What is the largest traditional advertising medium in the U.S.?" most would guess television, with its million-dollar 30-second commercials. They would be surprised to learn that the real leader is direct mail.

According to an analysis by the advertising agency McCann-Erickson, U.S. direct-mail expenditure rose from $7.6 billion (out of a total of $29.82 billion for all national advertising) in 1980 to $21.95 billion in 1990 (out of an overall national advertising total of $68.99 billion)* In each year of that decade of the eighties, the expenditure for direct mail was greater than those for national newspaper advertising, magazines, or national television advertising. And according to a 1994 forecast by Veronis, Suhler, and Associates, direct-mail expenditure was expected to keep on rising and reach $39.5 billion by 1998.

---

*Is all this requested and unsolicited mail wasteful? Ecologically, yes—but arguably less so than newspaper advertising. Half of your daily newspaper is occupied with advertising that is "junk" to you if it doesn't happen to be relevant to your current needs and interests. Discarded newspapers make up 20 percent of U.S. waste landfill. This means that roughly half of that, or 10 percent of the landfill, is made up of "junk advertising" in the newspapers. Direct mail amounts to only 2 percent of the landfill, or one-fifth as much.

This isn't meant to minimize the long-range ecological problem of printed advertising in any form. Perhaps someday, electronic communication will make it possible for our free-enterprise, post-industrial society to reduce the amount of paper produced, used, and discarded. But right now that day seems a long way off—and any possible answer is far beyond the scope of this book.

In terms of the cost-benefit ratio, direct mail is expensive but not wasteful. Indeed, it is the only medium (with the possible exception of the telephone) with a provable direct payback exceeding the combined cost of producing the mailing and the cost of what it is selling. It may rank highest in cost per thousand impressions, but it is lowest in cost per prospect or customer communication and response.

By far the greatest part of this expenditure, of course, will be for what is still quaintly called "mail-order" marketing—now a misnomer, in view of the fact that today's customers order by phone and fax (and now by computer) more often than by mail. Direct-order marketing is a more suitable term today.

And of course a huge part of that expenditure is accounted for by catalog marketing. In 1980, mail-order marketers mailed almost 6 billion catalogs. By 1994 that number had risen to almost 13 billion.

Other important direct-mail categories are business-to-business marketing; book, record, and CD-ROM clubs and continuity programs; fund-raising; promotions by department stores and other retailers; and publication subscription acquisition.

By and large this book is not concerned with pure "mail-order" direct mail, since that usage has *always* been forced by the stern rules of measurable payback to observe many of the principles of MaxiMarketing. Direct mail often *does* fall short of this ideal, however, when it is an integral part of a broader program of marketing and distribution. And there has been a significant increase in the last 10 years in this new use of direct mail for brand-building, prospect follow-up, and customer cultivation—where the direct-mail program's objective is not an immediate direct sale.

HEINZ SWITCHES FROM TV TO DIRECT MAIL IN THE U.K.

One of the most significant shifts in this direction by a leading brand advertiser occurred in the United Kingdom in May of 1994, when H.J. Heinz announced that it was eliminating $8 million in TV product advertising for its famous ketchup, beans, and other brands, and replacing it with a product-focused direct-mail campaign.

According to a company statement, Heinz will now be spending the $8 million on an umbrella corporate campaign, while individual products will be promoted with a totally new $8 million expenditure, earmarked for mailing directly to the best prospects for each brand.

It was a bombshell announcement that produced big head-lines in every business publication in the United Kingdom.

What was startling was that this wasn't just a tactical move in support of one or more products. It was a change in strate-gic direction formulated at the highest corporate level.

In the United Kingdom, store brands and private-label brands represent about 33 percent of supermarket sales (com-pared to about 18 percent in the United States). This makes the plight of mass-advertised brands that much more urgent. Retailers with their own store brands have become prime competitors with an important advantage: they know exactly who is buying what, in real time. What brought Heinz to the realization that changing times call for changing media choic-es was their earlier success in using direct mail to move their baby food brands.

A Heinz spokesperson in the United Kingdom said:

> With the baby food campaign, we addressed the fact that only a certain segment of the market is interested in baby food. We now recognize that the same principle applies to other categories. There are some people who only buy Heinz soups or beans. We want to build relationships with individ-ual customers.

INFOMERCIALS: LONG-FORMAT TV COMES OF AGE

Ten years ago we pointed out that half-hour and hour-long commercials were one of the unexplored frontiers of cable advertising. Clever entrepreneurs were even then buying pro-gram-length chunks of time to present a compelling self-help lecture interwoven with direct-response commercials for a home-study course on the same subject. Actually, of course, the entire program was a commercial.

At the time, we noted that image-conscious national adver-tisers could and would turn up their noses at the style and content of these brash and occasionally unscrupulous promo-tions. If they did, however, they would be missing the point: *A*

30- or 60-minute commercial, watched by comparatively few viewers who are prime prospects, may be a better buy than 30 seconds sprayed at everybody, including a few prime prospects.

Today, national advertisers such as Avon Products, Saturn, Eastman Kodak, Revlon, Apple Computer, and Coca-Cola have run infomercials, and the long-format TV segment was projected to add up to $900 million of paid time in 1993. Some 175 such programs ran in that year, more than twice the number that had run in 1988.

The industry also was given a certain legitimacy by presidential candidate Ross Perot's half-hour political programs on network television during the 1992 campaign. "Perot demonstrated that half-hour paid programming has tremendous power to influence people and keep their attention," says Steve Dworman, the publisher of *Infomercial Marketing Report*. "He's one reason you're going to see more traditional consumer-product companies using them."[27]

Advertising agencies have been gearing up to produce infomercials. In 1992, Saatchi & Saatchi formed Hudson Street Partners with infomercial producer Regal Communications. D'Arcy Masius Benton & Bowles, New York, formed Feldman & Associates to develop infomercials for Norelco Consumer Products Co. and Corning. J. Walter Thompson Direct created an infomercial for Eastman Kodak.

Infomercials are becoming more popular with marketers for several reasons. First, consumers respond to them. According to a 1992 Hudson Street Partners survey, 55 percent of all adults admitted to watching an infomercial during the previous year, a number that hits 70 percent among people age 18 to 24. The numbers are about equal for men and women, and there is a positive skew toward higher-income adults.

Some other reasons:

- Brand managers are looking for a competitive edge, and infomercials are relatively virgin territory.
- Marketers want advertising that is measurable and accountable, and a half-hour program can be both.

- Marketers also like the idea that an advertising campaign can actually pay for itself through TV revenue, by soliciting orders or inquiries for follow-up at the point-of-sale at the end of the show.

Apple's first 30-minute infomercial generated 100,000 phone calls, said company president Michael Spindler at their annual meeting. The program, produced by Tyee Productions and Hawthorne Communications, introduced the Macintosh Performa line of personal computers. It ran on national cable and on broadcast TV in 20 major metropolitan markets. The experience was so encouraging that Spindler told the stock-holders, "We are going to try to extend that type of media as we move forward in '95."[28]

A major breakthrough in the art of using the infomercial was made by Philips to introduce its Compact Disk-Interactive system in the fall of 1992. The multimedia player, the first of its kind, connects to a television set and stereo system. It can be used to play games, interact with educational programs, and show movies and CDs. Mark Toner, Philips' advertising director, has said that an initial image campaign coupled with direct-response spots obtained response and awareness, but that the spots did not convey the product's features—and dealers were spending as long as 40 minutes in the show-rooms trying to do so. Said Toner:

> We had to demystify the technology. With thousands of responses, our spots showed us the power of direct-response television. We thought that if a spot could generate that kind of response, imagine what a half-hour show highlighting such things as video games, educational programs, and full-length feature films could do.

Philips developed a "refer-to-dealer" infomercial, "The Great Wall," and spent $20 million to produce it and buy the time. Produced by Tyee Productions of Portland, Oregon, "The Great Wall" was so well done that broadcast stations as well as cable channels were willing to run it. KDKA, Pittsburgh, ran it after a prime-time Pirates game; WPLG,

Miami, ran it at 7:30 p.m. in place of *Wheel of Fortune*; KPIX, San Francisco, ran it at 8:30 p.m.; and KXTV, Sacramento, ran it on a Saturday at 6:30 p.m.

At the close, the show gave viewers an 800 number they could call to get the location of the retailer closest to their zip code. Philips sent callers a kit containing a letter, brochure, software catalog, and listing of additional retailers. According to Toner:

> In the first two weeks we started to see a marked impact on the retail level. Then everything started heading north— reorders, distribution, sell-throughs. Sales increased by hundreds of percentages during the six months "The Great Wall" ran. Our retailers saw the spike in sales, and now they are true believers in the power of infomercial advertising.

Among other benefits, salespeople no longer had to spend as much time demonstrating the product; it was cut to five minutes or less. By mid-1994, Philips had sold 250,000 CD-i units worldwide.

The potential of long-format programming for commercials to introduce new products and to detail the advantages of purchasing high-tech and high-ticket products, which was foreseen a decade ago in *MaxiMarketing,* is finally being realized by today's media explorers.

HOME-DELIVERED LONG-FORMAT VIDEO FOR LESS THAN $2

With VCRs in more than 80 percent of all television households, the time has come to take the videocassette seriously as an advertising medium. As such, it is an advertiser's dream. It offers all the power of television's hypnotic visual communication without its time and media expense limitations.

Instead of being forced to conform to the rigid time requirements of the 30-second commercial, you can take as long as you need to tell your story or show your wares. And instead of worrying about whether your captive audience will resent the intrusion, you can enjoy the deliciously unusual awareness that your viewers *want* to see and hear your advertising because they made an effort to get it!

The cost of duplicating and manufacturing videocassettes has dropped dramatically since we first recommended their use. It is now possible to manufacture and mail a videocassette for less than $2, or about the cost of printing and mailing an expensive brochure. (Production costs run from around $1500 to $2000 a minute.) Many advertisers are using videocassettes successfully today. It's a medium you will want to test if you are selling a product or service that could benefit from a live-action demonstration or visualization.

For example, the Smith Food & Drug grocery-store chain has produced a video that tells prospects about SF&D and gives them a walking tour of a typical store. Now when SF&D opens a new store, it mails these videocassettes to people in the surrounding zip codes. "We're showing people how the store looks before they have the opportunity to walk in," says SF&D spokesperson Shelly Thomas. Some 43 percent of the people who receive the video say it makes them more likely to shop at SF&D. The company has mailed more than 250,000 videos since it opened its first southern California store, and it now mails between 20,000 and 40,000 a year, some of which are recycled. The chain holds a drawing for a free VCR or TV, for those recipients who return their video to their local SF&D store.

Steamboat Springs, Colorado, has produced a video brochure that makes their vacation destination come alive. Steamboat Ski Resort has more than 100 trails on the mountain, computerized ski lifts, restaurants and live entertainment, and hot-air-balloon rides. Every January the resort hosts its annual "Cowboy Downhill" event, a unique rodeo on skis. "The videotape we produced on Steamboat really brings our resort alive," says Charlie Mayfield, the vice president of marketing. "It shows people having fun, the range of skiing opportunities and other kinds of recreational activity, plus the hospitality of the town. People are real friendly here—and on the video you can hear that in their voices." Just try to convey *that* in a brochure! Mayfield adds:

We distribute the video to ski clubs and individuals and to travel agents, who tell us it helps them to sell. Video gives you the advantage of face-to-face presentations where you control the message. It's immediate, it's comprehensive—you can show a lot more in a 15-minute video than you can in a three-page brochure—and it's been very successful for us.

Barry Johnson, CEO of the Duplication Factory, a leading producer of commercial videocassettes, tells us that the industry is producing about 60 million video-marketing cassettes a year, and predicts that this will rise to 80 million by 1997. Because 9 out of 10 households have a VCR, marketers now have "the capability of taking a television message, targeting it directly to the audience they want, and delivering it. Direct mail and television is a very powerful combination." Indeed, Select Comfort, which markets high-end air mattresses, makes a sale to about 2 of every 10 people to whom they send their tapes.

Johnson does point out that some "people are banking too much on the videocassette alone, which is a big mistake." Many marketers and agencies are forgetting the basis of direct marketing. A good advertising video should be accompanied by a personalized letter, a strong offer—not just on the videocassette, but in the printed material as well—an easy response mechanism, and all the other elements of a powerful package.

CD-ROM AS A CATALOG-ON-DISK

Is the CD-ROM the advertising medium of the future?

The answer right now is—nobody knows.

It depends on a lot of things, including improving the technology, installing more CD-ROM drives, and changing the habits of the public.

Here's the biggest concern of all: Once the novelty has worn off, will people (at least people of today's generation) really want to spend lots of their ever-more-precious leisure time roaming through an interactive *advertising* disk?

The answer to that is: It all depends.

If you are selling European tours on a CD-ROM that keenly interested prospects have requested, it can combine all the advantages of selling by computer and by videocassette. Viewers can enjoy both the motion-picture photography of a travel scenes, possible in a videocassette, and the select-and-search capabilities of the computer.

If a consumer is considering the purchase of a $50,000 automobile, then he or she may eagerly devour all the information, visuals, and persuasion about the car that you can offer.

Chrysler Corp. prepared a new-car buyer's guide on CD-ROM, to be distributed with copies of *Multimedia World.* It also passed out a CD-ROM demonstration of its Plymouth Neon model to college students, during its Jeep/Eagle Collegiate Health and Fitness Tour on 50 campuses during the school year.

Also, if a prospect knows exactly what item of merchandise he or she needs and is looking for, a vast mail-order catalog on CD-ROM makes it possible to instantly locate it on the disk, view it in color stills and movies, and learn everything about it he or she wishes to know.

Of course, CD-ROMs are a natural when it comes to selling computer software. One CD-ROM disk can store as much information as 1000 floppy disks, which means that CD-ROM can offer, very economically, demos of dozens of software titles. Or even include the complete software, to be "unlocked" after the prospect has tried the demo and decided to buy it.

When it comes to the development of the whole spectrum of specialty mail-order catalogs on CD-ROM however, there are good reasons for grave doubt, despite all the current hoopla.

The problem is that the vast majority of catalog sales are made to people who are *not* seriously looking for anything in particular, just browsing, perhaps for gift ideas. Again and again they end up getting hooked by something that they hadn't known they wanted, or even that it existed, until they stumbled across it.

With catalogs on CD-ROM, it's a different story. The catalog doesn't come right to your mailbox and your easy chair.

You have to consciously, deliberately seek out its contents on your computer. And it's a huge unanswered question whether people will really develop a fondness for browsing idly through hundreds of computer screens in the way that they flip and skip through hundreds of printed catalog pages—spending hours looking at screens of merchandise they haven't the least intention of buying, rather than watching *Seinfeld* or *ER* on television.

So when it comes to considering an investment in an advertising CD-ROM, we say watch closely, think carefully, and don't be swept away by the hype and hoopla. It may be great for you—but then again, this may be the one you let the other guy try first, with you sitting back to profit from his trial and error.

COMPUTER DISKS AS 3.5-INCH INTERACTIVE COMMERCIALS

Of course, you don't necessarily have to go "whole hog" and put your advertising on a CD-ROM in order to bring interactive advertising to personal computer owners. You can still accomplish a great deal with just a floppy disk, which is cheaper to produce and may be used by far more computer owners.

Since the cost of duplicating one is so modest—as low as $1—many advertisers can afford to send floppies "cold" to lists of carefully targeted prospects. America Online has been enrolling new subscribers by mailing a disk that includes all the software necessary to log onto the service plus five hours of free connect time.

The Buick division of General Motors was one of the first advertisers to discover the power of this new medium. Working with Paula George, who started The SoftAd Group precisely to create such interactive software, Buick ran a page ad offering the disk to readers of *MacWorld* magazine. The publication had a circulation of 200,000, and the ad obtained a 17 percent response. The home computer demonstration brought hundreds of buyers into Buick showrooms, prospects who had never considered owning a Buick automobile before. Eighty-four percent of them said they would show the disk to a friend; 10 percent said they would buy a Buick. In the first year, Buick distributed 67,000 disks, and it has repeated and expanded the program, offering IBM as well as Macintosh versions. By the end of 1993, Buick had given away more than a million disks.

"The software program has resulted in increased sales, test drives, and visits to the dealerships," said Bob Burnside, Buick's national advertising manager. Buick's studies show that because the disk is interactive—the user can request various features, see different models, and play with the disk— consumer retention of the message is higher than with other media, according to Nancy Newell, director of sales for the automotive division of Inmar Group and a former marketing manager at Buick.

Every year Buick sends a letter to people who had requested the software, asking if they would like the new disk. More than 60 percent of them say that they would, says Ms. Newell, adding that 90 percent of the users still have their disks a year later. A note encourages consumers to copy the disk and pass it along to friends, and users do give it to as many as four other people, Newell notes.[29]

THE BOOM IN TELEPHONE MARKETING

As we pointed out in the first edition of *MaxiMarketing*, the telephone is the third-largest advertising medium, having passed direct mail somewhere around 1984 to take its place just below television and newspapers. According to the Direct Marketing Association there are now around 900,000 people involved in telemarketing and telephone sales, one way or the other. Altogether it is estimated that telemarketing sales add up to more than $400 billion a year. Of course this includes inbound as well as outbound calls. At last report there were over 900 full-time telemarketing agencies, and more than 60 percent of them had at least 50 employees.

So what do these statistics mean to you? Simply that if you are not maximizing your use of the telephone in marketing the product, service, or business you are promoting, you are in real danger of being left behind. And if you are accustomed to thinking of telemarketing as simply calling up somebody to sell something, you're missing half the story. Inbound telemarketing is fully as important as outbound, perhaps more so for many businesses, and now it's easily within the reach of almost any business.

Even mass marketers are using inbound telemarketing. Early in 1993, Pepsi sent a direct-response follow-up mailing to 1 million Diet Coke households that had previously received a case of Diet Pepsi to sample. Recipients were invited to call an interactive 800 number and "talk" to the singer/musician Ray Charles. But that wasn't all. Pepsi also asked prospects to use their touch-tone phone to answer questions that would help Pepsi to gain valuable information about brand preference and frequency of purchase. Half a million Diet Coke users made the call.

To support its pharmaceutical business, Kmart has introduced an interactive telephone service called Healthcare Line, and the chain expects to receive 4 to 6 million inquiries of the service annually. The consumer phones a toll-free number and gets to select from 120 health-related subjects in 30 different categories. Along with health-care information, the service suggests an appropriate pharmaceutical product and provides cents-off coupons.

Many companies think that simply answering the phone isn't real marketing, but it is, and often they are overlooking many great opportunities.

REFERRING CUSTOMERS TO DEALERS, AND VICE VERSA

Chapter 8 discusses in detail the importance of building a bridge between the advertising and the sale. A basic way to do this, used by many advertisers with spotty distribution, is to include an 800 number in the print ads or TV commercials that readers or viewers can call for dealer information.

If you do this, be sure you do it well, or you may offend more people than you sell to. As a spot-check from time to time, try calling the number yourself, pretending to be a prospect, and see how you make out.

On a big-ticket item, it often pays to set up a system that sends the name of each phone inquirer to the nearest dealer and assists the dealer in establishing a local follow-up system.

In early 1994, SmithKline Beecham's Animal Health unit began to test an interactive phone service designed to direct consumers to nearby veterinarians. The company created two 30-second television commercials, one urging regular veterinary care for dogs and cats, the other informing cat owners about feline infectious peritonitis and encouraging them to talk to a vet about the virus. An 800 number appeared at the end of the spots.

Consumers who called in were directed through a series of prompts to the nearest participating vet, and they could be connected directly to a veterinary clinic or hospital. "New technologies are really broadening the possibilities for outreach and marketing," said Sarah German, manager of advertising for the unit. "The new program is a great way to focus in on specific consumers and specific vets."[30]

DATABASE BUILDING

Every incoming call is an opportunity to build your database of inquiries and prospects. The answers to a few tactful questions read by an operator from a phone-answering script will enable the operator to enter not only the name and address but also revealing demographic and psychographic details for later customized follow-up promotion.

MCI Telecommunications is offering MCI PromoLink, a service that captures qualified leads for you. The service not only captures caller names and addresses, it will develop mailing lists of qualified leads for you and deliver the information on disks, magnetic tape, hard copy, or all three. When you run a contest and want to pick random winners out of those who call, PromoLink can select the winners at the frequency you choose. And MCI provides documentation so that you can determine how well your promotional 800 number is working, reporting on the number of callers and the amount of time they each use, even identifying individual callers for specific promotions.

It can work like this. Let's say a regional women's apparel retailer has just gained the distribution rights to an exclusive line of clothing. Since several large department store chains also carry the line, the retailer needs to reach prospects quickly with a special promotion to increase visibility. The firm uses an MCI 800 number in its radio and print ads, inviting prospects to call in and become eligible for prize drawings. Winners, randomly selected by MCI PromoLink, receive an accessory item from the new clothing line. The retailer obtains a list of prospects interested in the merchandise.

Another example would be a food service company, currently delivering pizzas, that would like to expand its menu to include Italian entree selections. With a number from MCI— such as 1-800-ITALIAN—listed in the promotional flyer that it includes with pizza deliveries, the company would ask customers to call in to register to win free Italian entrees. Using MCI PromoLink, the company would encourage its customers to try its new offerings while developing a list for future promotions.

THE FAX BECOMES AN ADVERTISING MEDIUM

The fax machine is an entirely new and swiftly growing advertising medium, a medium that no one foresaw a generation ago, when the first office faxes appeared in the form of heavy, primitive, painfully slow, line-by-line scanner/transmitters.

Today fax machines are about as cheap as VCRs, and in 1995 it was expected that 1.4 million would be sold just for home (and home office) use in the United States.

Household fax penetration in the United States still lags far behind Japan, however, where it is around 30 percent. In Germany, which has installed more fiber-optic cable lines than the United States has, there are some 3 million fax machines and an estimated 500,000 are added annually, most of them in the consumer market. But in the United States, the household market is growing so rapidly that penetration is expected to rise as high as 50 percent by the end of the decade.

There are three main uses of the fax in marketing: as a substitute for (or improvement on) direct mail, as a way of placing an order, and as fax-on-demand.

THE FAX AS DIRECT MAIL

It is possible that some day "fax clutter" will be as big a problem as "mailbox clutter" has become. But until that happens, there are scenarios in which advertising "broadcast" by fax offers certain advantages over direct mail.

Instead of the weeks required for printing, inserting, and mailing a direct-mail piece, a fax advertisement can be delivered as soon as it is ready, and responses can come back by fax the same day.

A faxed page costs on average only about 24 cents, compared to twice that for a sales letter with first-class postage. You save again when the response comes back by fax rather than by the more costly business-reply mail.

However, a far broader use of the fax lies in its ability to provide an instant customized response to a request.

FAX-ON-DEMAND: INSTANT INTERACTIVE MARKETING

Fax-on-demand (FOD) is perhaps the first true example of that truly "customized marketing" that marketing experts have been predicting for years. Call a special interactive fax number from your fax phone, touch-tone the catalog number of the information sheet you want, and—presto!—it immediately comes rolling out of your fax machine.

The Macintosh software catalog MacWarehouse uses this capability to provide additional information on many of the items in its catalog. Call their FaxFacts number, punch in the code number of the item you want to know more about, and receive a whole page of additional information.

The Programmer's Shop in Hingham, Massachusetts, was in 1989 one of the first direct marketers to install FOD as a literature-fulfillment system. Other computer software vendors have followed suit. Today, travel-service providers, telecommunications equipment sellers, publishers, financial services, radio stations, pharmaceutical manufacturers, realtors, and the federal government are among the organizations that use FOD.

In 1994 the California Department of Tourism used FOD to instantly transmit encouraging news about travel conditions, to inquirers worried about the aftereffects of the Los Angeles earthquake of that year. It worked so well that the following year they conducted an improved FOD campaign—without an earthquake.

Doubleday lists 10 book titles of related interest on the back jacket of *The One-to-One Future* by Don Peppers and Martha Rogers. By calling the autofax number provided and punching in the numbers of the books chosen, readers immediately get back a fax providing more information on each selected title. The book jacket is free advertising since Doubleday has to print it anyway, and the faxes deliver ads to exactly the people the firm wants to reach.

If you are in any business where your prospects have fax machines, and if you want to offer more information about your products or services than you can easily fit into an advertisement or catalog or if you have to update specifications or prices frequently, you ought to be evaluating a fax-on-demand system.

ON-LINE SHOPPING: THE ELECTRONIC MALL OF THE NEW MARKETING

Clearly, the TV home-shopping networks we discussed previously are early examples of electronic shopping, but in the months and years ahead you're going to be bombarded by a steadily increasing crescendo of announcements and pronouncements about shopping with the click of a computer mouse—advertising sent to or accessed by personal computers through commercial on-line services and via access to the World Wide Web of the Internet.

America Online, with over 3 million subscribers, has its own shopping service, "2Market." When you go 2Market, you don't just go shopping electronically, you become part of an interactive shopping community. When introduced, it was your input that made this shopping environment so different. Behind the "Shop Talk" button, which appeared on all the screens throughout 2Market, the customer found "Message Boards" asking you to "Tell Us What You Think" and "Customer Service" buttons for chatting with AOL, the merchants, or other shoppers.

Worldwide there is the Internet, a vast web of computer networks. With easy access provided by commercial on-line services, such as CompuServe, America Online, Prodigy, and the Microsoft operating system connection, the Internet's tens of thousands of destinations are now within the reach of millions of computer users.

Currently there is a kind of code of honor among users of the Internet that forbids them from blatantly working an unrelated commercial plug into an on-line discussion group or message center. But an advertiser-sponsored service or site on-line is a different matter entirely. If an advertiser establishes a homesite or becomes an advertising sponsor of an information service on the Web (or on one of the commercial services), and interested users voluntarily seek it out, that is on-line advertising that isn't being condemned by Net surfers, and in fact represents a bright future for many advertisers.

The rush by marketers to establish World Wide Web sites (sort of like opening an electronic storefront) at times resembles the Gold Rush that sent the '49ers west in search of riches. Lens Express is selling eyeglasses and NordicTrack is marketing their exercise machines. In Santa Cruz, California, computer buffs are using their computers to order pizza from the local Pizza Hut. And a tiny company called Sandal Dudes is peddling rope sandals from its World Wide Web site and has attracted shoppers from 35 countries.

You can visit Holiday Inn in cyberspace, plan a trip on Southwest Airlines, get the latest spa news at the Reebok planet site, shop from the Spencer Gifts catalog, and check out the checking at Wells Fargo Bank.

In Europe, America Online and Bertelsmann, the giant German multimedia publisher, have established a $100 million joint venture to launch on-line services in Germany, France, and Britain and eventually in other European countries. Until now, services have been limited to national networks run by state telecommunication systems or small branches of U.S. providers.

According to *Time* magazine:

> Bertelsmann hopes to overwhelm the few existing on-line services in Europe with more appealing formats, combining international offerings with local content, custom and language. With that formula, Bertelsmann expects to generate $690 million in user fees from more than a million young, well-educated, and high-income subscribers by the year 2000.[31]

Toyota has engaged in an interesting pioneering effort at new-car promotion on-line. It involved a cross-match of their database of 8 million Toyota owners with Prodigy's database. They found that 140,000 Toyota owners also subscribed to Prodigy's on-line service. Toyota sent promotional e-mail via Prodigy to each of these owners, and 10,000 of them requested and received more information by mail. Of those prospects, 1.6 percent—160 people—have bought a new Toyota.

Japan's leading car manufacturer also offered other forms of interaction besides promoting immediately traceable sales. Toyota owners were exposed to a Prodigy screen where they could click on such menu choices as a "Toyota Bulletin Board—Talk with Toyota Owners across the Country"; "Tell Us What You Think—Your Opinion Is Important"; "Customer Assistance Center—Get a Personal Reply to Your Questions and Comments"; "Toyota Today"; "Caring for Your Toyota"; "Owner Services"; "The Toyota Line"; and "Free Brochure." Establishing a direct channel with just 140,000 Toyota owners out of a database of 8 million may not seem like a lot. But it foreshadows the day when car manufacturers will use on-line messages and bulletin boards to cultivate personalized relationships with millions of prospects and loyal owners.

What we are seeing is a great leap forward for the MaxiMarketing selective interaction model that may profoundly change the way goods and services are sold throughout the world. At this point it is extremely difficult to foresee where or how far it will go in the twenty-first century, but almost certainly it is wise to start experimenting with it.

THE BOTTOM LINE

When it comes to media, it's changing almost every minute. You need to keep informed as to what is available to help you reach your target audience, and you also must mobilize your creative resources to work out how to best use the bewildering variety of media choices available to you today.

Maximizing media exploration means learning how to make use both of the new media that have become available and of the existing media in new ways. Today's cornucopia of media options is overflowing with more opportunities than anyone could have envisioned even a few years ago. What is most exciting from a MaxiMarketing perspective is the interactive ease provided by so many of the new media options.

We strongly urge you to add a response element to all of your media explorations whenever and wherever that is possible. For this is just about the only completely accurate way in which you can compare the advertising effectiveness of a variety of media sources and decide definitively which can do the job for you. Better still, the responses you get will initiate a one-to-one relationship with a prime prospect or a new tryer whom you can then convert into a loyal, big-spending customer.

MAXIMIZED ACCOUNTABILITY

THE SEARCH FOR MAKING ADVERTISING TRULY ACCOUNTABLE

THE BIG PICTURE

*All advertising campaigns—even those seeking direct orders—
begin by fostering a favorable attitude toward the product or
service advertised. The big difference in this respect between
direct-response and brand-awareness advertising is that the
latter must create a lasting impression. A favorable perception
must linger on in the prospect's mind until the opportunity or
need arises at the point-of-sale to do something about it.*

*The MaxiMarketing model demands that all advertising—
whether for building a brand image or making an offer that
adds qualified prospects to a database—be fully and truly
accountable. When advertising calls for a direct response, we
know at once if the attempt we have made to create actionable
interest in what we are selling has been successful. By taking
immediate action, the respondent tells us right away. When we
fail to get a response, we can learn where we have failed by
isolating the various parts of the message and testing the
headline, the offer, and the positioning separately.*

*But in advertising designed only to build a lasting image of a
brand, a company, or a service, it takes much longer—in the
United States, the United Kingdom, Germany, or Japan*

sometimes $5 million, $10 million, or $20 million longer—to find out what has failed and why.

How often have you read in the weekly advertising press of the failure and abandonment of a campaign theme that had been introduced with such enthusiasm and confidence only a year or so before? How often have you winced at the embarrassing excesses of confusion and irrelevance in advertising, and wondered what was wrong with the advertiser's copy research?

The problem is that attitude changes over time are much tougher to measure than immediate actions. The predisposition-to-purchase and image-building effects of the advertising depend not only on its content but also on the breadth and frequency of its exposure over a period of time.

The search for a research method that will reliably indicate advertising effectiveness is as old as advertising itself. But even among the practitioners themselves, fundamental doubts remain about the value of any such method.

What is surprising is that a remarkably effective alternative to today's widely accepted and grossly imperfect copy-research methods does exist.* It makes possible exact comparisons of advertising alternatives, not just the old campaign versus the new, but comparisons of a number of possible new campaign approaches and of various ways of presenting different elements in the advertising tested one against the other. It is inexpensive. It takes place in the real world rather than in a simulated environment. And over and over again it has been proven to work reliably.

What is required of you is an open-minded willingness to put aside the failed copy-testing techniques of the mass-marketing era and to rediscover and update the effectiveness-measurement tool of the MaxiMarketing process.

---

*Chapter 4 discussed the value of adding a response element to your advertising, as a means of evaluating and ranking the cost-effectiveness of your media buys. Keep in mind as you read this chapter that everything we say in it about the worth of measuring copy effectiveness through direct response is equally true of measurement of media effectiveness.

While the advertising industry boomed throughout the late 1970s and most of the 1980s—total U.S. ad spending grew faster in most years than the gross national product—it stumbled badly at the beginning of the 1990s. There were no longer double-digit growth increases, and ad spending in certain media—notably network television and among large-circulation magazines—actually fell from one year to the next. A relatively mild economic recession provoked an advertising depression. How come? Here's what *Business Week* had to say:

> To many marketers, the reason is as simple as it is scary. The recession has laid bare forces that are giving advertising a permanently diminished role in the selling of goods and services. Cynical consumers are wearying of the constant barrage of marketing messages. They're becoming less receptive to the blandishments of Madison Avenue. And their loyalty to brands has eroded, as they see more products as commodities distinguished only by price.[1]

To boost quarterly sales, brand managers have shifted marketing money from image advertising to promotions: coupons, contests, and sweepstakes. The percentage of the marketing budget committed to advertising declined steadily over a decade until it represented less than one-third of all marketing dollars, almost a total reversal of the situation at the beginning of the 1980s. Then just when advertising was being written off, expenditures moved upward again as managers raced to protect the value of their brand equities. But the warning bell sounded by *Business Week* continues to haunt the halls of Madison Avenue.

Although the exact percentage would be difficult to come by, it seems fair to guess that as much as half of the roughly $150 billion that U.S. advertisers do spend annually in national measured media is devoted to pure, brand-awareness advertising. And yet despite the hundreds of millions of dollars that companies spend on advertising and marketing research, *no one has been able to accurately isolate and measure the direct effect on sales of any particular awareness advertising for a product or service.*

"Advertising, as a marketing and communications tool, will never command the respect it deserves until the correlation between share-of-voice and profitable growth is firmly established," said DeWitt F. Helm Jr., president of the Association of National Advertisers, at the group's 1993 annual meeting.[2]

THE NAKED EMPEROR: TODAY'S ADVERTISING RESEARCH

Christopher Whittle addressed this topic as the keynote speaker at the Advertising Research Foundation's 1991 annual meeting. While Whittle and his alternative media company have fallen on hard times, his observations about advertising remain as valid as when the company was the toast of Madison Avenue.

Early in the 1980s, Whittle said, he began to notice something unusual in the studies his company routinely conducted to measure advertising effectiveness in different vehicles. The studies looked at consumer awareness and other factors, before a campaign and after, as influenced by various media— Whittle's alternatives, plus the traditional television, magazine, and newspapers. Said Whittle:

> There would be long discussions between us and our clients about whether the movements in the test cells (which measured our new vehicles) were large enough, but nothing was ever said about the fact that the control cells (which represented all other spending) almost never moved.

At first, Whittle tentatively asked clients what they thought about this. Did it bother them that the $20 million they spent in the control cell showed no change? "Any time we brought this up, there was an almost noticeable discomfort, and the subject would invariably be changed," he told the ARF.

As time went on, Whittle noted the same pattern in study after study and became increasingly curious. One day, during a discussion of his test cell's response versus the control cell's inactivity, he suggested to the client, "Why don't you just pay us based on how we perform against the control cells? If we're better, pay us more, and if we're less, pay us less." No one was interested.

Whittle said he began to wonder why, after 20 years in the business, no one had ever shown him a piece of research that definitively demonstrated the effectiveness of their advertising in the traditional media—if only because it would have been a good negotiating tactic.

> Originally I had thought they *must* have this information. Why would they continue to spend all this money if they didn't? Then it struck me that perhaps it wasn't there. So I decided to do some investigating.

He met privately with a number of research and media executives of America's biggest advertising spenders and with the heads of some of their largest research suppliers. To a person they told him that they had no proof that the great bulk of advertising worked. Whittle quoted one as saying, "We don't measure one medium against another because we don't think either will work." Said another, "We stopped doing effectiveness research years ago."

In the end, Whittle's persistence uncovered a shocking truth that most advertisers would rather not talk about. *It is exceedingly difficult to predict before the fact or measure after the fact whether any given advertising effort is or is not successful.* True, anecdotal evidence of advertising effectiveness abounds: "We ran this campaign in a test market. Sales went up 10 percent. It must have been the advertising." But what was the competition doing? Had the economic climate changed in any way? Did the sales force get better shelf space?

What is missing is the capability to *improve* an advertising campaign by scientifically measuring the effectiveness of one single advertising message versus another. And by "measuring" we don't mean observing what people say they *intend* to do, or *seem* to have done, or *ought* to do based on the impact of the advertising. We mean precise measurement of their actual response to real advertising in a real-life situation. Many advertisers and agency executives throw up their hands and say that such measurement not only is impossible but would be meaningless if it *were* possible, because so many other factors affect a purchase.

Of course, there is one kind of advertising that has never had an effectiveness-measurement problem. Direct-response advertising has always had a secret weapon that has enabled direct-order marketing to grow from its modest beginnings— small mail-order ads in nineteenth-century farm publications—into the major selling force it has become today. According to the latest *Annual Guide to Mail Order Sales* by Arnold Fishman, U.S. mail-order and phone sales totaled an astounding $237 billion-plus in 1993.[3]

Why has direct marketing, driven by phone, fax, and mail response, grown so phenomenally? Precisely because the advertisers *could* tell how their ads were doing, and thereby improve on that performance. Michael Dell, when he began to sell personal computers directly to the end users in the 1980s, could measure precisely the actual responses he received to real ads in real-life situations. He could see what worked and what didn't work by counting the number of phone calls received and reply cards returned for each advertising insertion. He went on to build a $4 billion business totally dependent upon his direct-response advertising.

But when it comes to advertising that has not been shaped to lead directly to a sale, the use of direct response as a way of measuring and comparing effectiveness has been largely ignored. When it comes to advertising that is intended to position the product or improve its image, companies place great reliance on research methods that the experts themselves admit (as we shall see) to be woefully inadequate.

The truth is that a great deal both of advertising and of marketing research devoted to advertising effectiveness is a fairy-tale emperor who, as any child can see, has no clothes on—or at least one caught with his pants down and his knobbly knees showing. Sometimes it seems as if most advertising accountability research is conducted by an army of the blind leading the blind. They are brilliant, knowledgeable, and sophisticated, and they are equipped with fiendishly ingenious procedures and technology, but they are doing their darndest to observe and describe an elephant that they have never seen. So the answer may come out: "Very big; tough hide; and what appears to be two tails." And sometimes it turns out not to be an elephant at all—because it goes on to lay an egg....

Do we exaggerate? Of course we do. Marketing research related to advertising expenditures can yield large amounts of valuable information about desirable product attributes; about brand acceptance and positioning and ranking; about measurement of share of market and share of mind. About almost everything *except*

> "How effective is this advertisement going to be in producing sales?" OR
>
> "How many *more* sales would this *other* advertising approach produce?" OR
>
> "How does our advertising in *this* medium compare with this *other* medium, in its actual effect on the target audience?"

LIMITATIONS OF ADVERTISING COPY RESEARCH FRANKLY CONFESSED

In their never-ending quest for meaningful evaluation of advertising copy, researchers have used basal skin response, brain waves, eye movement, pupil dilation, physical activity, aided and unaided recall scores, noting scores, copy-point recall, visual and slogan recall—to name a few techniques. They have measured interest and attitudes toward the brand, product attributes and benefits, buying intentions, coupon redemption, and simulated sales response.

They have used a variety of research designs: "pre/post" versus "post" only, single versus multiple exposure, projectable versus nonprojectable samples, and natural exposure versus forced exposure. They have tested individuals and groups, done the research in homes, in malls, and in central facilities, and tried to simulate a natural setting by introducing competitive advertising and program material or simply by asking questions about the ads after showing them in a portfolio.

And *still* the question hangs in the air: "Will this proposed advertising help us to sell more product?" Here's an eminent authority on the subject, Dr. Edward M. Tauber of the University of Southern California, Los Angeles, writing in the *Journal of Advertising Research:*

> "How will this copy perform?" That is the never-ending question asked by advertisers around the world. It is a question that researchers must address *in spite of the inadequacies of our tools to give a thoroughly satisfactory answer.* [Emphasis added][4]

Remember Rosser Reeves (the advocate of the hard sell)? His type of commercial wouldn't score very well by today's standards—many, many people don't like them at all. But "a hard-sell advertisement," he preached to horrified ears, "like a diesel motor, must be judged on whether it performs what it was designed to do. Is a wrist bone ugly? An ear? Or are they beautifully functional?"[5] As Reeves later recalled, his Anacin boxes "were the most hated commercials in the history of advertising." But in 18 months they raised Anacin sales from $18 to $54 million.

Please don't misunderstand us—we are not arguing for a return to Rosser Reeves' pounding on our eardrums. Times have changed, and so have consumers. A television viewer with the remote control ever at the ready is much less willing to sit through an offensive commercial than one who has to get up from the couch and find another channel.

We are simply emphasizing that research often goes to great lengths to measure irrelevant things, including people's *opinions* about advertising or their *memories* of it rather than their *actions* as a result of it.

A recent cover story in *Fortune* carried a startling title: IGNORE YOUR CUSTOMER. What the business readers soon learned was that the author was telling them to ignore what people *say* they will do and pay more attention to what they actually *do*. Consumer taste-test panels insisted that they preferred New Coke to the original formula, but it bombed when it hit the market. Consumer research panels turned thumbs-down on fax machines, VCRs, Federal Express, and CNN before they were launched and became wildly successful.[6] One begins to wonder whether U.S. business isn't spending billions supporting a marketing-research establishment almost as wasteful as the Pentagon is, with its fabled cost overruns when dealing with some of our military defense contractors.

When Kevin Clancy (for years one of the principals of the renowned Yankelovich, Clancy and Shulman, and now the chairman of Copernicus, a marketing research consulting firm based in Westport, Connecticut) first went to work for the BBDO Advertising agency as a young marketing researcher in the late 1960s, the agency's executive vice president put him on a special assignment. BBDO wanted to publish a book on great advertising, featuring examples of ad campaigns that dramatically affected sales and produced a solid return on investment. The executive asked Clancy to scour the agency's files, talk to clients, read the academic and business literature, and even interview competitive agencies to find such examples for the book.

The executive assumed, of course, that Clancy would unearth these cases easily. Those were the days when advertising creativity was reaching new heights of marketing importance, and ordinary consumers frequently discussed ads at dinner and cocktail parties.

After months of research, Clancy turned in a depressing report. Great sales-producing advertising was hard to find. He had to report that "few cases existed....By and large, advertising with proven sales results was as rare as deer in Manhattan."[7] No book was written.

Larry Light, today president of Arcature Corp., a marketing consulting firm based in Stamford, Connecticut, said that when he was the BBDO research director a generation ago, "We learned that all copy-testing techniques have an inherent degree of unreliability greater than most users would like."

Suppliers, he observed, "assure us that their techniques are reliable, valid, and furthermore are a bargain at twice the price." But when he paired different testing techniques against each other, he found that no method could consistently pick a winning commercial. "We were concerned that research companies were getting richer than our clients."[8]

And has the situation improved of late? Alvin Achenbaum, as vice chairman of professional services at Backer Spielvogel Bates Worldwide, at a breakfast conference sponsored by the American Marketing Association in New York City, fired a volley that should have echoed up and down the canyons of Madison Avenue (and Park and Third, where more agencies are located today):

> Copy tests are in my opinion no better than market tests in their performance. To take the most prevalent technique used today—so-called "recall tests"—irrespective of the number of studies done which show that recall measurements are irrelevant, that they are not in fact related to consumer purchase proclivities or purchasing behavior, marketers continue to use and rely on that measuring stick.... But copy tests lack far more than a relevant measurement device. The fact is that they fail on almost every aspect of good research design—from the small samples they use to the unrealistic stimuli involved, to name only two.
>
> Frankly, the money spent on all of this foolish research is a waste, and, as such, a drag on marketing productivity. It may be a necessary lubricant for decision making, but it certainly is an expensive and misleading one.[9]

It would seem from the record that as far as copy research is concerned, never before has so much money been expended to so little effect.

NOW FOR A DOSE OF REALITY

When we were still running the Rapp & Collins advertising agency (which has now evolved into Rapp Collins Worldwide), we had a rare opportunity to compare the accuracy of predictive consumer-interview research and actual direct-response results. We were then working for a record club that hired a research company to conduct in-depth interviews of prime prospects and show them eight different direct-response member-enrollment ads under consideration for the club. The 104 prospects were all people who had bought records or tapes within the previous six months and had bought something by mail in the previous three years.

The researchers asked them to rank the eight ads according to "uniqueness," "interest in reading further," "believability," and "interest in responding." The results of this research predicted that the winners would be the ads nicknamed "Guarantee" and "No Fine Print." According to the research, "Headphones" ran a poor fifth and "Cartoon" a miserable last.

TV Guide inserts at the time offered the opportunity to do a simultaneous split-run test of a great many different direct-response ads. When we actually ran the ads in a *TV Guide* perfect eight-way split-run,* "Cartoon," a simplistic but very effective cartoon that had consistently beaten other approaches for years, decisively outpulled the ads that the research respondents had chosen as most likely to interest and persuade our record-club prospects.

The panel's responses had reflected more what they wanted the interviewer to think of them than what these record-buyers truly thought of the ads presented. At least some panel members undoubtedly ranked the lowbrow cartoon ad last because they didn't want to appear to be lowbrow themselves. If the company had relied on the predictive research, the profitability of their advertising would have been sharply reduced.

The Wall Street Journal reported that five of seven packaged-goods commercials identified by Video Storyboard Tests Inc. as being the most popular and best-remembered commer-

---

*The advertiser runs Control Ad A versus Test Ad B in alternate copies of Regional Edition 1, Control Ad A versus Test Ad C in Regional Edition 2, and so on. The ads can be printed either on-page or on supplied cardstock inserts. The winning ad is the one, if any, that outpulls the control ad in number of responses.

cials of 1993 were for brands that, according to Information Resources' InfoScan Service, had either flat or declining sales in supermarkets, drugstores, and mass-merchandise outlets.[10]

Pepsi-Cola's spot featuring basketball superstar Shaquille O'Neal was the second most popular commercial of that year according to Video Storyboard (McDonald's was first). While carbonated beverage sales in general were up 4.2 percent, Pepsi's sales fell 1.6 percent. In the same period, Coca-Cola sales were up 8 percent.

The real world and the copy-research world appear to occupy two distinct and separate planets.

THERE MUST BE A BETTER WAY

There has to be a better way to determine whether your advertising is reaching and affecting your intended target. And there is: Incorporate some form of direct-response offer in all of your advertising during the test phase. Then measure the difference between one advertising effort and another by comparing the number of responses received in a scientific A-B split-run test of the two efforts. (Better yet, test three, four, or five possibilities.)

In such a test, the advertiser might supply two different advertisements to a magazine, with the reply address (or phone number) in each one keyed differently, and the publication would then run both ads in the same position in alternating copies of the same issue. In a perfect A-B split, every other copy of the publication would contain ad A and the remaining copies would contain ad B. This advertising research technique meets the same requirements of the scientific method as those that Luther Burbank used when he was comparing the germination of different seeds under identical conditions.

Of course this split-run method can be used with direct mail as well. In fact it is the mainstay of improving direct-mail results—for book and record clubs, magazine subscriptions, charitable and political fund-raising, etc. It can also be used in retailers' direct mail, although such use is rare.

Staples, the chain office-products superstore, divides its customer list in two. "One will get a series of promotions, the other will not," says a spokesperson. "Purchasing behavior can then be measured over the next three months for each group." Staples can then determine the exact effect on sales.

It would be quite costly for direct-order catalog merchants to test one entirely different catalog treatment against another. But catalog firms often do split-test one catalog *cover* against another.

THE LONELY ADVOCATE OF SPLIT-RUN TESTING

Nearly three-quarters of a century ago, advertising pioneer John Caples explained the procedure for this method of precise advertising research. In his classic book *Tested Advertising Methods*, Caples showed how the question of effective advertising can be removed from the realm of opinion and be definitively determined by the actual response of the public.

But the system Caples described gradually fell into disuse. Except for its continued use by direct marketers, it became part of advertising history.

David Ogilvy, one of the great theorists as well as practitioners of advertising, deserves our thanks for having rekindled interest in what Caples advocated. In his foreword to the fourth edition of Caples' book, Ogilvy paid generous tribute to its value:

> On page 11 of this book, John Caples writes: "I have seen one advertisement sell 19½ times as much goods as another." This statement dramatizes the gigantic differences between good advertisements and bad ones....
>
> An earlier edition taught me most of what I know about writing advertisements. These discoveries...have been made by John Caples in the course of his long and distinguished career. He has been able to measure the results of every advertisement he has ever written.

The average manufacturer, who sells through a complex system of distribution, is unable to do this. He cannot isolate the results of individual advertisements from the other factors in his marketing mix. He is forced to fly blind....

The vast majority of people who work in agencies, and almost all their clients...skid helplessly about on the greasy surface of irrelevant brilliance. They waste millions on bad advertising, when good advertising could be selling 19½ times as much.[11] [Emphasis added.]

There are two main thrusts to Caples' book: (1) the testing method, and (2) the principles of effective advertising that he had derived by following that method.

Almost buried beneath the book's welter of practical principles of effective mail-order and direct-response advertising is that timeless but sorely neglected gem, the use of the A-B split approach to improve all advertising. Caples' approach applies the testing techniques of direct-order advertising to products not sold by mail or phone but rather at retail or by a salesperson—products and services usually supported by brand-image awareness advertising.

"WE DON'T KNOW, BUT WE CAN FIND OUT"

When we went into the ad-agency business 30 years ago, we began with an agency positioning that sounds really dumb in retrospect. Our attention-getting slogan was "We don't know, but we can find out"!

Of course, it didn't take us long to realize that an agency proclaiming "We don't know" isn't going anywhere. So we dropped that introductory slogan in favor of a more upbeat positioning. But the spirit that fired the agency's early days never faded for us. We never lost our passion for getting answers by sifting through lots of possibilities with split-run testing. In the first edition of *MaxiMarketing* we strongly advocated the utilization of this proven technique to make advertising more accountable. But in the ensuing 10 years we saw less split-run testing rather than more (except in direct-order direct mail, where it has always been the lifeblood).

You might think that testing is a truism that doesn't need any defenders. Think again. A quick look at the actions of today's breed of direct marketers will tell you differently. Joan Throckmorton, in her wise and witty column "The Creative Eye," carried by *Direct Marketing News,* put it this way:

> Testing is in danger. It's in danger because a lot of companies still don't get it. They think they're direct marketers because they acquire customers and keep a database. They send out direct mail, use print or broadcast, but fail totally to test.

Each month, mailboxes are filled to bursting with updates from a score of relationship marketers who want a slice of their prospects' discretionary income. The lockstep look of the packages received from all of those airlines, hotels, department stores, bank credit cards, and other modern-day direct-relationship marketers is a demonstration of how little testing they must be doing. When everyone in a category looks the same, standardized thinking has taken over.

The question every company newly engaged in direct interaction with the end user must face, whether in the mail, in print media, or on the Internet, is not *whether* to test copy, formats, offers, or other elements of their message—that should be beyond debate. The vital question is the one asked in the next heading.

HOW MUCH TESTING IS ENOUGH?

During the early years of Rapp & Collins we came up with a mathematical formula to calculate how much testing a client should do, then published a Schedule of Optimum Number of Alternatives, called the SONA chart, in one of the trade magazines. The approach we took then is still valid today.

What we found was that too much testing is as dangerous as too little. Either alternative can cut sharply into profitability. What follows are the elements we put into our formula for calculating the optimum number of test alternatives.

First, you want to determine the profit increase expected from a given improvement in results. What would be the impact on the bottom line of doing 10 percent better? What about a 30 percent improvement, or 50 percent, or even 100 percent? Second, what is the average cost for the test packages or test ad inserts you plan to use? Third, what would you estimate are your chances of coming up with a winner, based on your own past experience and the experience of other companies you can benchmark?

What we found was a geometric increase in profit at each increased response level. In one case a 30 percent increase in response brought about a 120 percent increase in profitability. Run your own numbers. You'll be amazed by the leverage hidden away in various incremental levels of response.

Here's a simple scenario. Let's suppose you are selling an item that, after subtracting your product and fulfillment cost and overhead, leaves you $25 per thousand for advertising and profit. If you do a mailing that costs $500 per thousand and obtain a 2.1 percent response, you will get back an advertising and profit contribution of $525, leaving you a profit of $25 per thousand mailed.

Now let's suppose that through testing you are able to improve that response by about 10 percent—you get just two more orders per thousand. Your advertising/profit contribution rises to $575, and your profit per-thousand-mailed rises to $75. So a 10 percent increase in response has resulted in a 300 percent increase in profit!

The more you test, the better your chance of hitting the jackpot. But there's a catch: The more you test, the greater the cost of testing. How do you strike a balance between a reasonable test investment and your chance of coming up with a big winner?

What you are looking for is the number of tests that will give you the best chance of finding a winner for the least investment—in other words, the optimum testing level. What we discovered in our early days at the agency was that we could expect to get an improvement of 30 percent or more from the winner out of the 7 well-conceived test advertising concepts for that product or service.

The moral: Just a little bit of testing may or may not accomplish something. But multiple testing can considerably improve the odds of your finding a better approach.

Once you do decide to step up testing activity, there are three guidelines that you must keep in mind.

1. *Don't substitute opinion for fact.*   If you develop several unusual new offers or totally new ways to position your proposition, don't trust focus groups to decide which you should adopt. People often do the opposite of what they say. To learn what the market thinks of your ideas, test them by exposing them in the real world of print and direct mail, then see which actually pulls more responses.

2. *The least likely is often the most likely.*   The beauty of testing a new approach 8 or 10 different ways is that you are going to include the least likely possibilities along with the most likely in the test grid. Be prepared to be surprised or even shocked by which one comes out the winner. We can recall at least two occasions on which the least promising ad, in our own seasoned professional estimation, came out No. 1.

3. *What is incidental is seldom monumental.*   Maybe you can cut costs while maintaining response, by going from three colors to two colors for the flyer in your direct-mail package. But it's not worth the effort. If it sounds like a good idea, just go ahead and do it and back-test the effect on results later on. Save most of your test cells for those variables that could have a great effect on sales.

    However, it must be admitted that what *is* monumental probably can't be tested. Chivas Regal inserted in a December issue of *The New Yorker* an ad with 13 light-emitting diodes and a switch and battery to run them. The ads, designed by Bronner Slosberg Humphrey, cost around $900,000 (or $3.33 each) to produce and place—more than the magazine's cover price. Absolut Vodka's Christmas ad in *New York* magazine included a pair of black gloves, designed by Donna Karan. The project, created by TBWA, cost about $1 million to produce and place, or $2.22 for each ad. Running ads like these requires an act of faith that they will break through the holiday clutter—as these did. But what a shame that so much money was spent for a single advertisement without adding a bound-in insert card with an offer that would add thousands of names to the prospect database for future targeted offers.

SO WHICH HALF IS WASTED?

Students of advertising are doubtless tired of hearing the famous quote attributed, on this side of the Atlantic, to department store magnate John Wanamaker: "Half of all the money I spend on advertising is wasted. The trouble is, I don't know which half."

We dare to repeat it one more time because we think we know the answer. It isn't *one* half or the *other* that many advertisers are wasting. Rather, *all* of their advertising money is being *half*-wasted, spent only half as effectively as it could be if its impact were doubled by finding out through split-run testing what works best.

We are talking about doing such testing early in the campaign, and if the competition is watching, quietly in a regional area. Why do advertisers in general resist this idea? What could be more important than improving advertising's performance?

By this time we are resigned to the fact that the ad-agency establishment would rather fly blind than be measured by responding consumers. But their loss can be your gain. By using this overlooked secret weapon, you can double or triple the impact of your ad budget and clobber your competitors.

HOW TO DO CAPLES TESTING

The essence of the method of scientifically comparing two advertisements, which Caples wrote about so long ago and which we highlighted in *MaxiMarketing* a decade ago, is the preparation of a number of different print advertisements, each with a single test variable: a different promise, a different positioning, a different form of presentation, even a totally different tone of voice. As a minor element in each advertisement, a direct-response offer is included that is identical in wording and presentation in every ad except for the key number in the mailing address or for use with the phone number.

The offer, which could be for a booklet, free sample, savings coupon, or simply an offer to supply the nearest dealer's name, can invite a response by reply coupon, by letter, by fax, or by calling a toll-free 800 number. The telecommunications breakthroughs that began in the 1970s have added an entirely new dimension to getting an advertising response. Toll-free 800-number phone calls are now an $8 billion industry and American consumers do not hesitate to pick up the phone when moved to action.

The ad that gets the most responses is—we say—also the ad that most likely made the best impression. Something about it made prospective customers in the test situation more interested in what the advertiser is selling. Even if the results are not taken as the final word as to which advertising approach is best, it most certainly provides valuable information. An expanded retest might be called for, or a modification in the direction formerly thought to be the way to go.

It is fascinating to read in the Caples book about a split-run test, done early in this century, of two different appeals for a product that is still around today: Milk Bone, the snack food for dogs.

Both ads carried coupons offering a free gift package of Milk Bone Snacks. Both ads carried the same message that feeding your dog table scraps in the summer is dangerous, and that you should give your dog healthful Milk Bone instead. One ad used a negative appeal, the other a positive one:

Ad A: Don't Poison Your Dog!

Ad B: Keep Your Dog Safe This Summer!

When the coupons had been counted, the advertiser found that Ad B had pulled 58 percent more requests.

Do you find it hard to believe that this was a meaningful result? If you were the marketing director for Milk Bone at that time, wouldn't you have found this to be extremely useful information? Wouldn't it have helped you to develop a sound copy platform? And wouldn't it still cost far less today to develop useful information about consumer reaction to copy claims in this way, than through dubious shopping-mall interviews or eye-movement measurements?

Obviously, you haven't solved everything with an A-B split. You haven't precisely measured the effect of the advertising on retail sales, or the long-term effect of repeated impressions (although you can arrive at some approximation). But you *have* provided yourself with a method for the scientific comparison of one advertising approach against another. You can even, as direct marketers so often do in their direct-response advertising, compare one advertising *element* to another—one headline to another, one graphic element to another, one endorser to another, and so on.

Combining the winning elements into a single advertising effort, as direct marketers so often do, can produce incremental improvements in response of 50 percent, 75 percent, 100 percent, and more.

In his *Confessions of an Advertising Man,* David Ogilvy recounts his use of the Caples technique to develop the best promise for a Dove toilet bar. He reported that "Creams your skin while you wash" pulled 63 percent more responses than did the next best promise, "and it became the fulcrum of every Dove advertisement that followed. This marvelous product made a profit at the end of its first year, a rare feat in the marketing world of today."[12]

If other brand advertisers and their agencies are using the same powerful research method for packaged goods today, it is one of the best-kept secrets in advertising.

WHAT ABOUT CUMULATIVE EFFECT?

One telling argument made against direct-response split-run

tests as a research method is that these tests cannot necessarily measure the power of a theme that depends on massive repetition for its effectiveness.

Take for instance the long-running, highly successful theme that Campbell Soup used for many years: "Soup is good food." The theme flunked the standard copy-testing research. Might it also have lost out in a direct-response split-run test against an ad with some other, more immediately compelling theme, each having the same buried offer?

Or to put it another way, is it possible that "Soup is good food" is a very mild, innocuous claim when heard only once, but grows steadily in power and persuasiveness the more often it is heard? If that were true, measuring comparative response to just one exposure might give a false impression of the appeal's strength.

Let us grant that possibility, even though over the years advertisers have wasted many, many millions of dollars by invoking this convenient explanation of an ad campaign's early lack of effectiveness. And let us also assume that your budget is large enough to achieve this wondrous cumulative effect of repetition. (Without the expenditure of huge sums for the constant repetition of your theme, your advertising isn't going to have *any* cumulative effect.)

Even so, there are still a great many ways that split-testing could develop and improve the *expression* of the "Soup is good food" theme. For example, do you get a better response showing people enjoying soup, or a steaming close-up of the dish itself? Does featuring one particular flavor attract more interest, and if so, which flavor is it? Does the use of a human-interest story featuring a real customer add meaningful impact? Direct-response split-testing can be useful in answering questions such as these at very little cost.

We also can't help wondering: If split-run testing had unearthed a theme that produced a response far *greater* than "Soup is good food," what might the sales impact have been for repetitive exposure of *that* theme? Alas, Campbell's will never know....

THE PROMISE OF ELECTRONIC TESTING

When we did the first edition of *MaxiMarketing*, electronic metering was in its infancy. But now we have a marvelous capability to actually find out how different expressions of the advertising will affect results at the point-of-sale. Unfortunately, for now this is limited to products sold in supermarkets and drugstore chains.

The advent of BehaviorScan has made possible A-B testing of the advertising of brand-name packaged goods in a way that measures the results at a supermarket or drugstore cash register. BehaviorScan permits the advertiser to set up two matched groups of households in six different cable markets. One group sees one advertisement, the other sees another. Because members of those households use a scannable card to identify themselves when they shop, the advertiser can immediately see which commercial had the greater effect.

A BehaviorScan spokesman says, however, that while advertisers spent almost $22 million on the service in 1993, most of them used it to test different advertising *weights* (amounts) rather than advertising *executions*. "They want to know whether additional sales will be worth the additional advertising expense." So there *still* appears to be resistance to letting the public vote with their actions on the issue of which ad approach is better!

Apparently, once the advertiser and the agency team have hit upon the advertising approach, there is little interest in any activity that might prove them wrong. If the anticipated lift in sales does not occur, it is better to blame it on the uncertainties of the marketplace.

CAN CAPLES COMPARISONS DEVELOP BETTER RADIO/TV SPOTS?

When we published the first edition of *MaxiMarketing* in 1986, it was rare to see 30-second commercials that included an invitation to respond by calling an 800-number. Today they are vastly more common. Yet we are not aware of a single television advertiser (except for an occasional direct-order marketer) who is making use of this capability as a copy research tool.

It is true that it is not yet possible to simultaneously expose two or more different test commercials containing an 800 number to two absolutely equal audiences. But you can give them roughly equal exposure by rotating the commercials and finding a way to source-code the replies.

If you spend $500,000 airing 800-number Commercial A, and $500,000 on air time for Commercial B with a different 800-number, the two as evenly intermixed as possible, there's a good chance you will begin to observe that one of the commercials is pulling more telephone calls than the other and generating more interest in the product or service.

We aren't talking here just about testing one commercial with a direct-response offer against another with a different offer, a situation in which testing is obviously a good idea. We are talking as well about testing different awareness advertising commercials in this way, by including in each an identical direct-response offer and coded-reply method.

There is a way this can be done without altering the content of each image-building approach in any manner. You can buy 30 seconds of time for a 15-second test commercial, or one minute for a 30-second commercial. The remaining time could be used for an emphatic, detailed exposition of the offer and for a repetition of the toll-free number. This would have the added advantage of providing a much larger, more measurable, more statistically significant response from each test commercial.

WHY WAS DIRECT-RESPONSE COPY TESTING ABANDONED?

If split-run testing of two or more different ads or commercials with the same direct-response offer is so effective, why has it fallen into such disuse today? The answer is shrouded in the mist of advertising history. But we can hazard a guess.

First, the development of radio and then of television seemed to require—and did produce—new, more elaborate forms of copy research that came to be accepted as the state of the art.

Second, advocates of other research methods bolstered their arguments against direct-response testing with what we believe to be a statistically fallacious argument. This argument was summarized in 1936 in a scholarly book, *Four Million Inquiries from Magazine Advertising,* by Harold J. Rudolph:

> It might be argued that replies do not constitute a representative sample of the magazine-reading population, since only a small percentage of any magazine's circulation is made up of potential coupon-clippers. For example, the average advertisement draws coupons from less than one-tenth of one percent of the readers to whom it is exposed. Therefore, in order to show an increase of 50 percent in replies, an advertisement need only secure responses from an additional one-twentieth of one percent of the circulation. Is this a significant margin? In other words, should one advertisement be considered superior to another because it has elicited response from one-twentieth of one percent more readers?[13]

The counterargument runs, by the immutable laws of chance, *a 50 percent increase in response cannot be explained away as a purely random result. It is a statistically significant difference.** It isn't the size of the circulation that matters, but the relative size of the response.

This is a very complicated question. We will spare you the ordeal of exploring it in detail.

It is useful to keep in mind that advertisers are not concerned with the entire readership of the magazine in which they are advertising, as Mr. Rudolph is. They are—or should

---

*Unless the total number of responses was extremely small. For example, if Ad A pulled 2 responses and Ad B pulled 3 responses, this wouldn't be a statistically significant difference. But if Ad A pulled 200 responses and Ad B pulled 300 responses, that *would* be a statistically significant difference.

be—concerned only with those readers who are prospective purchasers, a percentage that could range anywhere from 1 percent (for a business service) to 70 percent (for a headache remedy).

So the remaining question is this: *Are the responding prospects (the "coupon-clippers" or booklet requesters or dealers' name requirers) somehow different from and not representative of the far greater number of nonresponding prospects?*

What is clearly true is that respondents are different from nonrespondents in one obvious, outstanding respect: They respond! A survey of a cross-section of the population would undoubtedly reveal that some people are more responsive than others—they clip coupons, answer ads, and buy from mail-order catalogs more than people at the other end of the spectrum. It was once thought that such mail-order shoppers were a distinctly different breed of American. But today there are 100 million mail-and-phone shoppers in the United States.

We will grant that an ad devoted entirely to offering a free sample of a product might attract people who care more about getting something for free than do the rest of the audience. But if one advertising description of the free sample makes it seem more attractive and therefore invites more response than another, doesn't that provide a meaningful insight into the impression made on *all* of the prospects in the audience?

Taking this a step further, let us suppose that Campbell's soup has prepared and split-test two different ads. One amplifies with words and pictures the theme "Campbell's Soup Is Good Food." The other expands on a different theme, "Campbell's Soup—A Delicious Way to Save Time." At the bottom of both ads, in tiny type, there is an identical offer: "Write Dept. X [or Dept. Y] for a free booklet of soup-based recipes."

Let's say that "Save Time" pulls twice as many recipe-book requests as "Good Food." Wouldn't it then absolutely defy reason to believe that a survey of nonrespondents would indicate an opposite effect—that the Good Food promise made more of a lasting impression on prospects than the Save Time one—or that there was no difference?

This was the thinking that went into David Ogilvy's test of different advertising promises in introducing Dove toilet bar—and that led to the spectacular result we cited. But alas, in this as in so many other ways, Ogilvy was far ahead of the rest of the advertising world, and most of it still hasn't caught up.

It is true that like all other research methods (except for direct-order testing and possibly BehaviorScan), split-run testing of different ads with an identical offer cannot relate each advertising exposure directly to *an immediate sale.* But it *can* measure and compare public reaction to the advertising message at the precise moment when it is reaching the target audience in the real media environment. By testing A against B and the winner against C and the winner of that round against D and so on, split-run testing can build incremental improvement in the impact and believability of your advertising. Thus, given the glaring limitations of other kinds of copy research, one of the oldest forms of advertising research may become one of the newest. It could become an essential part of your complete MaxiMarketing system for outsmarting the competition.

HOW RESPONSE TESTING MAKES ADVERTISING MORE REALISTIC

Many ads that we see in magazines and newspapers are a product of what we call the "all you gotta do" school of advertising. "All you gotta do" to make an effective ad is to come up with a catchy headline, a striking visual, and a few provocative words. Usually there is some clever play on words that leaves it to the reader to figure out what is going on. (The graphic element may give you a hint, but only a tiny one.) This approach to advertising has perverted Bill Bernbach's "creative revolution," and thrusts its practitioners into a straitjacket of pseudo-creativity.

We believe that when advertisers put advertising creativity into the crucible of asking for a response, then carefully tabulate and compare the number of responses, reality begins to intrude. What you get is an entirely different view of what constitutes the best advertising. Rather than the advertising telling or showing the public what it *ought* to respond to, the public begins to tell the advertiser what it actually *does* respond to. Then "all you gotta do" advertising gives way to creating more responsive appeals, needed facts, desired information, persuasive explanation, unique positioning, buying motivation—and a new order of accountability.

THE BOTTOM LINE

We believe that the effectiveness of almost any kind of advertising, in just about any advertising medium, can be systematically and incrementally improved by (1) incorporating a direct-response element into the advertising, (2) split-testing a variety of approaches, each with the same offer, and (3) incorporating the discoveries thus made into the rollout of the campaign.

Split-run testing is the advertising panacea for "the rest of us"—we advertisers who don't have Nike's or McDonald's or Coca-Cola's megabucks to lavish on burning an indelible image into the public's mind whatever the message might be.

If you can afford an annual budget in the United States of only $5 million or $2 million or $1 million or $500,000—or the equivalent in another nation's economy—to convert your true prospects into future customers, can you afford anything less than sure and certain knowledge as to which of a number of different advertising approaches will move the people you most want to reach? Can you really afford not to use direct-response, split-run testing, to point you in the right direction?

True copy testing is so inexpensive that almost any advertiser can benefit from its use. It can add muscle to your advertising, and it can provide a simple method of verifying the case for whole-brain advertising that we make in the next chapter.

MAXIMIZED ADVERTISING IMPACT

APPEALING TO THE WHOLE BRAIN TO BUILD A BRAND

THE BIG PICTURE

For almost 100 years, two warring camps have struggled for the soul of advertising.

"Single out the prospect! Be persuasive! Present a convincing advantage or benefit!" is the battle cry of the first camp.

"Break through the clutter! Be creative! Be entertaining!" insists the second camp.

"Ridiculous!" snorts the first. "The public may be tickled to death with your advertising—but are you reaching the right people for your product with the right message?"

"Well, I'd rather have them tickled to death than bored to death! You can't save souls in an empty church!"

"Bah! You're just dabbling in creativity for creativity's sake!"

"You're living in the past! You're a slave to the linear, the literal, and the literary, in a whole new age of visual communication!"

Today, this familiar difference in approach (which has come close to causing fistfights in some advertising agencies and creative departments) is taking on new importance—because the stakes have been raised.

Given the exponential proliferation of new products and the dizzying blizzard of advertising messages, it is increasingly difficult for your advertising to be seen, noted, and remembered by your prospect—and it's more costly if you fail. Choosing the best way to present your message is more important now than it ever has been before.

But which way is "right"? The logical, left-brain argument, or the intuitive, right-brain appeal? The truth is, they both are. Each side appeals to a different side of the prospect. Together, they can appeal to the whole person.

Let's examine this historic left-brain versus right-brain conflict, as a prelude to developing a powerful "whole brain" approach and show you how to avoid the perilous pitfall of "No-Brain Advertising."

In our time, the concept of *left brain* and *right brain* has become a part of pop culture to such an extent that it occasionally works its way into comic strips and sitcoms. Perhaps because it is such a convenient explanation—the left hemisphere of the brain controls logic and language, says the theory; the right controls creativity and intuition—the concept became instantly popular. Men, according to popular stereotype, are mostly left-brained, women right. Men are logical; women are intuitive.

Well, as it turns out, that isn't exactly the case. A painter by the name of Lovis Corinth suffered right-hemisphere damage to his brain but continued to paint—more expressively and boldly than before. (We owe this observation to Jerre Levy, a biopsychologist who has spent most of her career studying this phenomenon.) Apparently both halves of the brain work together on tasks, and each is capable of doing the other's work, although perhaps not always as well. Some people—both men and women—tend to be more logical than creative; others tend to be more creative.

Regardless of the scientific truth, the concept of left brain and right brain has become a useful metaphor for the eternal duality in how human beings think and feel: yin and yang;

logic and intuition; impulse and analysis; dream and reality; art and science; fact and fiction; poetry and prose; realism and romance; linear thinking and lateral thinking.

This duality has frequently caused heated conflict between the advocates for one side or the other. Nowhere has this been more true than in the world of advertising and marketing.

THE VOICES OF LEFT-BRAIN AND RIGHT-BRAIN ADVERTISING

From the earliest beginnings of advertising theory, around the turn of the century, advocates for one side of the argument or the other have insisted that theirs is the one true path to successful communication with the advertiser's prospects.

Some of the arguments advanced in the early days still seem valid today. And some of the points-of-view expressed in our own time wouldn't have seemed out of place in 1910.

We have found it to be both entertaining and instructive to sort out and combine in a table some of the comments made throughout the years, according to whether they expressed a left- or a right-brain approach to advertising.

LEFT BRAIN	RIGHT BRAIN
"Print the news of the store. No 'catchy headlines,' no catches, no headlines, no smartness, no brag, no 'fine writing,' no fooling, no foolery, no attempt at advertising, no anxiety to sell, no mercenary admiration...."[1] —John O. Powers, advertising manager of Wanamaker's Department Store (1895)	Copy is not just the words but "that combination of text with design which produces a complete advertisement."[2] —Earnest Elmo Calkins, co-founder of Calkins & Holden (1907)
"'Keeping the name before the public' is wrong and 'salesmanship in print' is right."[3] —Lord & Thomas pamphlet, *The Book of Tests* (1905)	"They were almost all picture. It's the *atmosphere* in these that sells...the quality that gives prestige, the little imaginative sure touches that bring the thing before you."[4] —Cyrus Curtis, magazine publisher, referring to the Calkins & Holden campaigns for Arrow collars and Pierce-Arrow cars (1914)

LEFT BRAIN	RIGHT BRAIN
"True 'Reason-Why' copy is logic, plus simplicity, plus conviction, all woven into a certain simplicity of thought—predigested for the average mind, so that it is easier to *understand* than to *misunderstand*."[5] —John E. Kennedy, who taught Albert Lasker of Lord & Thomas that "Advertising is Salesmanship in Print" (1904) "Style is a handicap. Anything that takes attention from the subject reduces the impression."[7] —Claude Hopkins, *My Life in Advertising* (1927) "Present-day advertising research has a long way to go before it reaches the level of Claude Hopkins' contributions to efficient advertising."[9] —Alfred Politz, psychologist and advertising research consultant (1935) "Advertising began as an art...and too many advertising men want it to remain that way—a never-never land where they can say, 'This is right because we feel it's right.'"[11] —Rosser Reeves, *Reality in Advertising* (1961) "I have never admired the *belles lettres* school of advertising. I have always thought them absurd; they did not give the reader a single *fact*."[13] —David Ogilvy, *Confessions of an Advertising Man* (1963) "I think people want *information*. They don't get it from advertising. Say you're buying a tape deck. Well, you're up against it—especially if you read the ads. A double-entendre headline. Nice photo. But no *real meat* in the ad. Because the people who did the ad don't think you *really* want to know. Advertising people argue that it's good	"The actual effect of modern advertising is not so much to convince as to suggest."[6] —Walter Dill Scott of Northwestern University, *The Psychology of Advertising* (1917) "The psychoanalysts have learned this about humankind, that nearly all of the important decisions of the individual are really made *in the subconscious*."[8] —B. L. Dunn, advertising manager, Oneida Community Silver (1918) *Reason-why* advertising consists of "a clever and semi-scientific application of the thesis that all men are fools....I look upon the public as myself multiplied, and I have not yet reached that stage of diffidence and humility which permits me to write myself down as an Ass."[10] —Theodore F. MacManus, star copywriter for General Motors (1932) "It is not what is said but how it is said that influences us the most. Any copy in advertising is an argument. It is literally throwing down a challenge to the reader...saying: 'Let's argue about this.' The human reaction to any statement of claim is 'Wait a minute! Who says so?'"[12] —Pierre Martineau, research director of the *Chicago Tribune* (1957) "We are definitely again in the age of the eye. We have less time to read, browse, meditate, and muse. There is such a multiplicity of messages striking us from every side...that it seems sometimes that only the lightning message of a picture can strike deep and hit home when we have a moment to spare."[14] —Margot Sherman, vice president, McCann-Erickson (1959)

LEFT BRAIN	RIGHT BRAIN
to make it simple. But that's not the point. People want to know. Advertising ought to give them the information they need."[15] —Helmut Krone, executive vice president, Doyle Dane Bernbach, a member of the Art Directors Hall of Fame (1984)	"If an idea makes me laugh, that's a sure sign it's a good idea. All commercials should be entertaining, no exceptions made. Somebody's making the business too rational, which is wrong. Advertising is an emotional industry....Everybody ought to have fun....If you're not having fun, then you're getting screwed."[16] —Lou Centlivre, executive managing director–creative, Foote, Cone & Belding, Chicago (formerly Lord & Thomas!) (1985) "I never felt anyone bought anything from a teacher."[17] — Dan Wieden, Wieden & Kennedy (1995)

Fortunately advertising, like life, is a unity of opposites. Just as the two hemispheres of the brain work together, so can the two distinctly different approaches to advertising work together—and sometimes they *must*.

From the MaxiMarketing viewpoint, whether your advertising should stir up more activity in the prospect's left or right brain depends on what you are selling, to whom, and in which medium.

The following spectrum shows the correlation between left- and right-brain distinctions and product uniqueness, tangibility, and costs:

LEFT BRAIN ↔ RIGHT BRAIN

Unique product ↔ Parity product

High-involvement product ↔ Low-involvement product

Intangible product ↔ Tangible product

High-ticket sale ↔ Low-ticket sale

The diagram is only a starting point, not an infallible guide. Even though automobiles are a high-ticket, high-involvement, differentiated product, automakers can and often do turn to right-brain emotional communication, and often to good effect. However, when makers of high-ticket, high-involvement computers and software turn to lavish right-brain image-building rather than to left-brain information and persuasion, they are very likely to miss the mark.

WHY ADVERTISING IS SO LEFT-BRAIN FOR MARKETERS WHO SELL DIRECT

Direct-response advertising for direct-order marketers has historically been skewed sharply toward step-by-step left-brain communication—for a variety of reasons.

- To overcome the inertia of a prospect relaxing in a comfortable chair at home, the offer for the direct-order product or service needed to be *unique* and persuasive—to compel immediate action. Uniqueness calls for explanation and reason-why copy.

- The item advertised was often an *intangible* product or service, such as a home-study course or a novel appliance that could not be easily packaged and sold off a store shelf. It required lengthy explanation and motivation.

- The sale tended to be a *high-ticket* total, such as a Nordic-Track exercise machine or a library of recordings, because direct-order selling is expensive and requires a substantial margin for advertising and sales. So it was necessary to pile on sales argument after sales argument to overcome the price resistance.

- The item involved was frequently a *high-involvement* product or service with a strong promise of life-changing benefit, so hundreds of words were needed to persuasively spell out that promise.

- Direct-response advertising has needed copious left-brain persuasion also because the act of ordering from a distant source is a conscious and deliberate one, with a lot of skepticism to be overcome.

In recent years, however, the smartest direct-response advertisers have been finding ways to incorporate the warmth and excitement of a right-brain appeal into their advertising through powerful graphics and symbolism. For instance, an outstanding mail-order catalog from Lands' End, America's leading specialty catalog marketer, devoted the cover and four inside pages to a beautiful photo essay, with hand-tinted pictures, showing scenes from Christmas in Dodgeville, Wisconsin, the firm's home. The words and pictures of "Christmas Out Our Way" conveyed the idea that Lands' End is not a faceless corporation but a group of friends with kids and kitchens and sleigh rides and Christmas trees—the kind of people you'd like to do business with.

When MCI introduced the MCI Friends & Family member-get-a-member program, direct-response television commercials launched the program with a dazzling combination of left-brain facts and right-brain creativity.

The commercials focused on the *feelings* of people joining together with friends and family in a new experience and, at the same time, got viewers *thinking* about benefiting from a 20 percent discount for themselves and others close to them.

WHERE RIGHT-BRAIN CREATIVITY CONTINUES TO SHINE

At the right side of the spectrum, parity products such as facial tissue, beer, gasoline, mineral water, and cola drinks—where almost no discernible physical difference can be detected in a blindfold test—cry out for emotional right-brain advertising because there is so little that can be presented in the terms of logical argument.*

---

*But of course, there are exceptions. The essence of the MaxiMarketing approach is to give thoughtful consideration to *every* possibility. Many years ago a small regional brewery, Utica Club, ran one of the most powerful beer-brand advertisements ever written, a long-copy, highly persuasive ad headed, "Sometimes I wonder if it still pays to make beer this way."

This is especially true of parity products whose popularity is governed by fad or fashion. Fashionableness in consumer-product purchasing is a wonderland that defies logic and measurement, but it is an undeniable fact of life in marketing, and the devil must be given his due. Nike sports shoes won their fantastic success not just because of product superiority, although they do of course make a very good product, but because their massive advertising and public relations efforts somehow convinced Young America that it was absolutely the most "cool" shoe of all.

We see this same mysterious force of fashion at work in the marketing of designer jeans. Often one designer's jeans will outsell an almost identical product, made in the very same Asian sweatshops but marketed under another designer's label, simply because the first designer has been able to create more of an invincible aura of fashionableness around his or her line.

When J. Walter Thompson hired the noted behaviorist John B. Watson in 1927, one of Watson's contributions was a controlled blindfold test proving that smokers couldn't recognize their favorite brand of cigarettes. This helped to establish that such products could not be sold by means of rational left-brain arguments.

Indeed, it's hard to imagine any copy argument that could do as much for certain products as the all-picture ads that show a crowd of handsome young people having an absolutely marvelous time in a singles bar, ski lodge, or family kitchen. Such ads both attract the true prospects out of the mass of readers and touch a deep chord of yearning to belong, to feel at home, and to be accepted by the "right" crowd.

One tip-off that an ad has been designed to create an emotional, visual right-brain appeal is text set in tiny type against a black or color background. In such cases it is obvious that neither the advertiser nor the agency takes the left-brain copy seriously enough to make it easily readable. They are committed to a right-brain appeal only. One wonders why the advertiser bothered to include any copy at all if it is going to be made so unreadable. We often wonder the very same thing.

When there is an art director who regards the advertising copy as "just another design element," he or she is acting on the belief that the visual impact is everything. In which case the ad had better *be* a very strong, right-brain ad.

The problem is that so much advertising fails to communicate either a powerful visual message *or* a motivating verbal message and ends up in that great dust bin of creativity known as No-brain Advertising.

FOUR WAYS—NOT TWO—TO ADVERTISE

The fact of the matter is, there really aren't just two ways to do advertising, there are four: *left-brain, right-brain, whole-brain,* and *no-brain.* MaxiMarketing can find an appropriate place at times for any of the first three ways but is vehemently opposed to wasting an advertiser's money on the "no-brain" variety.

Beginning with Earnest Elmo Calkins at the beginning of the century, most of the greatest advertising theorists and practitioners have believed in appealing to the whole brain whenever possible and wherever appropriate. David Ogilvy loved facts and reasoning, but he also gave us "The Man in the Hathaway Shirt," the haughty Baron Wrangell wearing an eye patch. Running just in *The New Yorker,* the first ads had lots of wonderful Ogilvy prose. But the campaign was so powerful and so talked-about that eventually the ads could run without any copy at all, just displaying a fashion shot of Baron Wrangell, and Hathaway sales still boomed.

It is a mistaken notion to think of Bill Bernbach as being to visual advertising what Ogilvy is to verbal. "Advertising is the art of persuasion," said Bernbach, and he advocated stunning visual impact as a means not only of grabbing the reader's attention but also of enhancing the power of persuasion: "The device I use to attract the reader's attention also tells the story."[18] Thus his agency's famous ad for the Volkswagen "Bug," headlined "Think Small," was illustrated by a very small photo of the car in a sea of white space. The left-brain message was fully developed in compelling copy, but it was rendered unforgettable by the stunningly creative right-brain visual expression.

Whole-brain communication that combines the dream image and the persuasive argument is the secret ingredient that is so often missing in brand-building awareness advertising, and that can do so much to increase its effectiveness.

WHOLE-BRAIN-PLUS ADVERTISING BY HELEN RESOR

An early pioneer in whole-brain advertising was Helen Lansdowne Resor, Stanley Resor's wife and creative director during his 40-year reign at J. Walter Thompson. Her advertising increased sales of Woodbury facial soap by 1000 percent in eight years. Helen Resor was far ahead of her time—adding the plus of a direct-response offer to her mastery of whole-brain creativity.

Her most famous Woodbury ad is a classic example of the MaxiMarketing approach to creating successful advertising. Although it ran well over three-quarters of a century ago, many brand advertisers could profitably study and emulate it today. It was striking, tasteful, and extraordinarily effective. Just look at how many elements she had working for it:

1. A headline with a succinct USP that became part of the American language: "The Skin You Love To Touch."

2. For right-brain appeal, a painting of a beautiful woman being nuzzled by the man of her dreams. The illustration does far more than reinforce the headline. There is an associative message here that runs silent and deep, far below the level of conscious reasoning.

3. Copy containing a reason-why explanation of how new skin forms, a preemptive claim that washing with Woodbury soap "can keep this new skin so active that it cannot help taking on the greater loveliness you have longed for," and a supporting message telling exactly how to use the product.

4. In one lower corner, a direct-response form offering both an eight-color reproduction of the painting (by a well-known artist of the day) and a week's supply of the soap to sample for 10 cents.

5. In the other corner, a picture of the product and a fine-print suggestion, "Tear out this cake as a reminder to get Woodbury's today at your druggist's or toiletries counter." (What a wonderful idea: a tear-out shopping reminder! It's surprising it wasn't widely adopted.)

Building awareness, sampling the product, encouraging a purchase, and motivating a response—all for the price of a single whole-brain advertisement.

ONLY YOU CAN DECIDE WHICH IS BEST FOR YOU (BUT THE PUBLIC CAN HELP)

Are we advocating that *all* advertising be whole-brain? No. The puzzle, the paradox, and the challenge is that some purely rational, verbally persuasive ads, with *no* visual symbolism, have been extraordinarily successful. (The longest-running mail-order ad in history was a long-copy logical argument headed "Do You Make These Mistakes in English?") On the other hand, some purely emotional, associative, nonverbal communication (such as the visually brilliant "Absolut Vodka" advertising in magazines and at New York City bus shelters) has also been extraordinarily successful.

The MaxiMarketing solution is *not* "Thou shalt include both left-brain and right-brain communication in all thy advertising." Rather, we urge you simply to be acutely *aware of* and to *consider* both the left-brain and right-brain possibilities when you are engaged in the creative process or review.

On the one hand, are you neglecting the presentation of a fascinating, unique, and persuasive selling proposition that might boost your advertising's degree of memorableness? On the other, are you so involved in the rational argument your advertising is presenting that you have failed to build in an appeal to those deep, primitive, wordless wellsprings of human emotion that move people to action and often have nothing to do with logic?

Only you, the advertiser, can decide. But you can receive valuable help from the very people your advertising is targeting. Let the public tell you what makes them respond—not through their opinions *but their actual, measured responses.* (People's *opinions* about advertising, such as "I would never read that much copy," can be quite misleading.) If you run the kind of split-run copy testing described in the previous chapter, testing left-brain, right-brain, and whole-brain variations, you may be amazed at the difference in response—and equally amazed by what rolling out the winner does for your sales curve.

However you achieve success, and wherever you decide to place the emphasis, the important thing is to avoid the deadliest of advertising sins: *no-brain advertising.* It is a sin you can observe being committed every day in the advertising pages of your favorite magazines, and in the commercial breaks as you watch television. And it's easy to spot.

It clearly has no thought-out Unique Selling Proposition, or at least none that is apparent; no easily understood message; no relevant visual symbolism, demonstration, or association with a powerful emotional appeal. And, we are sadly tempted to add, as far as we can see *no point of view,* except that the ad is supposed to be "clever," "catchy," and "creative," and "makes you laugh."

THE WASTEFULNESS OF NO-BRAIN ADVERTISING

Going right back to its earliest days, the trail of advertising history is littered with the bones of campaigns that tickled the public mightily but failed to sell the product.

In 1902, a new cereal called Force was launched through a series of full-page ads in the Sunday newspapers. The ads used drawings and poems to introduce a character named Jim

Dumps who was "a most unfriendly man"—until he started to eat Force cereal. "Since then they've called him 'Sunny Jim.'"

After a few months, Stephen Fox tells us in *The Mirror Makers,* the campaign was assigned to Calkins & Holden. Calkins himself wrote hundreds of the jingles. The public sent in thousands more. Songs, musical comedies, and vaudeville skits were written about Sunny Jim. Any cheerful fellow with the moniker of James was likely to be called "Sunny Jim" by his friends.

Soon *Printer's Ink* was able to proclaim that Sunny Jim "is as well known as President [Theodore] Roosevelt or J. Pierpont Morgan." There was just one problem, and you can guess what it was. "The advertising absolutely sold 'Sunny Jim' to the public," Calkins confessed years later, "but it did not sell Force."[19]

Over half a century later, the same fate befell the creators of Bert and Harry Piel, the delightful cartoon characters who peddled Piels beer on television, with voices provided by those incomparable comedians Bob and Ray.

The trouble—and the thing that makes clever advertising such a temptation—is that it sometimes works *too well.* The advertising is remembered, but the product isn't.

Of course, every so often a clever new advertising concept does hit the cash register with the same impact as it does the funny bone. When Wendy's introduced the Clara Peller "Where's the Beef?" commercials, sales went up by 30 percent. But for every Clara Peller breakthrough, how many thousands of overly clever, overproduced "creative" commercials have there been, with no visible sales effect and no impact on market share?

Trying to pull off a Clara Peller coup with an award-winning flight of wild fancy that has *no clear point of view* is simply playing high-stakes roulette with the client's money. (And remember, "Where's the Beef?" contained a meaty argument within its entertaining enactment.)

Harry MacMahan did a survey to discover what happens after an agency's commercial wins a Clio, the most prestigious award in the business. (A competition, by the way, that gives no points for the commercial's *sales success!*) Of 81 past winners, he found that 36 of the agencies involved had either lost the account or gone out of business. This poor record may simply reflect the ingratitude or boredom of clients (a not completely unknown phenomenon), but it doesn't seem plausible that this could be the whole explanation. More likely, the agency's work simply was not making a difference in the client's sales.

Yet, it would not be fair to suggest that all of the too many no-brain advertising campaigns are entirely the fault of the advertising agencies that created them. It is the clients who okay and pay for the advertising. It is they who bear the final responsibility for its strength or weakness. And it is they who stand to gain the most from carefully considering whether it is sufficiently right-brain, left-brain, or whole-brain in its approach.

NO-BRAIN COPY: THE DECLINE OF PRINT-ADVERTISING SKILL

There is some excuse, however slim, for advertising excesses in television, where marketers delve into the mysteries of visually dominant communication (motion! sound! music!) and of the generations that grew up on it. Each new wave of emerging consumers nurtured by MTV, video games, and now the interactive computer screen develops its own special language of animated communication shorthand.

In print advertising, however, there is no excuse for no-brain messages, especially when it's so simple to call for and compare responses. And yet we see tens of millions of dollars being frittered away on advertising that doesn't effectively speak to and persuade the left brain, the right brain, or any part of the whole brain.

Alvin Achenbaum, as vice chairman of professional services at Backer Spielvogel Bates Worldwide, once said:

> Let's face it, print is boring to create, evaluate, and service. Television is exciting; it's the movies. Moreover, it takes a lot fewer television than print units to spend a million dollars in the media.[20]

So television has tended to command the most attention and the highest-priced creative talent, whereas print advertising often comes off second-best.

But the glamour of being associated with big-money TV commercials is not wholly to blame. Bad advertising can come from talented people in large and small agencies with or without big-budget television accounts. It also can—and often does—come from the orders of inexperienced clients, overriding the agency's best judgment. The common denominator is the absence of any *point of view,* other than that advertising first and foremost must do whatever it takes to break through the clutter and look in step with the latest fashion or fad in advertising. What an ad says or does *after* it gets noticed often seems to be a minor consideration.

"Merely to let your imagination run riot, to dream unrelated dreams, to indulge in graphic acrobatics and verbal gymnastics is *not* being creative," argued Bill Bernbach, the guiding genius of the original Doyle Dane Bernbach, in a company pamphlet.

> The creative person has harnessed his imagination. He has disciplined it so that every thought, every idea, every word he puts down, every line he draws, every light and shadow in every photograph he takes, makes more vivid, more believable, more persuasive the original theme or product advantage he has decided he must convey.

Clients would be smart to make an enlarged poster of Bill Bernbach's words and display the advice prominently in the boardroom when the agency comes in to present its great new "creative" campaign.

SOME DEPRESSING EXAMPLES

Often we have personally been involved in the struggle for an advertising idea. Therefore we are painfully familiar with, and sympathetic to, the pressures under which creative people work daily. Because of this awareness in our own careers, we have largely refrained from speaking critically in public about the advertising efforts of others.

But in writing and now updating *MaxiMarketing,* as we see the huge amounts of money being wasted on advertising that talks to itself about itself without even a remote connection to answering any real consumer need, we feel compelled to make a few nominations to the "No-Brain Hall of Fame."

- *"Innovation is easy. You simply create the exact opposite of everything people wanted the day before."* This is the headline and subhead for what seems to be an ad for a large-screen Toshiba television set. The body copy spends almost as much space congratulating the company on past and future products as on the current product. What the innovation does for the *consumer* is totally lost in the orgy of self-congratulation.

- *"Where Do I Work?"* Aramark says that it works at businesses large and small, near and far, in nine time zones, in hospitals, schools, colleges, and child-care centers. "I work where America works. I work where America plays. I work for 10 million people every day." But it never says what it *does,* or what it might do for the ad's reader.

- *"The First Supper for a good solid start."* This was obviously the ad-person's clever (although offensive to many) takeoff on da Vinci's "The Last Supper," selling Mead Johnson's Pablum baby cereal. Instead of 12 disciples at a long table, there were 12 babies in high chairs—we kid you not! And no body copy at all. The advertiser or the agency could not or would not consider what might be said about the product that would be of great interest to new parents, or what offer might help to build the company's database—but it could spend its money to lose ground with art-lovers and to lose altogether people who take their religious faith seriously.

- *A Discover Private Issue credit card page* has no headline, only five lines of dialogue under a picture of two men at a backyard barbecue:

MAN #1: Where'd you get steaks like that?

MAN #2: They came with the grill.

MAN #1: Come on, where'd they come from?

MAN #2: Private Issue.

MAN #1: We're having one of those "Who's on first?" conversations, aren't we?

The "who's on first?" line is a reference to a famous Abbott and Costello comedy routine. Think about the ad long enough, and it starts to make sense. But few prospects *are* going to think about it long enough. Are they going through the magazine to ponder and puzzle over what each advertiser actually means, or are they going to move along to the magazine's editorial content?

- *A Mass Mutual two-page ad* also has no headline. (Maybe we've stumbled across a new Madison Avenue "creative" trend.) One page is a picture of a couple reading the newspaper; the facing page has three lines of type and a small block of copy. The three lines of 12-point type say:

A promise to stand behind your story even when the going gets tough.

A promise to make your health insurance an asset instead of an issue.

A promise you'll retire with more than a scrapbook of bylines.

The copy begins:

Nothing binds us one to the other like a promise kept. For more than 140 years, we've been helping people keep their promises by ensuring we have the financial strength to keep ours. That's why families and businesses rely on us to insure their lives, their health and their financial future.

Who is promising what here? Mass Mutual is going to stand behind "our story"? *What* story? They're going to make our health insurance an asset? Could be; they're an insurance company, after all. But *how* are they going to do that? We'd like to know. And how are they going to ensure that we'll retire with more than that metaphorical scrapbook? And by this point, does anyone *care*?

These may seem like extreme examples. But if ads of this muddled type account for only 10 percent of all U.S. advertising today, we are talking about the wasteful expenditure of more than $15 *billion.* The actual cost to business is probably far larger.

What is astonishing is how little has changed in the 10 years since the original edition of *MaxiMarketing* appeared. What strikes us as we look at current print media advertising in North America, Europe, and to an even greater extent the emerging markets of Latin America, Southeast Asia, India, and South Africa, is the continuing power of an advertising establishment that so often values self-serving cleverness over meaningful content.

NO-BRAIN ART DIRECTION CAN DEFEAT WHOLE-BRAIN COPY

Sometimes great right-brain copy is betrayed by no-brain art direction—and very often the advertising trade publications support the betrayers. For instance, the editors of *Art Direction/ The Magazine of Visual Communication* once proclaimed:

> Body copy—it comes in all shapes and sizes. But many art directors consider copy a nuisance and try to shunt it off into some obscure corner. But hard as it may be to believe, body text can not only decorate but [be] an integral part of the design. Type, a very flexible variable, can be molded into nearly any form. Sure, lots of art directors choose to wrap it around product shots, but in some respects that's merely an example of accommodating the visual. Why not make the copy a visual? *Art Direction* has come across many ads that do just that, ads that make the copy an extension of the design.[21]

Alongside this essay appeared, as an example, an ad for Zyderm Collagen cream, a facial treatment offered only through dermatologists and plastic surgeons. The photographic illustration was a cropped photograph of the head of a statue of Aphrodite, and the body copy below it had been "molded" into a kind of reverse S-shaped swath running down through a sea of white space.

The copy had *no paragraphing,* obviously because it would interfere with making the body text "not only decorate but [be] an integral part of the design."

To the left of the swath, floating in the white space, was a small headline: "Aging Beautifully." On the right side was a subhead, actually in smaller type than the body copy: "A new kind of program for aging skin that only a doctor can provide."

How the copywriter must have wept to see the USP, the rather carefully constructed, informative argument, and the offer of more information, all so artfully concealed behind a wall of pure design!

Ogilvy writes of a fund-raising organization whose entire ad was set in "reverse"—white type on black. When, at his suggestion, they tested the identical copy using black type on white, they *doubled* their results.

We clipped a page ad by Metromedia Technologies, a firm that is apparently in the business of graphic communication ("indoor and outdoor murals, banners, backlight displays, on-premise signage..."). The virtually unreadable body copy is printed in a sickly maroon color on a black background.

If copy isn't meant to be read, why bother to include it in the ad? And why pay copywriters in the United States $100,000 a year and more to write the stuff? If it *is* meant to be read, doesn't it deserve, at the very least, to be *legible?* Find out for yourself how unreadable or uninviting a great deal of advertising text can be. Open any magazine and see how many candidates you can nominate to the "No-brain Hall of Fame."

TODAY'S SPECIAL NEED FOR LEFT-BRAIN COMMUNICATION

Perhaps because we live in an age of breathtaking video imagery, left-brain persuasion isn't as admired as it once was.

In 1957, when video was beginning to feel its oats, Pierre Martineau, research director of the *Chicago Tribune*, declared that we were "wrong in considering copy, or logic, sacred. Words more often than not play a minor role in what is actually happening."[22]

What Martineau overlooked is the matter of what is being sold, and to whom. Were you ever sold an insurance policy by an agent using pictures only?

As a point of fact, the need for ad-people with a knack for purely verbal persuasion has never been so great. Why? Because the introduction of new services and so many new high-tech products demands words—skillfully crafted words.

As we move further and deeper into the Information Age and the Service Economy, we find that many of the new products flooding the market are not *products* in the usual kick-the-tires sense; rather, they are packaged information and services sometimes wrapped around physical products. It took less than a decade for lawn-care *services* like Chemlawn and Lawn Doctor to wipe out 40 percent of the sales of off-the-shelf lawn-care *products*.

Until such products and services have become fully embedded in the public mind, the advertiser must provide prospective customers with *information, facts, explanation, rational and emotional persuasion*—in other words, left-brain communication.

APPLE'S EARLY WHOLE-BRAIN TRIUMPH

Apple Computer skillfully used both right-brain and left-brain advertising to introduce the Macintosh computer, which today, despite its having lost the race with Microsoft's Windows for the dominant position in systems software, still has reached annual sales of more than $10 billion.

On New Year's Day, 1984, during the telecast of the Super Bowl game, Apple fired a blast of pure right-brain communication with its famous "George Orwell" commercial. One million dollars was spent to produce the commercial, it was said, and another million to air it—*once!*

Ten years later, the trade press still makes admiring references to that single commercial. It was an outstanding example of the power of celebrating an event that benefits as much from the public relations effect as from the actual impact of the advertising message.

But Apple didn't stop with the emotional impact of the right-brain "1984" commercial. It followed up a few months later with a 30-page, left-brain ad in *Newsweek* that told readers everything they had ever wanted to know about why they should purchase a Macintosh computer. It accomplished what that wise direct-marketing pioneer, Victor Schwab, used to advocate: "taking you [the reader] by the hand and leading you from where you are to where the advertiser wants you to be." With words and pictures that were models of simplicity, clarity, and completeness, the ad told people who didn't know anything about computers just about everything they needed to know about the Macintosh computer. Pure—and brilliant— left-brain advertising.*

EMULATING APPLE'S LEFT-BRAIN BLOCKBUSTER FOR A FRACTION OF ITS COST

Okay, so you can't afford to buy out an entire issue of *Newsweek*. But there is nothing that Apple did in *Newsweek* that a niche marketer with a smaller budget cannot profitably emulate for a fraction of the cost.

How? By preparing a brochure or a video (which costs less than $2 to duplicate and mail) that can be just as detailed, just as clear, and just as long (if necessary) as the 30-page Macintosh ad. You can mail it to rented lists of clearly identified prime prospects. Or you can mail it to your own prime prospects, identified by invited inquiries from interested

---

*Too bad Apple didn't stick with this left-brain approach in their print advertising. In the years following the Macintosh debut, the company's advertising often suffered from many of the ills we have described.

When Microsoft first overlaid MS-DOS with an inferior imitation of Macintosh called Windows, in order to grab away the market for user-friendly system software, Apple missed a golden opportunity to slug it out with Windows in print. They could have proven the superiority of Macintosh with powerful left-brain comparisons between the two systems. But they failed to do so, and an improved Windows 95 became the most widely used system by far.

readers of your newspaper or magazine advertising or viewers of a strategically placed commercial on independent television stations in your market area. This approach will be discussed further in Chapter 8.

EVEN IN THE TELECOMPUTING GENERATION, THERE ARE MORE READERS OUT THERE THAN YOU THINK

You may be concerned—and well-meaning experts may tell you—that in this electronic age, with its short attention span, "Nobody will read long copy anymore." It is a paradox, however, that along with the impressive growth of television viewing since 1950 has come an equally impressive growth in the book-publishing business—from a few hundred million dollars then to over $13 billion 40 years later.

It is true that the large general-interest magazines, such as the old *Life, Look,* and *The Saturday Evening Post,* were wiped out as television gained media dominance. But a surprising fact is that the total number of magazine titles published, and of copies per issue, is far greater today than it was a generation ago.

The number of bookstores in the United States has grown from roughly 5000 in the mid-1960s to almost 30,000 today, including many giant superstores devoted entirely to selling books and offering a comfortable corner to indulge in coffee and snacks. All this isn't so surprising, when you consider the considerably raised level of average education. Between 1950 and 1992 the number of Americans with at least some amount of college education took off from a little over 6 million to hit nearly 70 million.

So somebody out there still can read. And does read. And *will* read your copy about the product or service you are advertising, as we move ever deeper into the Information Age. As long as you are providing the clear information that the prospect needs and wants to know, *and* as long as you understand and empathize with the prospect's deepest hopes and fears.

Herbert D. Maneloveg, a consultant who held top media and marketing positions with several famous agencies, once wrote a commentary on this issue that is as relevant today as the day he wrote it. We wish we had room to reprint every word. In part, here is what he had to say:

> We are presently in a promotionally oriented marketing mode, where a more knowledgeable, more discerning public will wisely, calmly wait out a purchase until the marketer puts it on sale or offers a "deal." What we're seeing is the slow, inexorable erosion of brand loyalty for many product categories, the public now selecting from the numerous product lines it senses as all similar, with price break being the sole determining factor. Thus a growing number of product managers, faced with sales below planned objectives, are turning to a series of short-term promotional flights that indeed move product, but at a much lower profit margin: a kind of Catch-22 situation that perpetuates the dilemma rather than solving it.

> Unfortunately, much of today's advertising communications (and the ad community) has become an unplanned culprit in this situation, perhaps a larger part of the problem than we'd wish to admit. Why? Because many are just not reading our public correctly; they're not facing up to the fact that *today's upscale, more educated consumer wants to learn more about a product rather than less....*

> Take the untold hundreds of millions spent on soft-drink and fast-food advertising. How much of a marked difference in market share has there been from one year to the next? You name the category—coffee, beer, shampoo, liquor, cigarettes—and try to count on the fingers of both hands those product campaigns that truly educate and convince rather than merely remind and entertain.

> Accordingly, the public...watches an annual avalanche of national advertising, elects not to be loyal to almost anything because few marketers have offered any communications reason to be loyal. The consumers wait to buy when they're

ready, not when the marketer would like them to purchase, and the magic of advertising just doesn't work today.

Yet it can work....We must learn to adroitly blend short-message impact with compelling reasons, longer-length copy and expanded ideas to sell in the current marketplace; to make our people brand-loyal again.[23]

Chapter 7 discusses other ways to deal with this phenomenon of brand-franchise erosion, caused by too much promotion and too little persuasion. All we want to do here is simply shout "Hallelujah!", in joyous response to Maneloveg's plea for, in effect, more left-brain advertising. (However, we think he goes too far in saying, "The magic of advertising doesn't work today." It still does—sometimes.)

THE NEW GENERATION ISN'T THAT DIFFERENT

All right, so the new generation is different. But it isn't all *that* different. In *Ogilvy on Advertising,* the author says that shortly before Bill Bernbach died he was asked what changes he expected there would be in advertising in the future. He replied:

Human nature hasn't changed for a billion years. It won't even vary in the next billion years. Only the superficial things have changed. It is fashionable to talk about *changing* man. A communicator must be concerned with *unchanging* man—what compulsions drive him, what instincts dominate his every action....For if you know these things about a man, you can touch him at the core of his being.[24]

"A gentleman with brains," commented Ogilvy admiringly.

More than that, we would say: a gentleman with a *whole* brain, a brain with unusually well-developed and well-integrated left and right hemispheres. And though Bill Bernbach's talent for moving markets with words and pictures was one-of-a-kind, you too can use both sides of *your* brain to communicate with both sides of your prospect's brain.

Then you will be fully in tune with the MaxiMarketing approach to communicating the Unique Selling Proposition and the Extra-Value Proposition of your product or service.

THE BOTTOM LINE

Whether your next advertising campaign should be predominately left-brain, right-brain, or whole-brain depends on what you are selling and to whom, and how the competitive climate is shaping up. Each advertising direction has its uses, and the measured responses to your advertising from the target audience can help you determine the right mix. Measured response also will help you to avoid the deadly sin of no-brain advertising—messages that put cleverness ahead of content, and art direction that is more interested in following the current vogue than in communicating your current strategy.

Today, the proliferation of amazing new products and services has created a need for highly skillful explanatory left-brain and whole-brain communication. And don't let anyone tell you, "Nobody will read all that copy." There are more readers today than there have ever been before, and often they want to learn more than many advertisers are willing to provide for them.

Your advertising need not—and often cannot, at least not affordably—tell your whole story up-front. But it must break through the clutter to reach a true prospect, and to leave behind a meaningful impression of the advantage or benefit of the product or service you are advertising.

As you plan or review the creative strategy and execution of your company's advertising, here are some questions you must remember to ask:

- *Will it attract and communicate with the prospects we are trying to reach?*
- *Does what we are selling call for left-brain, right-brain, or whole-brain communication?*

- *Should we—and is there some way we can—add whole-brain appeal to this proposed left-brain or right-brain advertising?*

- *Does the headline reach out to our true prospects? Will the body copy in this print advertising be clearly legible and inviting to read? Do the design and illustration reinforce the message implicit in the words?*

- *Is there an appropriate offer we can make in the copy that will enable us to measure the impact of the advertising, extend and deepen our contact with the reader or viewer, and add valuable information to our database?*

Whatever your responsibility in the marketing management chain—from product manager to research director to advertising director to chief executive officer—you can have an impact on the effectiveness of your company's advertising by asking pointed questions about left-brain and right-brain orientation, and by steering your company away from disastrous no-brainers. There's too much at stake for you not to do so.

MAXIMIZED PROMOTION RESULTS

FINDING A BETTER WAY IN THE INFORMATION AGE

THE BIG PICTURE

So what happens after your prospect has been made aware of what you are advertising, and has shown an interest in it? More often than not, the advertiser turns to sales promotion to make something happen.

Sales promotion is the art and science of converting a favorable attitude toward your product or service into an immediate stimulated purchase. As William A. Robinson, president of the sales promotion agency bearing his name, has put it: "Advertising creates an acceptable environment, and we push the products through the pipeline. I know it sounds corny, but promotions ring the cash register."

Today's sales promotion is the child of the demassified market. Product proliferation has inevitably led to intensified competition and intensified sales promotion. (In 1994, over 20,000 new consumer products appeared on the shelves of America's supermarkets and drugstores—a 214 percent increase over the previous year.) But today's sales promotion can be a problem child: greedy, costly to feed, often bad-mannered, and sometimes downright destructive—yet an essential member of the marketing family, handy to have available when needed and at times a brilliant performer.

We believe that by demanding the same accountability from the activation process of promotion that we urged for brand awareness advertising, and by adopting the MaxiMarketing information-driven focus, you can maximize the usefulness and profitability of your sales promotion activity. The new sales promotion of the Information Age will increasingly be seen as "datamotion"—the use of information in a database to direct the right weight of promotion to each prospect or customer and to get the best immediate response for the least money.

Along with a fresh look at sales promotion must come an effective plan for generating other forms of moving the prospect to becoming a customer. We call this "bridging"—everything you do from the moment a prospect raises her hand to say I'm interested to the moment you close the sale—and we cover that in the chapter following this one.

Sales promotion is big business. While the change in American advertising spending—a 5.75 percent compound annual growth rate during the 1976–88 period—actually turned negative during the 1989–91 recession, promotions as a share of marketing budgets have continued to grow. *Business Week* reported that companies now spent 70 percent of their marketing dollars on promotion, leaving just 30 percent for media advertising. "Ten years ago, advertising got 43 percent vs. 57 percent for promotion."[1]

And yet for packaged-goods (known in Europe as "fast-moving consumer goods") manufacturers, the results can be astonishingly unrewarding. Studies have shown again and again that an expensive promotion campaign can produce a short-term lift in market share. However, as the effects of the promotion die away and the competition launches its own return salvo, brand share often returns to its pre-promotion level—*or lower.*

Even worse is the situation identified by Magid M. Abraham, a vice chairman at Information Resources Inc., and

Leonard M. Lodish, a professor of marketing at the Wharton School. Using single-source marketing data, the two found that only 16 percent of the 360 trade promotions they studied were profitable. "For many promotions, the cost of racking up an incremental dollar of sales was *greater* than one dollar."[2]

Over the long term, excessive promotion has been shown to erode and even destroy brand share. Tryers attracted by special promotions are often brand-hoppers who shop for the best price, not the best brand. And regular users become accustomed to getting a direct or disguised discount, and refuse to buy when the brand returns to its regular price.

HOW EXCESSIVE PROMOTION CAN ERODE PROFITS

Professor Roger Strang of the University of Southern California has suggested that long-term sales begin to decline when the ratio of advertising to promotion falls below a certain "threshold"—probably 60 to 40. He cited a study by R. J. Weber to show what happens when brands get sucked into a promotional war.[3]

The product manager for Company A, the leader in its category, began to cut back on television advertising and pour money into promotion. The next two nearest competitors followed suit. All three just about doubled their total advertising and marketing expenditures, but the percentage devoted to advertising dropped dramatically.

After three years, the market share of each brand was about the same as or less than it had been at the start of the war. But the profit contribution per-case-shipped had declined sharply. The analysis showed that the higher the promotion-to-advertising ratio, the greater the revenue decline! Thus Company A, whose percentage of expenditure devoted to brand advertising declined from 64 to 32 percent, experienced a drop in per-case profits from $3.36 to $2.33—a 44 percent fall.

But Company C, whose brand advertising dropped to just 9 percent of its total marketing budget, saw its per-case profits drop from $2.58 to just 74 cents—a 249 percent plunge.

Not long ago a product-manager friend shared some of his concerns with us:

> Direct marketers never did convince me that spending $350 per thousand or more on direct mail to target competitive-brand users or to build a relationship was better than spending $6 per thousand to reach 52 million people in the Sunday papers. But how much longer can I live with the low readership, a 2.5 percent or less redemption rate, sky-high misredemptions, and the insanity of being buried every quarter in an avalanche of 75 billion coupons aimed at bargain hunters in America?

He told us that he ran some numbers, and that this is what he found:

> After adding up all my costs, I'm paying 50 cents to get a 25-cent discount coupon redeemed...and well over half the buyers would have bought my product at the full price anyway. That's about three times my net margin. So I spend over $300,000 on just one promotion to lose 34 cents on every sale. Of course, I tell myself I make the money back on additional sales from the redeemers, and the ability to load up the retailer with my product when I announce the promotional effort. But then in the next quarter I'm hit with my competition coming in and doing to me what I did to them. How can I afford to go on this way?

SO WHY DO IT?

Why *do* manufacturers and service companies spend so much on promotion, often more than on brand-image advertising? There are a number of reasons, some of them valid, some questionable.

1. A new-product launch needs all the help it can get, including aggressive promotion. Promotion can help to entice curious consumers into a trial, and it can pressure retailers for shelf space.

2. The product-manager system tends to favor short-term gains. Spectacular increases in share points due to heavy promotion can make the product manager look like a hero in the short term. And in the long term, when share of market and profits per case may have declined because of over-promotion, the same product manager usually isn't around to receive the blame because he or she has moved on to a better job!

3. Top management may be under pressure to demonstrate sales gains to Wall Street in a quarterly or annual statement, and may succumb to the temptation to inflate sales by any means possible.

4. Retailers may have come to expect the benefits of promotion and to demand it, even though it may accomplish very little for the manufacturer in the long run.

5. It's hard to resist engaging in defensive discounting, when the competition is out there giving away the store. This is true, even though, as Don Shultz and William Robinson wryly observe in their book *Sales Promotion Management*, "No one wins a sales promotion war."[4]

6. The company, intently focused on current performance, simply may not have done the kind of long-term, hard-nosed analysis needed to determine what over-promotion is doing to brand share and case profit over the long term.

If at some level you are involved in decision making in advertising and promotion, especially of mass-marketed products or services, always remember that your strategic planning must look to reduce your dependency on sales promotions that reduce margins and that may be eroding your brand franchise. As you strengthen your communications and your total relationship with your best customers by following the MaxiMarketing model, you will feel less need for a promotional "fix."

Whatever the vagaries of the promotion process, there are ways to make your sales promotion both more *productive* and more *accountable*. If you are involved in management or marketing in a category other than mass-marketed packaged goods, sales promotion may actually be underutilized. In that situation your promotions are less likely to be neutralized by a competitor's counter-promotion, and your opportunities to realize the benefits of a carefully conceived sales promotion effort may be far greater.

Often, part of the problem with developing effective sales promotion is that management looks down on the process as being a much-needed, hard-working scullery maid rather than one of the favored members of the marketing family. Thus it fails to command the intense attention and interest inside the company, and at the advertising agency, that the production of a dazzling new television commercial or the development of a new product for a niche market do command. Too often, marketers see promotion as being a separate, necessary, but routine activity rather than an integral part of the corporate brand-building strategy.

Even the language used in Europe for years, and gaining favor in the United States, is revealing. Brand-building image advertising is "above the line"; sales promotion and direct marketing are "below the line." "The line" is the separation between "measured media advertising" and everything else. The "above" and "below" designations have become a counterproductive putdown of the importance of promotion and direct marketing relative to media advertising.

BEGINNING TO FIND A BETTER WAY

The first step in maximizing the effectiveness of sales promotion is to treat it with the utmost respect—to put it not "below the line" but alongside awareness advertising as an equally respected marketing partner.

As we see it, a complete rethinking of the role of sales promotion, as a new-and-improved force for sales and profits in today's information-driven economy, must include three main components.

1. More and better testing of promotional options.

2. Wherever possible, using promotion not only to lead to a direct sale but also to help build a proprietary database for a continuing relationship with the customer. Promotion can play a primary role in gathering the names of customers and relevant information about them.

   The House of Seagram built its proprietary database of 10 million users of alcoholic beverages almost entirely from promotional offers for individual bottles of Chivas Regal, Crown Royal, Martel Cordials, and its other brands. General Foods (later to become Kraft General Foods and now Kraft Foods) put together its initial consumer database of 3 million households in the late 1980s by compiling the data from past promotional offers for more than 70 brands. Now, by continuing to add information obtained as a side-benefit of ongoing promotions, the Kraft database has grown to such a point that it holds comprehensive buying-behavior information on 30 million households. How Seagram, Kraft, and other marketers use their proprietary databases as a launchpad for highly cost-effective promotions will be looked at in greater detail in Chapter 9.

3. Making promotion an important part of your multifunctional advertising. By making the promotional offer part of the advertising, the ad budget becomes a double-duty expenditure. Too few advertisers ask how they can combine the promotion, the advertising, and the accumulation of information for the direct-marketing database into a single blockbuster effort. When done properly, the promotion also becomes the message that builds brand preference.

   British Airways launched its "Biggest Offer Ever" promotion to get people flying again after the "Desert Storm" Gulf War, with full-page and double-page newspaper ads in 35 countries. Not only did the offer of two free tickets for everyone flying British Airways on a given day attract media attention worldwide, but the direct-response reply form in the ads, used as the entry in the drawing for lucky winners, created an instant database of 3.5 million air travelers. Shortly after the campaign, air traffic picked up, and British Airways got more than its share. "Biggest Offer Ever" then became the theme of British Airways' advertising in the months following the promotion.

THE NEED FOR MORE AND BETTER REAL-WORLD TESTING

Substantial improvements can be made in sales promotion efficiency and profitability through more and better testing of promotional alternatives.

Shultz and Robinson say that if you mention testing to a group of sales promotion managers, you will probably get a nod of agreement and a comment along the lines of "We know we need to do it, but we don't have the time, money, people, or [you fill in the blank] to do it."[5]

Roger Strang surveyed 55 large-volume manufacturers and found that 20 percent of them budgeted no money at all for sales promotion research. From the MaxiMarketing point of view, this is a costly mistake. We discussed in Chapter 2 how adding a response element to advertising and promotion causes the various parts of MaxiMarketing to work together to produce a "learning curve" that leads to improved performance. In the case of sales promotion, it can accomplish several valuable objectives.

1. *Comparative measurement.* Measuring the number of direct responses from each of your sales promotion efforts in each of your media buys can allow you to compare precisely the *comparative* efficiency of one promotional effort or media source to another. The cumulative effect of a series of tests, each set of findings building on the previous set, can greatly increase the likelihood of your reaching the campaign objectives.

2. *Speed and economy.* Compared to other forms of marketing research, direct-response testing can be relatively quick and inexpensive.

3. *A sense of reality.*   Direct-response testing happens in the real world, not in a questionable simulation.

4. *Potential secrecy.*   If you choose, testing can be done privately (via direct mail, with an offer redeemed at the point of sale) so that you don't tip off your competition, upset your retailers, or confuse the public.

5. *Database building.*   Finally, capturing the names and addresses of prospects and customers through sales promotion can feed vital information into the customer database.

As we examine the practices, problems, and opportunities associated with each of the principal kinds of sales promotion advertised in media—couponing, premiums, sampling, and sweepstakes—we will see how this approach could have prevented some failed promotions, salvaged some doubtful ones, and made some good ones even better. Let's take a look.

THE PERILS OF COUPONING

Couponing is a good place to start, because it "consumes" (some would say *burns up*) so many dollars.

When one examines the current state of discounting in the form of cents-off redemption coupons, it's hard to avoid being struck by a paradox: Use of couponing continues to increase in the United States, right along with doubts about its value. From the brand marketer's point of view, there are an uncomfortably high number of points of resemblance to addictive behavior.

It's expensive.

It makes you feel good for a while, but then you need some more.

You don't really want to do it, but the other fellows are doing it and you don't want to be left out.

You know it's not good for your health in the long run, but you're too busy worrying about your next fix to worry about the long run.

It was back in the 1970s that money-back redemption coupons began to zoom in popularity with manufacturers, retailers, and consumers. Manufacturers liked them as a way to force the growing number of new products through the pipeline, and to get the dealer to stock and display them. Retailers liked them as a way to build store traffic. And consumers began to clip and hoard them because they offered a way to fight inflation and recession, and to stretch the family budget further.

Coupon use rose from 58 percent of households in 1970 to 76 percent in 1993. Even though the number of coupons issued by all U.S. companies dropped to 298 billion in 1994 (the first drop in 23 years), that remains a staggering number to contemplate. The key question is: How many of the 6.8 billion coupons that consumers redeemed in 1994 actually represented desirable activity?

THE DOUBTS ABOUT COUPONING

Robert Evans, director of promotional services for the Gillette Company and former chairman of the Promotion Marketing Association of America, was one of the early doubters. Over a decade ago he warned:

> One of the things that is starting to become a problem is that media costs are skyrocketing and are starting to knock out the smaller brands and causing those brands to devote almost their entire marketing budget to promotional expenditures. As a result they are not building the brand identity they might have in the past, and the question being raised frequently is, *"Does the consumer really know who you are, or are they buying the brand that is being promoted this week?"* [Emphasis added.][6]

Around the same time, Len Daykin, editor of *Brand Management Report,* wrote:

> When coupon use was just growing, it was used selectively by the manufacturer. Now it's almost automatic—if there's a promotion pushing into the warehouse, there's usually a

coupon device to pull it out. And that has a negative effect, because in any given week, a consumer with a sharp eye can find coupons in almost any product group. *I think what's being created is a very large group of consumers who are loyal to coupons, not brand.* [Emphasis added.][7]

The trouble is, so many coupon redeemers are existing customers and cheaters. And nobody seems to know how many. (Of course, couponing to present users has some value in preventing defection to a competing brand.)

"You can measure how many coupons are redeemed," points out Robert Blattenberg, a University of Chicago professor who has developed a computer model to evaluate sales promotion. "But it's very hard to analyze what real impact you've had. You don't know if the coupons have led to increased sales or just deferred sales. You don't know if you are getting purchases from an existing user or a new user." Or from a cheater.

THE CASE OF THE CHEATING CONSUMER.   Most of the expressed concern about misredemption has been focused on the large-scale fraud perpetrated by gangs who buy and clip from bundles of newspapers, or even reproduce coupons which they then redeem through larcenous retailers. But as far back as the early 1980s, Management Decision Systems was uncovering strong evidence that one coupon out of every three submitted was being improperly redeemed not by organized crime but by consumers themselves, costing marketers more than $500 million a year.

The company said it stumbled across this intelligence by accident: "We were trying to see if people switched brands as a result of a coupon, or if they bought their normal brand or nothing." But they found that about a third were using the coupon to buy a competing brand (with the collusion of store personnel, obviously).[8]

Their conclusion roughly coincides with the findings of a study by K. C. Blair, showing that consumer misredemption of coupons ranged from a low of 14 percent to a high of 54 percent, with an average of 33 percent.

WHAT ABOUT REDEMPTION BY PRESENT USERS?   There are no
meaningful figures on how many coupons are redeemed by
loyal existing customers, because that would vary with the
product's share of market. But it's reasonable to assume that
the larger the share, the larger the percentage of redeemed
coupons that come from existing users.

According to Irene Park,

> the competition's users with an historic pattern of "other
> brand use" can be lured away only with the highest level of
> discounted pricing. However, *even at the highest coupon val-*
> *ues, current users account for more than 60 percent of the*
> *coupon redeemers.*[9] [Emphasis added.]

If that were true, and if it were also true that 30 percent of
the redemptions come from cheaters who use the coupons to
buy a different brand, a pathetic 10 percent of the redemption
would be coming from thrifty brand shoppers and genuinely
interested triers. Shocking, if true. But what may be even
more shocking is that marketers for the most part really don't
know, and judging by their behavior don't seem to *care.*

In short, by the time you add up the existing users who
just want a discount, the cheaters who intend to remain loyal
to some other brand, and the bargain hunters who don't give a
hoot about what brands they choose, the conclusion is
inescapable that mass couponing adds little if any real value to
the brand.

It may cost only half a cent to distribute a coupon, but the
true cost of putting a coupon into the hands of a non-user
who redeems it and thereby becomes a regular product user
may be several hundred times that much. Isn't it time to find a
better way to encourage purchasing, in an age of pinpointed
targeting capabilities and selective interaction with a better-
informed consumer?

THE POPULARITY—AND WASTEFULNESS—OF COUPONING IN FSI'S

And yet, despite the problems inherent in traditional couponing and the new opportunities made possible for targeting

known competitive brand users in a proprietary or public database, brand product managers remain, for the most part, trapped in the wasteful system.

Moreover, most of the money for couponing goes into a comparatively inefficient method of coupon distribution, Sunday newspaper freestanding inserts (fsi's). Fsi's account for more than 3 out of 4 of all grocery product coupons (and almost 9 out of 10 of all health and beauty aid product coupons). Direct-mail distribution of coupons has remained stuck around 4 percent for the past 10 years, even though it offers much better targeting capability.

Couponing with fsi's seems especially wasteful because it offers no opportunity to screen out existing users or to treat them differently—and little opportunity to deliver a meaningful advertising message in the midst of the much-deplored clutter of these inserts. (Depending on the season, some Sunday papers carry as many as four or five fsi sections, each containing more than 20 pages.)

There has been some improvement in this area in recent years. Companies that distribute fsi's now use demographic and regional information to target different buyers. Vallasis Inserts, for example, can break distribution in certain cities into different sections, and marketers can test price points against age, gender, and demographics.[10]

The proponents of couponing argue that, while it may seem ridiculous to give discounts to bargain hunters and to people who would buy your brand anyway, it's still better to get those sales than pass them up. And they also make the case for the brand-building value of fsi's.

A coupon-clipper studying the fsi, they say, may note your product's picture and read the copy and be influenced by it, even though she doesn't clip your coupon. This seemed to be confirmed in a recent study by three professors of A.C. Nielsen scanner data. According to a story in *The Wall Street Journal*, "The researchers say that while looking for the coupons they do use, shoppers pick up on the messages conveyed by other coupons—even if they don't actually clip them and use them."

But note the curious ending on the *Journal* item: "This means that the incremental sales to noncoupon users *can help offset any reduced profit margin caused by coupon redemption.*" [Emphasis added.] In other words, couponing is cutting manufacturers' profits, but maybe not as much as they had previously thought. That's pretty feeble encouragement.

On balance, the mass-market approach to couponing must inevitably give way in the remaining years of this decade to new and better alternatives more consistent with the overall trend to more individualized marketing.

DATABASING COMES TO COUPONING: THE KRAFT STORY

Perhaps the packaged-goods company that has done the most to overcome the long-standing problems associated with couponing-as-usual is Kraft Foods (formerly Kraft General Foods). In the mid-1980s the company created a new position, Director of Direct Marketing, and hired John Kuendig to fill it. When he arrived, Kuendig began to draw together into an organized database all the loose threads of household and product-usage data derived from the company's many promotions, and to test programs designed to make profitable use of this treasury of information. Kraft was determined to bring their product promotion into the Information Age.

They ended up with, in effect, two databases. First came the "overall" database, with information on a total of more than 35 million households. But they found that this was too unwieldy and costly to maintain as a dynamic, relational database. So they pared it down to a functional, on-line database profiling 25 million households.

Surprisingly, Kuendig told us that it cost Kraft relatively little to create the database. The corporation already had the hardware in-house. They bought a software package for about $500,000. They were already keypunching all of their premium requests and sweepstakes entries. It cost "next to nothing," compared to the cost of a big-time advertising budget, to turn this information into a usable relational database, Kuendig said.

Now, as they receive and enter data on a new household, they overlay information (demographics and lifestyle) from Polk-NDL, and use Donnelley Cluster Plus to add demographic information. They then record additional behavioral data as time goes on, as the household responds to additional Kraft offers and promotions. Still more information is obtained and entered by including a questionnaire in all promotional offer fulfillment packages. (An astonishing 20 to 25 percent of recipients complete and return the questionnaire, even without an incentive.) They also mail survey questionnaires annually to 10 million database households, to further update demographic and behavioral information.

Kuendig can put together his own direct mail co-op cheaper than buying into an outside co-op mailing service like Carol Wright—and his past histories of all households are more relevant. "By putting a value-added offer into my co-op package, I can build goodwill for Kraft while delivering my promotional incentive," says Kuendig. "After a while, the consumer will look for my promotional mailings because they offer what she wants and needs, and because the value-added extra is custom-tailored to her lifestyle and shopping habits."

Everything that Kuendig sends to the consumer reflects the information in the database about the household. "I can create co-ops that make sense," rather than simply offer discounts. For example, he has run a "light foods" co-op featuring 13 different brands appealing to health-conscious families. "Then I can continue the dialogue by asking for additional meaningful information." Kuendig says that all Kraft redemption promotions can now take into account the promotion's effect on the subsequent buying behavior of coupon nonredeemers. They can measure share-of-mind impact on the total audience contacted, not just the respondents, just as they would do for an awareness advertising campaign.

ELECTRONIC COUPONING: THE VISION VALUE STORY

The Vision Value Network attempts to overcome many of the problems associated with wasteful fsi couponing by turning to "electronic couponing." The concept was developed by Advanced Promotion Technologies, a public company headquartered in Pompano Beach, Florida, and formed in 1987 as a joint venture between Procter & Gamble, Dun & Bradstreet, CheckRobot, Schlumberger Technologies, PNC Company, and GTE Interactive Services.

The Vision Value Network works in three ways that reflect an understanding of the selective and individualized MaxiMarketing approach.

1. The Vision Value interactive terminal at supermarket checkout lanes is a high-tech wonder. The terminal has a touch-sensitive color video monitor, printing capabilities, and a card reader that supports the Vision Value Club frequent-shopper program, as well as a variety of electronic financial services (credit, debit, check-cashing approval). The terminal screen shows deductions for credits and refunds as it scans promoted items. The thermal printer built into the terminal can print out paper coupons, recipes, and appropriate messages when a product price is scanned or when the shopper touches the screen in response to a prompt. Special offers redeemed automatically at the checkout counter are flagged in the product displays throughout the store.

2. The Vision Value Club is a frequent-shopper program that uses a "smart" card to keep track of points. The shopper inserts his or her card into the terminal card reader and can accumulate points for buying participating brands as well as for the total dollar purchase. The program builds loyalty for both the promoted brands and the supermarket's loyalty program. The accumulated point total appears on the terminal screen, and the member can redeem gifts from a special catalog.

3. Vision Value Financial Services permits the card member to access payment options such as credit, debit, or automated check approval. Shoppers also may earn additional points by applying for a Vision Value Visa or MasterCard through a participating bank.

What it all comes down to is providing a participating manufacturer with an uncanny ability to track an individual consumer's purchasing history and to target marketing messages based on family characteristics and buying behavior. You can tailor your discounts to frequent buyers or to prospects—or to users of competitors' brands. You can deliver an advertising message—or cross-sell a related product—on the video monitor. For example, it is possible to give a shopper buying baby food a coupon for diapers, or a customer who buys a diet soft drink a coupon for a low-calorie frozen entree.

Each time the consumer uses his or her Frequent Shopper Club Card at checkout, the system can access the demographic information and purchase history for that particular shopper so as to make the right promotional offer to the right person at the right time. It is possible to have multiple offers to different targeted shoppers going on in the same store at the same time.

Vision Value transmits marketing messages by satellite to each store. The system has the ability to vary the promotion by market, region, chain, or individual store. Says Advanced Promotion Technologies' CEO Robert Wientzen, "You only pay for what is actually delivered to your target audience, so your promotion is affordable as well as efficient. Plus we can give you total exclusivity in your product category. While we're running a Vision Value promotion on your brand, no other brand can compete."

It would be premature to hail Vision Value as an unqualified success, even though early returns are impressive. It certainly represents an important opening to what could become a customized world of sales promotion. Two Drake University professors conducted a follow-up to a 1990 study. In 1994, they concluded that the system is successful in generating shopper loyalty in participating stores. Of club members surveyed, 9 out of 10 said that they use their Vision Value Club card on all or most shopping trips, a 21 percent increase from the 1990 study.

Supermarket chains that have installed the terminals include Vons, SuperValu, Fleming, Big Bear, Megafoods, Kroger, Furrs, Smitty's, Super Foods, X-TRA, and Lunds.

Major packaged-goods marketers such as Keebler, Jimmy Dean Foods, Procter & Gamble, Lever Brothers, Kimberly-Clark, Scott Paper Products, Duracell, Kraft, Ralston Purina, Tropicana, and others are learning how to make electronic couponing a better way to deliver product discounting than old-fashioned mass-distributed cents-off couponing. With the Vision Value Network, you can glimpse the future of the supermarket checkout.

The overwhelming dependence on couponing and price incentives is not going to go away overnight. And if your company is a packaged-goods advertiser involved in the practice, it will be well worth your while to consider ways in which the couponing effort can be made more efficient at a time when every business practice is becoming more accountable.

TRY "UNDERCOVER" COUPONING

There is now a way to skip current product users when couponing. It has two limitations: It costs more than fsi's, and it can't reach as many people. When you consider the hidden costs of having a high percentage of fsi coupon redemption by users, however, this other way begins to look not only attractive but also cost-effective.

It is what *Marketing Communications* magazine has dubbed "undercover marketing," or what Gary Blau of Select & Save has chosen to call "guerrilla marketing—before your competition figures out what's going on, it's too late, you've already communicated with their hard-core users."[11]

From the perspective of MaxiMarketing, it is an important step in the process of moving modern-day promotion in the cost-effective direction of selective interaction with known prospects. We provided an example in Chapter 3 of how Metromail, Infobase, and other public databases make it possible to send samples by mail, or coupons in a co-op mailing, to consumers known to use a competitor's brand in your product's category. And, if you wish, to skip households known to be using your brand already.

As we saw in the Ecotrin pain tablets case history, although the cost per distribution in this kind of direct mail may seem high, the cost per redemption can be at least as low as that of coupons in fsi's. And by building in a direct-response element and relating the tabulated responses to known characteristics of the responders, you can gain priceless marketing information about your best prospects.

Another way to achieve the same result is Catalina's Checkout Coupon, which issues a coupon only to those people who buy a certain item at the supermarket checkout. The coupon could be triggered by the purchase of a competitor's product to encourage trial, or for the next purchase of the same item to encourage loyalty. Catalina Marketing Network, headquartered in St. Petersburg, Florida, says that its printers are in 8000 supermarkets in the top 25 U.S. markets.

OSCAR MAYER'S EARLY USE OF "DATAMOTION"

What if you want to vary the weight of your promotional incentive to nonusers, users, and competitive brand users? You can use the data in your database or information available from an outside source to send different strokes to different folks. This can show dramatic results in controlling the program's overall cost. Keep in mind that, while we are focusing on couponing, the same variable-incentive "datamotion" concept also applies to many other forms of promotion in this age of database-driven marketing.

Oscar Mayer provided an early example of this method in a direct-mail couponing test. The firm divided the market into three cells: Oscar Mayer users, competitive-product users, and non-users of the category. Each cell received a different letter and a coupon with a different incentive value. The users got the lowest-value coupon and the competitive-product users a higher-value one, while the non-users received a full-value certificate, in effect redeemable for a free sample.

The letter to current users thanked them for buying the product and expressed the hope that they would continue to buy it. (After all, existing customers are important too! Indeed, they are your most valuable asset.) The letter to users of a competitive product sought to define the attributes and benefits of the Oscar Mayer product as compared to other brands.

And the letter to nonbuyers in the category introduced them to the product and invited them to try it at no cost.

The greatest number of redemptions occurred in the groups at both ends, the Oscar Mayer users and the non-users, both with redemption rates of 55 percent. Understandably, the competitive-product users were the most difficult to penetrate, and came in with a redemption rate of around 14 percent.

The Oscar Mayer campaign demonstrated the power of customization, segmentation, and variable incentives in sales promotion. The users were encouraged to remain loyal but were not wastefully over-rewarded. The non-users were tempted to try Oscar Mayer at no charge, and almost 15 percent of them accepted.

This is really a new kind of advertising communication: "private advertising." You talk to your best customers and prospects privately, and what you say depends on what you know about them. And even if your competitors find out what you are doing, it will probably be too late for them to neutralize your targeted, individualized promotion strategy with a counter-campaign.

OTHER FORMS OF DISCOUNTING IN OTHER CATEGORIES

Of course, the offering of a discount with a coupon is an option not just for packaged-goods manufacturers and fast-food chains. Almost any kind of selling by or through retailers can use coupons and rebate offers—usually without the saturation problem that is such a factor in neutralizing the value of couponing for established packaged-goods brands.

Professor Thomas Nagle of The University of Chicago says:

> The industries that are using [sales promotion tactics] most intensively now realize that they have gone overboard, and are trying to cut back. But that is going to be more than made up for by the expansion of sales promotion techniques into industries that have never used them before, like financial services, the airline industry, and alcoholic beverages.[12]

WALDENBOOKS APPROACH.   When Waldenbooks opened a book-store on Manhattan's Lexington Avenue, it blasted off the launchpad with a full-page ad in *The New York Times* containing not one, not two, not three, but *five* coupons:

1. "Thirty-five percent off book purchases (same-day only)."
2. "Free Membership in Waldenbooks Romance Book Club—for Romance Book lovers—a bimonthly newsletter, free books, and special offers."
3. "Free membership in Waldenbooks Otherworlds Club. For SF/Fantasy buffs—a newsletter, exclusive offers, and a huge selection of books."
4. "Free membership in Waldenbooks Happy Birthday Club. For kids 14 and under—a birthday card and a birthday bonus."
5. "Free" (picture of a cup of coffee).

While not every retailer can afford a full-page ad in *The New York Times*, there is nothing in this vigorous promotion that couldn't be emulated *in principle* by any retailer, no matter how small.

The ad was a logical extension of the earlier move by Waldenbooks into the wonderful world of having a MaxiMarketing relationship with book buyers. In 1990 they established the Preferred Reader program, which attracted 3.8 million members in its first year. Preferred Readers pay a $10 annual fee and receive 10 percent off their purchases and a $5 coupon for every $100 in purchases at Waldenbooks. In its first year the program accounted for 35 percent of the chain's sales, a figure the company expected to rise to 50 percent.

Most important of all, Waldenbooks now can track which books each member of the program is buying. The membership card must be presented to get the 10 percent discount and to earn the rebate. This is couponing by membership only, and it builds an invaluable storehouse of buyer-behavior information on each individual customer.

In an initial effort shortly after launching the program, Waldenbooks mailed a postcard to 10,000 Preferred Readers who might be interested in *Voice of the Eagle,* a novel set in prehistoric times. The chain built the list from members who had bought the author's first book, or who had bought Jean Auel (*Clan of the Cave Bear*) titles, or were attracted in some other way to the category. The card included information about the book, a blurb from Auel, and a $2 discount coupon for the book (in addition to the 10 percent discount for Preferred Readers).[13]

Waldenbooks Preferred Reader Program has become a model for other booksellers, who now can see how promotion and database marketing became a natural fit to maximize sales and profits. It's a high-powered example of how the various parts of a MaxiMarketing strategy can work together in an ongoing relationship-marketing program.

HIGH-TICKET "COUPONING."   In advertising a high-ticket purchase, it is possible to offer a coupon with a dramatically high face value (although if it's too large, it runs some risk of losing credibility). Of course when the discount gets big enough, you can switch to calling it a "rebate."

During the rebate craze that swept Detroit in the 1980s, all of the car manufacturers were offering big cash discounts, and just as with couponing in the packaged-goods field, the offers tended to cancel each other out and leave everybody in the same place—lower profit margins.

So Chrysler came up with a rebate that the company insisted was *not* a rebate. The car company sent an elegant direct-mail piece, gold-embossed and printed on heavy stock, and bearing a message from company chairman Lee Iacocca, to nearly 4 million people. In appreciation for customers' having had enough faith in Chrysler products to have bought the car during the company's dark days, they were presented in the mailing with a "Thank You, America" certificate worth $500 toward the purchase of any Chrysler vehicle.

A company spokesperson said the promotion was "eminently successful." Within a few months, Chrysler's year-to-date sales of domestic cars were up 30 percent over the previous year. More than 2 percent of the certificates were redeemed at dealerships, and Chrysler attributed the sale of 130,000 cars and trucks directly to the program. Once again, targeting a known database of likely buyers (their own past purchases) with a personalized direct-by-mail message breathed new life into promotional discounting.

A universal law of merchandising is that *the better a new promotion concept works, the greater the likelihood of ultimate saturation usage by an entire category.* As a MaxiMarketer, you need to look at who is doing what discounting in your category. Is there a new game in town, or is the common practice at a mature or saturated level? Choose the discounting or rebating coupon strategy which fits your product or service best and which will make you stand out from the crowd. And to gain the biggest possible competitive advantage, consider turning your promotion into an exciting relationship-marketing program. Waldenbooks did it, and you'll find several other examples in Chapter 9.

MAYBE IT'S TIME FOR ANOTHER LOOK AT TRIED-AND-TRUE SAMPLING

That old marketing standby, sampling, when done properly, can still be very effective. It's surprising companies don't use it more often. Even if your company has not had its own positive experience with sampling, it's worth taking a fresh look at a promotion tool you may want to try again.

To make the best use of sampling, you should either have a product advantage that can be demonstrated or be introducing a new product.

Aaron Cohen Marketing Services of Scarsdale, New York, did a study to determine how a user of a particular product would react after receiving a sample of a brand he or she did not already use.

The firm studied the sales impact of 10 products in John Blair Marketing's sample pack. The sampled products experienced market-share increases ranging from 5 percent for a brand with over half the volume in its category to 3533 percent for a new product that started with an exceptionally low base.

"COLD" DISTRIBUTION VERSUS REQUESTED SAMPLES

In sales promotion advertising, should you mail unsolicited free samples directly to targeted prospects, or merely *offer* a free sample? The advantage of the first approach is that your sample will reach a far greater number of people at far less cost *per person* when compared with the cost of soliciting and then fulfilling a sample request. But the second approach may cost less *per interested prospect* sampled, and provides a prospect's name and address and perhaps other data for your database as well. It also permits you to combine sampling with advertising research, using the Caples copy-testing method described in the previous chapter and making your direct-response offer a free sample.

General Mills showed just how powerful a free-sample offer can be when the cereal company went on prime-time network TV in 1994 to offer a free sample of Total Raisin Bran. More than a million breakfast-cereal lovers picked up the phone and called the toll-free 800-number to request a sample-size box. Did it work? General Mills was back a year later repeating the promotion, and this time offering a full-size box. Evidently, they had found a way to convert a good number of the competitor's customers.

SPECTACULAR SAMPLING SUCCESS BY HELENE CURTIS

One of the most spectacular sampling successes by means of "cold" sample distribution was the introduction of Finesse shampoo and conditioner.

Helene Curtis spent $10.5 million to mail out 70 million little blue packets (backed by $18 million in television advertising) to middle- and upper-income women. Within six months Finesse conditioner had become number-one in its category, with a 12.2 percent market share. And these percentages were expected to increase, because the company had not yet been able to get enough product into the stores to meet the demand.

What do you think would have happened if Helene Curtis had skipped the sampling and spent all $28.5 million on television advertising? Our guess is not nearly as much. There have often been new-product introductions with $20 million or $30 million or more spent on television advertising and very little to show for it in traceable results.

If you are concerned about the cost of sampling, consider this: If the cost is evaluated in terms of weighing the advertising cost *per new customer acquired* rather than the cost per advertising impression, sampling could come out as one of the most economic forms of advertising rather than one of the costliest.

As the ability to target prime prospects via direct mail continues to improve, the cost-effectiveness of sampling becomes even more attractive. With today's vast databases of households accurately audited for individual interests, habits, and current brand usage, you can distribute your samples precisely where they will do you the most good.

SAMPLING VIA NEWSPAPER DELIVERY

Chesebrough-Ponds delivered a sample of Mentadent Fluoride Toothpaste with Baking Soda & Peroxide, plus a 75-cent coupon, with the morning newspaper. The promotion company, Sunflower Select Sampling of Overland Park, Kansas, provided imprinted plastic wrappers into which delivery people put the newspaper plus a separate sealed pouch containing the sample, the coupon, and an ad. The headline on the ad, which the consumer could read through the clear plastic, said, "You Already Know About Tartar Control Toothpaste. What You Don't Know Is..." When you open the plastic and unfold the ad, you get the product news: "New Tartar Control Mentadent Has It *All*...Effective Tartar Protection. Fluoride, Baking Soda & Peroxide. The Ingredients Dentists Recommend Most for the Care of Teeth and Gums." The readable copy gave the reasons why Tartar Control Mentadent is different from (and better than) other toothpastes.

The illustrations included the distinctive paste dispenser (no old-fashioned tube for Mentadent), and the Mentadent box (so that the consumer would know exactly what to look for in the toothpaste department).

This Chesebrough-Ponds' marketing expenditure has a lot going for it. It

1. Strengthens the brand image
2. Heightens interest by including a product sample
3. Gives those prospects who like the taste/effect a reason to buy the product
4. Includes a high-value coupon to move the product off store shelves and start the buying habit

All that was missing from the Mentadent blockbuster was a brief questionnaire on the coupon, to help them learn more about the user and to capture the redeemer's name for their database.

Sampling by CD-ROM

A new chapter, or perhaps even a whole new book, on how sampling can turn your desktop computer into a retail store has been written by the personal computer industry. MacZone, a mail-order computer and software retailer, has offered a free CD-ROM that contains more than 150 software programs from more than 70 publishers. Pop the disk into your Mac-compatible CD-ROM drive, and explore the software through multimedia guided tours, working demonstrations, and information on each application. If, having sampled the features, you found a program that you liked and wanted to buy, you simply called MacZone's special toll-free access number and charged your purchase. They gave you an access code number that would unlock the software so that you could download it immediately from the CD to your hard drive. MacZone then sent you any manuals or documentation by overnight carrier.

How about Testing Promotional Television?

Why not experiment with harnessing the reach of television to the appeal of sampling and other activation promotional offers? The public is now thoroughly familiar and comfortable with the use of the toll-free 800-number. Through purchase of an additional 15 or 30 seconds you could add an offer of a trial coupon, a relevant premium, or a sample to an existing 30-second brand-image commercial and invite responses. By asking a few questions when the respondent calls, you could identify your best prospects by individual characteristics.

Phone operators could be trained to screen the calls and separate present users from non-users. The information generated for your database would provide an invaluable storehouse of information.

The computer could print each cents-off coupon mailed out with the name and address of the respondent or with a UPC symbol, and comparison of the redeemed coupons to the database would reveal who was using the coupons and eventually the sales volume resulting from the promotion.

How Not to Do Sampling

Someone had a bright idea for Celestial Seasonings Tea. Why not do a two-minute direct-marketing television commercial, on cable, offering a sampler pack of a variety of Celestial Seasonings tea bags for $10 (high enough to help pay for the advertising), with founder Mo Siegel as the spokesperson?

They did break new ground carrying out the idea. But then the payoff of a great concept was sabotaged by the way they delivered the sample. The fulfillment package had no letter, no booklet, no inspirational sayings (except the one on each of the canisters), none of the charm and romance of the Celestial Seasonings Tea story to heighten the perceived value of the samples.

The package contained three bags of each of six kinds of tea, two enameled, oblong, metal tea canisters, and four 25-cent coupons with a brief thank-you note. It certainly didn't seem like a $10 value. It may have won some new customers (even as it turned off other prospects), but not nearly as many as a stronger resell and a better fulfillment package surely would have done.

Furthermore, the economics of the offer were questionable. It may have seemed like a good idea to somebody to charge $10 in order to cover the cost of merchandise and fulfillment. But look at it from a MaxiMarketing perspective. The stiffer the price, the fewer the responses. The $10 price might have yielded an advertising cost per order of $15, resulting in a $5 deficit to be added to the fulfillment cost. But a $1 offer might have pulled so many more responses that the advertising cost per response would be only $2, resulting in a deficit of only $1.

Quietly testing different offers before launching the campaign could have produced a far more satisfactory result.

SLOW DELIVERY OF REQUESTED SAMPLES HURTS

Like most of today's promotional offers, a 12-page Coty ad in a recent *Good Housekeeping* warns "allow 4 to 6 weeks for delivery," although you order the five sample fragrances by phone. The reasons for the slow delivery are likely to be (1) "that's the way we always do it" and (2) a valid economic consideration: the use of cheap bulk-mail postage rates for delivery.

But we know from past experience with direct-marketing clients that slow delivery mars the effectiveness of follow-up. When correspondence schools offering free information about their courses would mail out the information booklet by first-class mail rather than the much slower third class, the rate of conversion to sales of the inquiries was always far higher—and more than justified the additional cost. People want what they want when they want it!

One of our agency's direct-order clients once examined the total sales to test cells of customers whose first shipment had been sent within 24 hours of receipt of the order, within two days, within three days, and so on. He found that eventual sales to each test cell were in inverse proportion to how long the customers had had to wait for their first order. First impressions count.

When requested samples arrive six weeks later, the recipients probably have forgotten all about the offer, and their original enthusiasm is likely to have been replaced by other interests and concerns.

PREMIUMS: THE "SOMETHING EXTRA" PROMOTION TOOL

Premium promotion often suffers from many of the same ills as the other major categories of sales promotion. It seems obvious, but apparently it isn't, that good premium promotion needs to:

1. Strengthen the image of the brand's unique benefit or positioning or personality
2. Encourage continued use of the brand
3. Stimulate the widest possible response from real prospects

The marketplace abounds with examples of advertisers who did—and did not—observe these reasonable guidelines.

We came across a four-color bleed advertisement from *Woman's Day* that illustrates exactly how a MaxiMarketer would *not* run a premium promotion:

The makers of
MOP & GLO WILL SEND YOU
THE PERSONAL TOUCH RAZOR
FREE when you buy Mop & Glo

The ad did nothing for the product other than remind consumers of its existence with a big product picture and the copy line: "Get a beautiful shine on your regular or no-wax floor." The body copy was devoted almost entirely to the deal.

The premium had no logical connection to the product, other than that many women use both items—at very different times and for very different reasons.

There were two coupons at the bottom, a cents-off coupon for Mop & Glo floor-care products and a mail-order coupon for the ordering of the razor. To get the razor, the consumer had to send proof-of-purchase (part of the label *plus* cash-register receipt) *plus* 50 cents for handling and return postage. *And* buy first-class postage for the outside envelope! Note how much the consumer has to go through just to get this very mundane, unrelated, uninteresting little premium.

We cite this particular ad as just one example of the all-too-common practice of treating the consumer thoughtlessly or indifferently in a costly premium promotion.

The cartoonist Borth has effectively satirized this odd way of winning the hearts and minds of prospects. The cartoon shows the manufacturer conferring with his marketing advisor:

> MANUFACTURER: How can we get more people to buy our product?
>
> ADVISOR: Easy! Offer them a $1 refund coupon with each purchase of a large bottle.
>
> MANUFACTURER: That could cost us a million dollars if a million people used those coupons!
>
> ADVISOR: So we tell them they have to send along the label which is glued on the bottle...
> ...which means they have to remember not to throw out the bottle after it's empty...
> ...then soaking off the label in one piece and drying it. Then we tell them to include the cash-register tape which they probably lost...
> ...then use their own envelope, put a stamp on it, and mail it, then wait eight weeks. Who's going to do all that for 80 cents?
>
> MANUFACTURER: Okay...but make sure they can only have one refund per family![14]

Too exaggerated? What do *you* think? The obstacle course depicted in the cartoon bears an uncanny resemblance to many premium offers we see that seem to have as their goal the *discouragement* of response.

COMMON MISTAKES IN ADS OFFERING A PREMIUM

A common error we encounter in premium ads pulling for response is that they ignore the basic principles for maximizing response.

Carnation's Come 'N Get It dog food, for instance, ran a premium-offer ad that included a 50-cent coupon and a reply form for requesting (with proof of purchase) the paperback edition of the best-selling book *No Bad Dogs the Woodhouse Way* as a free premium. So far, so good—a soundly conceived, relevant premium and sampling promotion.

The ad shows a dog with the book in its mouth and the clever headline, "Take it from me, FREE!" But nowhere in the ad is there *any* selling copy about either the dog food or the book! The "all you gotta do is..." school of advertising strikes again. All our direct-response advertising experience tells us that specific, interesting, persuasive selling copy about the book could have doubled or tripled the response from dog lovers.

Anacin ran a baffling ad headed "Save $100!" The opportunity offered was to return the direct-reply form with 50 cents and proof of purchase for a "new 32-page book packed with coupons, discounts, and rebates to save you money, plus exciting articles that can make your life easier, healthier, and more fun."

But there was no explanation—none—about the editorial content of either the booklet or the value coupons. Were the coupons good for three nights in a modest Florida hotel? For a 10-year supply of Anacin tablets? The reader was left to guess.

This is still another example of what Alvin Achenbaum once called "marketing strategy erosion."

> This is the situation where the strategy of a market communication is eroded in its execution because of faulty and incompetent oversight. Although it exists in advertising, it is most prevalent in the merchandising and sales promotion areas.
>
> Despite the large sums spent on merchandising and sales promotion, they have continued to be treated by most marketers as a secondary factor—not totally integrated into the marketing program; not consistent with its strategic thrust; and usually not properly evaluated as to their real effect on annual sales.[15]

But not everybody is going in the wrong direction. Along with disappointing examples like Mop & Glo and Anacin, we can cite examples of premium promotion that meet at least some of our guidelines.

For example, in Chapter 3 we described the brilliant series of mailings that Seagram sent out to persuade known users of competing Canadian whiskies and Jack Daniel's to switch to Crown Royal. The first mailing offered a pair of Crown Royal on-the-rocks glasses as a premium, redeemable by submitted proof-of-purchase. The second mailing offered two sets of Crown Royal playing cards.

Both premiums were quite appropriate for the product. In addition, the direct-mail copy and art was so compelling and charming that it heightened the premium's perceived value, in much the same way as vivid accompanying copy can enhance the value of a free sample. By association, this enhanced value of the premium then added to the image of the product itself.

Using predictive modeling and no-waste targeting of competitive brand users, the Seagram campaign was able to recoup its entire cost with attributable sales within nine months, and then by redefining the program was able to convert 1 out of 4 competitive-brand users to Crown Royal.

How Can More Powerful Premiums Be Developed?

An underutilized tool of premium promotion is PreTesting. *Not* through asking consumer panels for their opinions—a practice that is filled with booby traps—but rather through direct-response testing of a number of promising possibilities.

You can do this publicly, with split-run inserts in selected magazines or A-B split runs in newspapers, or privately, via surveys or direct mail. This MaxiMarketing step can be performed in either of two ways:

1. A multiple split-run of a number of different advertisements, each one offering a different premium for the required payment.

2. A self-contained multiple offer, in which the same adver-
    tisement or direct-mail copy lists and describes a number
    of premium possibilities and the respondent is invited to
    choose one.

In either case, the public will inform you by way of its
responses which is the most appealing premium for you to
offer in future ads.

Sounds like it might be too much trouble? Take a moment
to check out how many advertising dollars your company is
devoting to premium promotion this year. Then calculate what
it would mean in revenues if prior split-run testing of premium possibilities had resulted in a doubling or tripling of the
sales effectiveness of the promotion.

You can also test different price-points for a self-liquidating
premium via direct response. You may find that you can charge
enough to cover the premium *and* the advertising that offers it.
Then you could run, in effect, "free" advertising for your product!
It would be like uncovering a promotional gold mine.

RELATIONSHIP MARKETERS TAKE A DIFFERENT APPROACH

One rich vein that is increasingly being mined by database-
minded marketers is the ongoing award of premiums, to be
earned partially or entirely by continued purchase of the product or family of products.

The classic Betty Crocker premium redemption program,
run for generations by General Mills, is the all-time king of
ongoing premium continuity programs. Buyers of General
Mills cereals and other packaged-goods products collect on-
pack "stamps" that are worth points toward the redemption of
free household gifts such as silverware and tableware.

A few years back the operation was dramatically rejuvenat-
ed, under the guidance of catalog consultant Katie Muldoon.

Beginning around 1990, the redemption point system was
revised to make it possible to acquire merchandise more

quickly with a combination of cash and points. Staff was increased to answer customer queries, and a customer database was created to make possible targeted catalog mailings. The catalog grew to 80 pages of a broader assortment of merchandise, with a number of discount coupons for General Mills products bound into the center.

As a result the catalog premium business began to grow 10 percent a year, surpassing $27 million by 1992.

But to an $8 billion corporation like General Mills, a mere $27 million in annual sales volume can't be very important. The operation is neither big enough to be a significant profit center, nor pushed with sufficient vigor to make it a major promotional vehicle.

In 1994, General Mills spent $210 million on measured advertising media. Just think what might happen if they chipped away 10 percent of that amount for a heavyweight $20 million advertising campaign to promote the catalog and the redemption system more vigorously. Additional catalog redemption revenues would help to pay for the cost of advertising it, and wider distribution and dramatization of the catalog would stimulate sales across the board of lesser brands like Fruity Yummy Mummy and Nature Valley Granola Bars that can't afford much of a budget on their own.

Now what if they got *really* serious about making the program a key corporate strategy, and put a miniature Betty Crocker catalog in every one of the 200 General Mills products that comes in a box, bag, or wrapper?

In short, we think that General Mills is overlooking a golden opportunity to build on the Betty Crocker relationship marketing program—and to stay a step ahead of packaged-goods rivals who are just now getting into database marketing in a serious way.

PREMIUM-DRIVEN FREQUENCY MARKETING BY A RETAILER

Zellers, Canada's largest department store chain in terms of market share, offers a dazzling 156-page premium merchandise catalog through a frequent-buyer program called Club Z.

Club points earned by purchases (100 points per dollar of purchase) represent an additional discount on top of the everyday low prices. (If you buy at Zellers and then find a lower price within 30 days, Zellers will refund the difference.) Club Z members obtain gift merchandise from the rewards catalog either through points alone or through a smaller number of points and cash.

Membership in Club Z stood at over 7 million in 1994—a staggering 63 percent of all the households in Canada! Around 75 to 80 percent of Zellers shoppers have become members of the club. This mass merchandiser mails out 7 million circulars *a week* to draw club members into the stores. What they have done is to carry promotion to a higher plane by making it part of the image and strategic positioning of the store itself. How they did this, and turned Club Z into a profit center in the process, will be covered in Chapter 9, when the awesome power unleashed by transforming promotion into "datamotion" as part of a relationship marketing blitz is discussed.

THE MAXIMARKETING APPROACH TO SWEEPSTAKES PROMOTIONS

By this time the power of a well-planned sweepstakes is legendary, and the appetite of the U.S. public and consumers around the world for entering a sweepstakes appears to be insatiable. But many sweepstakes promotions seem perfunctory, and unrealistic in their expectations of how to motivate entries and, more important, increase sales.

Remember that barely 20 percent of the U.S. population has ever sent in a contest or sweepstakes entry. Of those who have, over 75 percent accompanied their entries with facsimiles rather than proofs-of-purchase. And many were professional entrants who make going after a prize a way of life. Since many of the proof-of-purchase entries came from present customers who will buy your product regardless, you are left with a tiny percentage of entrants who were persuaded by your sweepstakes to try your product.

One final problem: You can't test a million-dollar sweepstakes in Peoria, then abandon it without awarding the prizes if the sales results are disappointing. So pretesting a big national sweepstakes simply isn't feasible.

IMAGINE THE CLOUT OF A NEVER-ENDING SWEEPSTAKES!

To have an impact in sales, a sweepstakes has to be imaginative, fun, appropriate, and brand-reinforcing. Edgar's, a department store chain headquartered in Johannesburg, South Africa, runs one of the best sweepstakes promotions we've ever seen. Edgar's has made entry into a monthly sweepstakes a privilege of membership in its relationship-building continuity club. The store has signed up 1.3 million members for The Club, more than a quarter of the South African households in its target market.

Members pay to belong. Each month there's a charge of about $2 on the credit card statement. This provides Edgar's with about $24 million to cover member benefits and leave something over for profit. The club is run as a separate profit center with its own financial plan and its own headquarters. Club members receive a slick monthly magazine and discount vouchers worth more than twice the annual membership fees, and they are surveyed to learn what they do and don't like about the chain and new club benefits. But the biggest inducement is the monthly sweepstakes.

A million rands (about $285,000) in prize money goes to winners each month. First prize is 250,000 rands. There are 620 prizes in all. The big difference is the automatic entry of members in a new sweepstakes each month, and the additional amount of prize money that winners can donate to education. The top five prizewinners get to make a donation, provided by Edgar's, to meet the needs of schools chosen by the winners themselves. It adds up to 3 million rands (almost $1 million) a year, and helps to close some of the critical gaps in education at every level of South African society.

Edgar's employs a full-time person to find the most useful educational "giving opportunities" each month and thereby to help prizewinners make a wise choice. Television commercials show dramatic examples of improved facilities, computer workstations, aid for schools devoted to handicapped children, and other outcomes. Prizewinner days are celebrated at local schools and at the chain's stores. Every month *The Club* magazine shows how schools are benefiting, and all Club members take pride in what they are achieving.

The Edgar's experience demonstrates that even in the conceptualization of sweepstakes prizes, there is plenty of room for true customer-involvement creativity. Once you start thinking about what you can do to extend the bond with the customer, not just get an immediate boost in sales, you begin to think differently about the whole art and science of sweepstakes promotion.

THE SELF-PRIZE SWEEPSTAKES

This type of sweepstakes sometimes offers a way to get a lot of benefit out of a modest prize structure. Your prizes become... the products you are selling. Thus you attract as entrants the people who are most interested in what you have to sell, and the possibility of winning can cause them to study and dream about your product's outstanding features.

Lanier Business Machines (now Lanier Worldwide) once asked our agency to develop a direct-mail campaign to business firms that would increase the quantity of sales leads for its pocket dictating machines without eroding the quality of the leads. To have offered a typical nonrelated extravaganza of prizes to a business audience would have been harmful to Lanier's image as a manufacturer of quality business machines. But by conducting a tasteful sweepstakes in which the prizes were the Lanier dictating machines the sales reps hoped to sell, we were able to double its flow of leads with no deterioration in lead quality.

One of the most dramatic examples we have seen of the self-prize sweepstakes was British Airways' "Everybody Flies Free" promotion, described earlier. By giving away all the seats on all their planes on a given day, British Aiways captured the attention of the world.

In November 1993, Budget Rent-a-Car ran a similar promotion, letting everyone who called (and who was a qualified
driver) have a car rent-free for 24 hours. Most (but not all) of
the firm's 1015 locations participated in the event. The free
day was two days before Thanksgiving, and customers had to
return the car, available on a first-come, first-served basis, to
the same location. "The idea is to drive our customers home
for the holidays," said a Budget spokeswoman. Once again,
the publicity generated made every dollar spent on the promotion do double-duty.

CREATING WINNING PROMOTIONS FOR SMALL BUSINESS

Lest more modest advertisers be staggered and intimidated by
the astronomical sums cited in some of our examples, we
remind you that promotional successes achieved with millions
of dollars can be emulated with budgets of only thousands of
dollars—or even less. It isn't difficult to imagine a local merchant working up a dramatic sweepstakes bonanza made possible by the suppliers of the products usually carried in his or
her store.

In fact, we can't think of a single promotional device used
by giant companies that couldn't be successfully adapted by
the smallest business. An appropriate and brand-reinforcing
premium? How about a T-shirt or baseball cap, emblazoned
with the name of your product or store? A free sample? The
most modest delicatessen can put a sign in the window: "Stop
in for a free taste of our fantastic Virginia ham or potato
salad." Even better, we passed a little bakery in Lower
Manhattan that had spread out bite-sized samples of its baked
goods on a card table, sitting right out on the sidewalk!

If you run a small business, try studying the sales promotion advertisements of the national advertisers and playing
"What if?" with the promotion strategies and devices you see
featured in them. You may be surprised by the profitable ideas
that emerge. And when you are ready to launch your own program, keep in mind all of the do's and don'ts that have been

distilled in this chapter from the lifework of those who have gone before you.

THE BOTTOM LINE

There is a better way to maximize the effectiveness of your promotion budget.

Mastering the new tools of one-to-one marketing and the tried-and-true principles of direct-response advertising can move you in the right direction and keep you on the right track. As we move farther into the Information Age, old-fashioned, scatter-shot sales promotion increasingly will be replaced by customized information-driven "datamotion."

If you're slugging it out in the packaged-goods field—up against similar products and similar promotions, working with promotional pennies per sale rather than dollars—traditional couponing may be providing the illusion of success while providing little positive or even some negative effect on profits.

But problems are opportunities in disguise. The tougher the race, the bigger the hero you will be if you win it. There are new ways you can make your sales promotion deliver the right results: by strengthening the brand-image content of your promotion; by targeting your promotion more sharply to heavy users and selected prospects; by conducting split-run direct-response tests to get the best premium or the best way to showcase and enhance your free sample; by having your promotions generate valuable information for your prospect and customer database.

What is most promising today is your ability to pick and choose who receives the promotion and to send just the right promotion to just the right person at just the right time. On the horizon, and already being pioneered by trendsetting marketers, is the movement away from one-shot promotions to relationship-building continuity promotional programs.

And if you have a small business, even a tiny one, you can adopt and adapt some of the secrets of the biggest kids on the block so as to put promotion to work maximizing your own sales and profits.

MAXIMIZED PROSPECT INVOLVEMENT

BUILDING A BRIDGE BETWEEN THE ADVERTISING AND THE SALE

THE BIG PICTURE

With today's trend toward customized production and customized marketing, the role of advertising is inevitably changing. Rather than trying to influence "everybody" in the media audience, its more proper function will be to attract, interest, sift out, identify, and gather together the comparative few who are the immediate or ultimate best prospects for the advertised product or service.

What happens after that becomes as important as what went before. The marketer converts this identified group into a committed buying group by sending additional advertising and promotion material of equal quality directly to the home or office of the selected prospect—whether by letter, brochure, voice-mail, fax, videocassette, audiocassette, CD-ROM, on-line site, World Wide Web homesite, follow-up salesperson, or any combination of these.

We call this vital marketing activity bridging. *It completes the selling process by means of additional facts, arguments, benefits, incentives, etc., that the up-front advertising didn't have the space, time, or capability to include.*

Allocating this bridging process more serious attention and funding must—and will—become an increasingly important part of the marketing process at the smartest companies.

Of course, we realize that the idea of inviting an inquiry and then providing more information in response to it is almost as old as advertising itself. Today, however, this key ingredient in total marketing communication is assuming a new importance.

Too many advertisers still treat both the offer of more information and the manner in which it is provided as a kind of casual afterthought. Often they view it as a routine action rather than as the vital function of building a bridge between the up-front connection with a prospect and the completion of the sale.

We checked this out recently by answering a number of ads. Frequently we saw no evidence that the firm was giving the same kind of thought and care and creativity that had gone into the up-front advertising to the planning and preparation of the the next step: the initiation of a direct relationship with a real, live prospect.

In the MaxiMarketing model, this scorned Cinderella of marketing is invited to step up and share the throne with the stalwarts of the marketing process, media advertising and sales promotion.

In this chapter we look at how advertisers are failing to bridge the gap between advertising and the sale, how you can focus more marketing power on those in the total media audience who are your best prospects and potentially your best customers.

As we noted in Chapter 2, direct-order selling involves essentially the same process that brand advertisers use in selling their products through retailers, but it compresses it into a one-step process. A single advertisement or direct-mail package contains the why-you-should-have-it, why-you-should-get-it-now, here-it-is, and how-to-get-it message. The store is right there in your hand or on your television or computer screen.

The skillful direct-order advertiser tries to keep the entire process flowing as one uninterrupted stream, from attracting the prospect's attention all the way to putting an order form in his or her hand. When the marketing process is viewed in this light, a costly fault is exposed in the practice of many advertisers who distribute their products through retail channels or offer a service: *They fail to bridge the gap between the advertising and the sale.*

When awareness advertising seeks to drive the prospect toward making and acting on a buying decision, it confronts a deep gap of time and physical distance between the advertising impression and the cash register, very much like a moat around a medieval castle.

Instead of constructing a bridge and leading the reader or viewer by the hand across that bridge and into the castle, where the advertised product hopefully awaits, many advertising campaigns abandon the prospect-traveler on the wrong side of the moat and hope for the best. No wonder many interested prospects never make it into the castle but wander away, puzzled and frustrated.

NOBODY IS IN CHARGE OF LOVING THE PROSPECT

We think it can partly be explained by an over-fascination with advertising as an end in itself, rather than as just one important step in an ongoing process.

Week after week, the advertising trade journals fill their pages with critical acclaim for the latest breathtaking flights of fancy in print and broadcast advertising. These tributes rarely tell you whether the advertising successfully led many consumers into the retailer's castle to purchase the product. To put it another way: Company management usually insists on loving its advertising, but it neglects to put anybody in charge of loving the prospect.

As companies grow, they tend to become compartmentalized and departmentalized. Responsibilities are divvied up and parceled out. The chief executive is busy planning for the future, worrying about cashflow, and making the most of the company's assets. The marketing director is busy trying to improve market share, allocating and approving budgets, and seeking that breakthrough new product. The product managers are busy tracking sales, supervising the ad agency's campaigns, and building up advertising recall scores. The sales promotion manager is busy pushing the goods through the retail pipeline by means of redemptions or rebates or premium offers, making deals with retailers, or coming up with yet another sweepstakes promotion.

But nobody—or so it would seem—is busy worrying about where the prospect stands, and about building a bridge that will help him or her to travel from the advertising or promotion contact to the cash register.

We are talking here about much more than what usually comes under the heading of "customer satisfaction programs." We are talking about raising prospect-handling to the same level of attention and care that customer-handling has received in recent years. Imagine for a moment the effect on your bottom line if just 10 or 20 percent *more* of those who are mildly attracted by your advertising were to become convinced that they should come over from the competition and become *your* customers.

THE CASE OF THE UNBUYABLE DRESS

A reporter in *The Wall Street Journal* once told of a maddening experience which, although somewhat extreme, dramatizes and typifies the problem:

> Two weeks ago, *The New York Times Magazine* carried an ad for an off-the-shoulder black-and-white formal that some women readers thought they might die for. One of them, this reporter, naively assumed the dress could be bought, and set out to buy it.
>
> The first stop was Bloomingdale's in the Short Hills Mall in New Jersey. Although the sales help there breathlessly

admired the picture of the dress, they said they didn't have it. Nor did the B. Altman & Co. or Abraham and Strauss department stores in the mall.

The next day, this now suspicious reporter went into Manhattan to Macy's at Herald Square. The saleswoman was not amused. "If one more person shows me that picture..." she said peevishly. "We don't have it, never had it and aren't going to get it," she continued, very, very calmly.

The next day, a call went out to the manufacturer, Leslie Fay Co. The dress had been ordered by Saks Fifth Avenue in New York and Marshall Field in Chicago, they said.

At Saks, the subject of the dress brought weariness to the voice of the saleswoman. "I know the dress, but we don't have it—never did," she said.[1]

And so it went. We'll spare you the painful additional details, other than to say that when the reporter learned that she absolutely, positively could not buy the dress, she called and asked a spokesperson for the company what the point of the advertising was. "It wasn't really an ad," he said. "It just showed products that Leslie Fay makes."

More recently, USSB (the United States Satellite Broadcasting Company) ran an eight-page, tabloid-size insert in *The Wall Street Journal*. In all that space, it still was not made entirely clear what the company wanted the reader to *do*. The first page of copy talked about a new small satellite dish, the second two pages of copy talked about the available programming (obviously not free programs, because they tell you that you get one free month when you purchase a Digital Satellite System), the fourth page of copy promoted multichannel programming, the fifth page of copy explained that the system includes a way that parents can censor children's viewing, and the last page discussed customer service (if you have a problem, call the customer service center "where professionals—real, live, actual people—are ready to answer your questions or to get you someone who can; 24 hours a day, 365 days a year").

But, if you are not already a customer able to call the customer service center, don't try calling USSB for more information. There is no phone number listed anywhere in the eight pages. Don't think of writing to them, either. There's no address. So what *are* you supposed to do? "For details, ask your local RCA retailer, and tell them USSB sent you." What if you don't know who your local RCA retailer is? If you're the persevering type, you can go looking for him in the Yellow Pages—although nowhere in the eight pages do we find that useful hint.

Our local RCA dealer, once located, was helpful. He told us over the phone that the satellite receiver comes in two flavors, $700 and $900, and that the service costs $30 a month. He didn't ask for our name or address, however, and didn't offer to send more information. Having been stopped short by an eight-page supplement—and then finding our own way to a dealer—we were finally left high-and-dry on the wrong side of the moat.

Wouldn't it have made sense to devote some of the advertising and promotion budget to capturing the prospect's name and address, taking him or her by the hand and leading him or her to the moment of buying decision? We're talking about a pretty serious family investment here, $700, plus a commitment to spend $30 a month—that comes to $360, year in and year out!

Friendly, informative, complete, reassuring direct-mail follow-up could have answered questions, removed doubts, explained and depicted benefits, instilled confidence, and stimulated immediate action with a tempting reward for action.

Of course, direct-mail follow-up doesn't even have to be done through direct mail anymore. To sell today's high-ticket, high-tech products, videocassette demonstrations and autofax printouts are doing a bang-up job of converting undecided prospects. And now, advertising on CD-ROMs is emerging, and many companies are beginning to provide more detailed information, plus opportunities for interaction, on the home computer screen via the Internet's World Wide Web.

We wish that the "lost" dress or the satellite-dish advertising stories were isolated examples, but you know they are not. Stop for a moment and think of your own personal experiences being disappointed, frustrated, or confused when trying to learn more about advertised products or services.

Page through your favorite magazine. Notice how often the hard-to-read copy or tricky ad design makes it difficult for you to get interested in what the advertising is trying to tell you. And then if you *do* get interested, watch how the communication stops abruptly or trails off, providing you with no pathway toward deeper involvement. You, the reader, are left with nowhere to go—just another victim of the *discontinuity* of so much of today's advertising.

FIVE STRUCTURAL COMPONENTS OF GOOD BRIDGE-BUILDING

What does the ideal bridge look like, the one that will lead your prospect from an advertising or other message to a final sale? It is constructed of the very same components as those found in a successful direct-marketing selling effort.

1. *Activation.* The first step must be to engage the prospect in a *dialogue,* in two-way communication. There must be some reason included in your advertising for the interested prospect to respond—an offer of where-to-find-it or of more information, a sample, a premium, a rebate, etc.

The invitation to respond shouldn't seem to be a casual afterthought, such as a toll-free phone number displayed quick as an eye-blink at the end of a 30-second commercial, or an offer concealed in tiny type at the bottom of a magazine or newspaper ad. It should be an integral part of your marketing and advertising strategy and communication.

Once you have accepted this premise, logic dictates that the goal is to not only invite and encourage response but also to maximize it.

2. *Information.* Next comes the transmission of warm, friendly, persuasive, detailed follow-up information about the product—all those things that you'd like to tell your prospect but didn't have enough time for in a 30-second commercial or enough room for in an ad mostly occupied with a huge photograph used to grab the reader's attention.

And don't listen to those proponents of right-brain advertising, whispering in your ear that "nobody will read all that copy." Think of "all that copy" in your follow-up as *smorgasbörd,* a feast of information spread out before your prospects from which each can take just what he or she wants or needs. Some, who are hungry for information, will pig out on all of it. Others will pick out just a morsel here or a morsel there.

3. *Persuasion.*   Information alone is never enough. Ideally, your follow-up should take the reader by the hand and lead him or her emotionally from a present problem to the ultimate benefit—whether by means of a long letter, a powerhouse brochure, a booklet, a faxback, or even an advertising video (which today can cost as little as $1.50 to duplicate).

What is important is to send the right message to the right person when his or her interest is at its most intense.

4. *Propulsion.*   Direct marketers have learned the hard way that one of the greatest enemies of sales success is the human tendency toward inertia and procrastination. "Oh yes," says the prospect, "that sounds like it might be worthwhile, and I really must do something about it sometime." But too often the impulse slips away, never to be revived.

To turn that "sometime" into *right now,* direct marketers use what they call "the hot potato": they put something in the prospect's hand that he or she *must* do something about. A deadline. An early-bird discount. A reward for acting at once. The propellant to move the prospect to action *now.*

We would like to see more mainstream marketers using the hot-potato form of activation promotion. You can use promotion and "datamotion" to *propel* the prospect forward, to get her or him to go out and buy the product.

Of course, your bridging material can provide a list of all your dealers—or better yet, a customized computer printout of the names and addresses and phone numbers of the dealers nearest to the prospect's home address. And the ultimate bridge is likely to be a site on the Internet where you can begin an ongoing dialogue customized to each prospect's needs in real time.

5. *Completion.* Direct marketers try to make it as easy as possible to order. They exercise great care in designing a clear, simple, inviting, friendly order form. The retail equivalent is a sales clerk who understands what you, the advertiser, have made the customer want, and who is prepared to provide it promptly, pleasantly, and correctly.

The brand or product advertiser, alas, has no such sales clerk to rely upon. But filling that gap from afar as well as you can is a key element in the marketing process, part of loving the product and the prospect. Failure to do so can result in "disadvertising"—advertising that creates enemies, not customers, as the Leslie Fay experience suggests.

Obviously, the urgent need for bridge-building will vary in direct proportion to the price and availability of the product. Bridge-building may be neither practical nor necessary for a 49-cent product that is on sale next to every drugstore cash register in the country and is purchased by users only a few times a year. But it can be crucially important in the case of a product or service that is selling for $30, $300, $3000, or $30,000 at just a few locations in each area, or through a sales force calling on business prospects. It could also be important for a product that costs under $5 but that a good customer may purchase as often as 50 times a year.

FOUR COMMON FAILINGS IN FOLLOW-UP LITERATURE

In order to monitor the bridge-building performance of advertisers, from time to time we answer ads that invite a request for more information by toll-free phone call, fax, or reply form. More often than not, the fulfillment package we receive reflects poorly on the name and reputation of the company that sent it to us. It makes us wonder who is in charge of creating such a negative impression, at a company that has just spent $10 million or more in advertising to attract our interest. The following are the most common failures to love the prospect or respect the product that we have encountered.

1. *No letter, or only an amateurish letter, included.*   We have to place this at the top of our list of complaints about company communication with prospects and customers.

The importance of including a letter has been proven conclusively many times over in direct-order mailings. It is simply the most important component when it comes to generating a response. It is what the recipient reads first and most carefully.

But promotional mail is frequently guilty of going out with no letter inside at all. You wanted a booklet? Okay, here's the booklet. You asked for a cents-off coupon? Okay, here's the coupon. You wanted a free sample? Okay, here it is. *But no letter.*

Or if there is a letter, it's likely to be a short, blunt, poorly worded piece of business correspondence; often it has no salutation and is typeset in "cold" printer's type rather than familiar, friendly "typewriter type."

A common error is to think that if the enclosed booklet tells the whole story, there is nothing more for a letter to say. But direct marketers know that a letter gives you a priceless opportunity to tell your story a second time—in warm, human terms.

People have been known to read and respond to a letter that is 8, 10, or even 15 pages long—but only if it is a compelling piece of copy by a master of the art, a skilled professional who loves the prospect and loves the product. "Ah, but *my* problem is different," we hear you saying. "I can image an interesting letter about a Caribbean cruise or an exercise machine. But who wants to read a letter about *toilet tissue?!*"

Sounds like a tough problem, doesn't it? That's because it *is!* But if slice-of-life commercials can present consumers talking with excitement and genuine interest about their favorite brand of laxative (as they sure do), then surely a creative copywriter can compose a pleasant, persuasive note to accompany a cents-off coupon for such a product.

2. *Hard-to-read typography.*   This may seem like an odd item to place on this list, but it very much belongs in any consideration of loving the prospect. We have received brochures with a bad case of "art director-itis," in which long stretches of text type are set in small, unreadable white letters on a black background. Or worse, are superimposed on a full-color photograph or illustration with great variations in tone, so that the reader must struggle to make out the white letters printed on a background of white clouds!

Some other common typographic sins:

1. Type too small to be read easily, surrounded by acres of "artistic" white space
2. Type set in a measure that is too short or too long
3. Pale, thin, sans-serif type
4. Grotesquely exaggerated line spacing
5. Type that curves around the visual element with such flair and style that it's impossible to read without great effort

In contrast, take a look at an article in *Reader's Digest* or *Newsweek,* and notice how effortlessly your eye glides into and through the text. Then take a look at your company's product literature and see if it's equally easy to read.

3. *Slow response.* We mentioned this in Chapter 7, but it applies here as well. *Boardroom Reports* once reported:

> Recent industrial advertising monitoring shows only 44 percent of advertisers responding within 60 days to inquiries prompted by ads or publicity releases. About 30 percent of the remaining 56 percent fail to respond even within 16 weeks. Result: potential customers are turned away by lack of interest in their needs.[2]

Modern technologies such as instant-reply faxback can be of some help here, but they are not the whole answer. Recently we responded to a trade magazine ad and got back a fax with the information requested virtually instantaneously. It was another two weeks after that, however, before a marketing consultant to the company finally called to ask if we had any questions. When we told her about our project, she promised to have the company send us more information. Which it did—a full month after our first request, and long after we had found our way to the competitor's door.

The same situation too frequently prevails in consumer advertising. Some companies we contacted did fairly well with their promptness of response, especially advertisers of high-ticket items. Others were shockingly and inexcusably slow, so slow that most inquirers would have forgotten that they had inquired. Indeed, we responded to an ad by the American Plastics Council offering a free booklet that, 11 weeks later, still had not arrived.

A case can be made for the cost-saving need to use the slower delivery of third-class mail instead of fast (well, relatively fast) first-class mail, in sending out a low-value coupon for a low-price packaged-goods product. But is it always a *good* case?

The cost of just one prime-time airing of a TV commercial, if rechanneled into better bridging, can buy an awful lot of first-class postage. And a reply in the prospect's mailbox just four or five days after his or her request is a wonderful way to say to that person, "We respect you! We take you seriously! We care about you! We want you!" Especially if it's accompanied by a warm, chatty letter.

When it does take six weeks to receive a reply to a promotional offer, the Postal Service cannot be assigned all the blame. In America, business mail (third class) takes two to three weeks at the most. What really holds up the mail is the turnaround time at the fulfillment house. Today, the six-week pace is totally unacceptable, and entirely unnecessary.

4. *Unclear or inadequate purchasing alternatives.*   Some companies do fairly well when it comes to enclosing a list of dealers. Few go so far as to set up a complete program, in which the computer prints out the name of the nearest dealer for the inquirer and also sends the name of the inquirer to the nearest dealer.

Then there are those two magic words that are not used as often as they could be: *either* and *or*. The prospect can *either* obtain the product from the nearby dealer listed *or* can order direct. The incremental business obtainable in this way—not merely accepted but positively encouraged by means of clear ordering instructions, order form, money-back guaranteed, incentive, etc.—can produce extra income that can pay for more advertising, which in turn can stimulate retail as well as direct purchases. Everybody wins.

There was a time when companies fretted that their dealers would boycott them if they accepted direct orders, even quietly and privately. This is far less true today. As retailers compete more and more directly with manufacturers by selling their own house brands—and as dealers stagger under far more inventory than they can possibly monitor in the marketing world—the case against dual-channel distribution for the manufacturer has been substantially weakened.

However, if there *is* a legitimate reason for concern about dealer reaction—and admittedly there sometimes is—you may be able to assuage it by offering to provide via direct sale only those items in your full line that are not carried by most dealers. Pfaltzgraff dinnerware built a thriving catalog operation in precisely that way. Far from weakening retail sales, it may have strengthened them, since it meant that shoppers could buy Pfaltzgraff patterns with the assurance that they could always add anything from the full line to their dinner set later on, no matter how limited their dealer's stock.

SOME EXAMPLES FROM OUR MAILBOX

Come along and look over our shoulders, as we examine some of the follow-up material that has arrived in our mailboxes.

We're going to skip the two extremes. At one extreme there is the lonely, naked, cents-off coupon, either in an envelope all by itself or with a curt note. This practice is inexcusable, but so common and standardized that even a single illustration of it would seem self-serving.

At the other extreme is literature from companies whose survival depends on follow-up, such as resort vacation packages and financial services, and whose mailings can be expected to—and do—exhibit a high degree of professionalism.

Instead we're going to look at advertisers positioned between these two extremes. The examples were chosen more or less at random, and we are *not* singling out the advertisers for special criticism. Whatever shortfalls we may have found, they are far more often the rule rather than the exception across the marketing spectrum.

IBM

Big Blue was offering demo disks of OS/2 Warp, "The new 32-bit, multitasking, multimedia, Internet-accessed, crash-protected, Windows-friendly, totally cool way to run your computer." When we called 1-800-3-IBM-OS2 we reached a real person who asked only for our phone number, name and address, and where we had heard about the product.

A week later the disk arrived in a 9" × 12" envelope with an all-purpose letter:

> Dear Valued IBM Customer:
>
> I appreciate your interest in our software solutions and am pleased to provide you with the materials you have requested.

That's the brisk language of business correspondence, not the effective, conversational, one-to-one language of outstanding direct mail.

Since IBM had to generate a label with our name and address, it couldn't have been that much more difficult for the computer company to generate a personalized letter, addressed by name. And if Big Blue, the granddaddy of computer companies, *can't* figure out how to send us a computer-personalized letter, how come? Furthermore, while the letter does tell us how to order the program, it doesn't attempt to *sell* the program at all, nor is there any inducement to act promptly.

When we popped the disk into our computer, the demonstration itself was interesting as a demonstration: the vivid color, the graphics, the movement as pictures and letters faded in and out on the screen. But the message throughout was "We're wonderful," not, "Here's what we can do for you." It wasn't clear to someone unfamiliar with the older OS/2 or the DOS operating system just why the new OS/2 Warp is such a big improvement.

Just imagine the cost of the advertising, plus the cost of delivering the 9" × 12" package including the computer disk, and wonder along with us how any company could fail to have every element in the follow-up work 100 percent to move the recipient to make a purchase. Instead, the IBM package rates at best a 35 on a scale of 100.

Royal Copenhagen Porcelain; Georg Jensen Silversmiths

We once answered an ad headed "Come Dine with Kings," which showed Royal Copenhagen Blue Line porcelain dinnerware, a Jensen candlestick, Gotham flatware, Holme Gaard glassware, and several Georg Jensen patterns. The ad invited: "Send $1 for the complete color folio."

We received two four-page color folders, and a price list that had been copied on an office machine—you could see where the staples and binder holes had been.

The two folders showed all the pieces in the Blue Fluted Plain and the Blue Fluted Full Lace patterns of Royal Copenhagen porcelain dinnerware. There was a brief blurb in three languages on the back page of each folder. The price list covered *only* the Blue Fluted Plain Border line.

There was no letter.

There was *nothing* about Gotham flatware *or* Georg Jensen silver plate *or* Holme Gaard glassware.

We felt like asking for our dollar back. Apparently the purpose of the $1 charge wasn't really to defray the cost of the follow-up. It was to discourage response.

Total Raisin Bran

As mentioned earlier in this book, General Mills ran a television campaign not long ago for Total Raisin Bran. It was a powerful direct-response commercial, inviting viewers to call for a free sample. The company received a *million* calls, a staggering number. It was a daring and effective way to sample the product, but the fulfillment left a great deal to be desired.

The telephone operators asked only for the caller's name and address. There were no questions about the caller's current product usage or demographic information for the database.

We waited *six weeks* for the box to arrive. It came in a plain brown carton, crushed, and without a letter, although it did include a slip of paper that said in effect "Here's your box of cereal" plus a 75¢ discount coupon for a regular box.

A personalized letter could have thanked the respondent for her or his interest, and explained why Total Raisin Bran is so much better for you than other brands. (Not only do you get the sweet, plump raisins specially grown for Total, and the crunchy, flavorful bran, but you get your Total recommended daily supply of vitamins and minerals.) Even a well-done non-personalized letter would have added greatly to the impact of the shipment, while surely adding only a tiny fraction to its total cost.

Obviously the promotion did work as a sampling strategy, because General Mills repeated it again a year later. But rather than just being an effective promotion, it could have been a far more effective MaxiMarketing program, through a strong "bridging" package and then further use of the database acquired by handling the requests properly.

Whatever position you hold in your company, dig out your most recent advertising and take a look at it. If it includes an offer of more information, play consumer and answer the ad yourself. You may get a shock when you wait and wait for it to arrive, and then see in what condition it arrives.

Today, when all of us are faced with sharply escalating media costs, paying more attention to your communications with interested prospects is more than just desirable. It's a marketing necessity. If your company's marketing is *really* going to be customer-focused (as so many companies claim they already are), then giving your prospects all the information and help they need becomes truly critical.

A new day is dawning, a day in which the fulfillment of offers and information available by phone or mail will not be a casual afterthought to up-front advertising efforts, but rather an integral part of winning and keeping customers.

The advertising material sent in response to requests will be conceived and executed with the same care and professional skill as the up-front advertising, and it will take its place as an important link in the marketing process—a bridge between the advertising and the sale. Here are two striking examples.

ROGAINE WRITES A NEW CHAPTER

In the late eighties, a new approach to the art of bridging was demonstrated by the pharmaceutical company, Upjohn. It was a radical marketing technique to promote sales of its new baldness-fighting product, Rogaine, Upjohn's brand name for minoxidil.

Traditionally, pharmaceutical companies don't advertise prescription drugs to the public at all, only to doctors. But of course in most cases a doctor isn't going to voluntarily tell patients that a new drug is available that might do something for their baldness, and patients might not think to ask. That meant that Upjohn would have to reverse the usual process, and get the patient to ask the doctor about it.

Upjohn began with television ads in November of 1988. The ads were limited in what they could say by U.S. Food and Drug Administration regulations. They merely told interested viewers that a new product might help them with their male-pattern baldness, and suggested that anyone who was interested should consult a physician. The object was simply to build awareness among consumers and doctors.

But this approach wasn't sufficiently productive. The following year, Upjohn tried tacking an 800-number onto an image commercial, and the flood of responses quickly changed their way of thinking. Soon the company shifted Rogaine heavily into genuine direct-response advertising, both on television and in print media. The commercials invited interested people to call a toll-free number for more information. Now, in true MaxiMarketing fashion, the advertising was being designed from the ground up to maximize response from interested prospects.

By 1994 the Rogaine campaign was generating more than one million calls a year, and annual U.S. sales had hit $103 million.

Now when a call comes into Upjohn's fulfillment center, the customer service representative enters the caller's name and address into the computer, which then issues instructions to the lettershop to ship a 20-minute video and one of 35 versions of a computer-generated personalized letter. The phone representative asks the caller if he or she would like the names of three nearby dermatologists or other physicians who treat hair loss. If the answer is affirmative, the computer automatically plucks these names from a databank and inserts them into the personal letter.

To test this system, we answered a Rogaine ad. The Upjohn Hair-Loss Information Center sent us a personalized letter and brochure in a window envelope, with the videotape shipped separately. The videotape showed six men, initially strangers, rafting down the rapids of Colorado's Eagle River. They talked about hair loss, their feelings about it, and their experiences with Rogaine, which in their judgment had resulted in hair growth ranging from minimal to dense. The film was very involving and, given the six different individuals, covered a wide range of life situations—far more than a TV campaign of 30-second commercials could ever cover.

The brochure answered all of the obvious questions about Rogaine, and included all of the FDA-required data about the drug. It also included two business-reply cards that the recipient could pass along to a friend also concerned about hair loss.

The letter not only was personalized by means of the name and address originally given to the customer representative, it also included the names, addresses, and phone numbers of three doctors "randomly selected from among the doctors in your area who have told us they treat hair loss." Everything we were led to believe would happen when we spoke to Upjohn was happening. To encourage the doctor visit, the bottom of the letter carried a certificate that both patient and doctor fill out; Upjohn sends a $10 check back to the patient after the visit to the doctor, whether the patient decides to use Rogaine, do something else, elect surgery, or do nothing. The letter concludes:

> Studies also show that using Rogaine at the first signs of hair loss greatly increases the chances that it will regrow hair. To find out if Rogaine is right for *you*, schedule an appointment with a dermatologist or another doctor experienced in treating hair loss *today!*

What balding person could resist all of *that?*

TOYOTA BUILDS SOLID BRIDGES

When we called 1-800-GO-TOYOTA for a brochure and the location of our nearest dealer, the operator asked our name, address, phone number, current car make, year, and model. When were we likely to purchase or lease our next vehicle? Had we ever considered leasing? Would we like the name and address of the dealer in the area? Would we like the dealer's phone number? As a final question she asked: "Is there anything else we can help you with?" We asked what else she had in mind. "Information on other models," she said. We had been responding to a Corolla ad and were to receive a Corolla brochure. We asked about other models and she said she would include a full-line brochure in the package, adding that it would take 5 to 10 working days to reach us.

She was wrong. It took only *four* working days. The personalized covering letter said, among other things:

> There's nothing like a test drive to give you the feeling of owning a Toyota. And to help you choose the Toyota that's right for you, there's nothing like the assistance that you'll get from our courteous and knowledgeable dealers. That's why we encourage you to contact your nearest Toyota dealer soon. [The dealer's name and address followed.] We have notified our dealer of your inquiry, so please consider this letter your invitation to visit the showroom.

The four-color brochures included were as impressive as anything we've seen from an auto company. They featured dazzling photography, and the information was easy to follow and to understand.

What *truly* impressed us, however, was the call we received the very next day from a salesperson at our local Toyota dealership. He invited us in for a test drive and offered to send even more literature. All in all, an exceptional demonstration of exactly what *bridging* is meant to be. Nothing is more important than coddling, cultivating, and converting your prime prospects, the ones who have taken the trouble to tell you, "Here I am. Help me." (See Figure 8.)

PROSPECT INVOLVEMENT: AN AFFORDABLE SOLUTION

What if you saw a news article in *Advertising Age* headlined like this:

Magazine Advertising That Costs One Million Dollars or More— Yours for Only a Fraction of That Amount

Wouldn't it be wonderful if it were true? Here's how it *can* be.

In 1995 it cost about $78,000 to reach the roughly 3 million subscribers of *Newsweek* through one black-and-white page. But let's suppose that you have an outstanding story to tell, and yearn for lots of room to tell it in. And let's suppose that your fairy godmother has granted your wish.

Suppose that, instead of being confined to a single page, you have been allowed to fill 12 pages, or 16 pages, or even 32 pages with powerful photographs, details of laboratory tests, favorable press comment, customer raves, dealer listings, everything. And this additional advertising will *not* cost you the $936,000 to $2.5 million that such an insertion might cost in *Newsweek*. It would amount to only a fraction of the cost of your single black-and-white page.

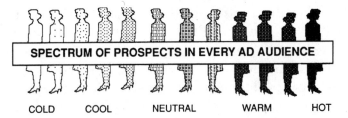

In any mass medium, there is a broad spectrum of interest in and need for the product or service being advertised, that is, you can't sell baby food to readers or listeners or viewers who are childless. And it is difficult to convert people who are totally devoted to another brand.

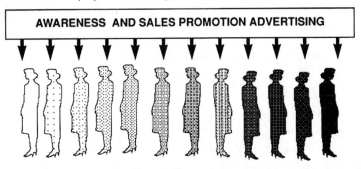

Awareness advertising and sales promotion in any such medium is necessarily spread out over the entire spectrum, which means that much of it is wasted on nonprospects and unlikely prospects.

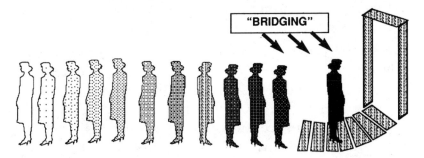

By means of featuring or including a direct-response element in the advertising, "bridging" separates out and identifies the best prospects—then builds them a bridge between the advertising and the sale through additional private advertising, promotion, and interaction.

FIGURE 8.   How "Bridging" Identifies, Separates, and Converts True Prospects.

There's just one catch, and not a very serious one. Your 32-page advertisement will not be read by all of the 3 million subscribers to *Newsweek,* but only by the comparative few—perhaps 1 percent?—who are keenly interested in what you are offering, eager to read about it, ready to buy.

This is the magic of bridging. Instead of running your 32-page advertisement in *Newsweek,* you *mail* it to those readers who saw your fraction-of-a-page advertisement and then mailed a reply form or called to say, "Tell me more!"

Instead of being limited to shouting your wares outside of every house as your wagon rolls down the street, you are invited to enter the homes of the really interested prospects, sit down in the living room, and carry on a leisurely, persuasive conversation. This metaphor is useful in more ways than one. Let us examine it more closely.

WHEN IS PROSPECT INVOLVEMENT APPROPRIATE?

Perhaps some products and services don't *deserve* such lavish attention. Perhaps busy prospects wouldn't be interested in sitting down with you to discuss paper towels or candy bars for half an hour. There's the possibility that you, the advertiser, really don't have enough to say to fill up the time anyway.

So we concede that prospect involvement may not be practical and desirable in the marketing of *all* the thousands and thousands of advertised products and services. What we *do* say is that it is applicable far more often than most marketers realize.

CHECK THE ASSESSMENT GRID. To help you determine whether you should be using the power of direct interaction with prospects and customers in your selling efforts, we have constructed The Prospect/Customer Involvement-Potential Grid (Fig. 9). (The same considerations are involved in deciding the feasibility of database-driven marketing for Prospect Involvement *before* the first sale, the subject of this chapter, as they are for Customer Cultivation *after* the first sale, discussed in the next chapter.)

Where the product or service you are selling falls on the grid indicates the likely desirability of using database information and interaction with individual prospects or customers.

Important: Using this grid is not an exact science. Rather it is a kind of mental exercise or game, to stretch your mind and get you to focus on the extent of your opportunities for database marketing. A lot of it is based on your own "gut instinct." It is just a way of helping you to think about the issue and to get a handle on it.

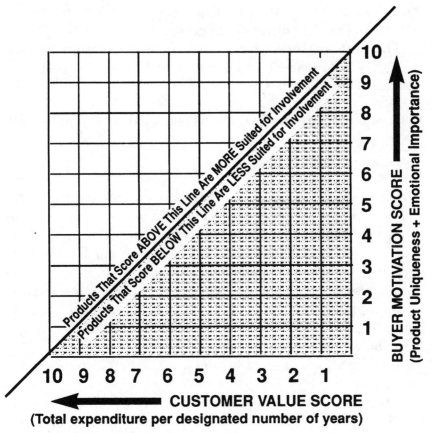

FIGURE 9. The Prospect/Customer Involvement-Potential Grid.

Here's how it works. You assign a total point value to whatever you are selling, and that number determines where it falls on the grid. A product or service that scores in the upper left quarter of the grid is a promising candidate for extensive customer involvement, either before or after the first sale is made.

Your product's position on the grid is determined by a combination of two scores: a "Buyer Motivation" score from 1 to 10 on a vertical axis, and a "Customer Value" score from 1 to 10 on the horizontal. Thus if you decide to assign your product a Motivation Score of 7 and a Customer Value Score of 9, your product will be positioned where horizontal line 7 intersects vertical line 9—deep in the favorable zone. The highest score—a 10 and a 10—would position your product in the extreme upper left corner of the grid.

The Buyer Motivation score is an expression of how strongly your prospect or customer feels about buying your product. This has two parts to it:

1. How strong are the prospect's feelings about the *problem?*

2. How strong is your product's claim to provide a unique *solution* to that problem?

Let's take cat food as an example. Certainly the prospect's feelings about the family cat or cats run very deep—most cat-owners will do *anything* for their beloved pets. But that alone isn't enough for a high score. Suppose your cat food is ordinary, and competitors offer something similar. That lack of uniqueness drags down the Motivation score. On the other hand, suppose your cat food has an exclusive magic ingredient, one proven by laboratory tests to make cats live longer. Now you've got a Motivation score of 10!

Next let's look at the horizontal axis, the Customer Value score.

No matter how high your Motivation score, you are still going to have a hard time financially affording direct interaction with the prospective customer if your "customer value" is too low. This simply means you must ask: "If we win and keep a new customer, how much will that repay us, in hard cash, for advertising and profit over a purchase cycle measured in months and years?"

On the grid, we left the number of months or years blank because it depends on your company's unique situation, management philosophy, return on investment requirements, and accounting practices.

A mail-order book club may cheerfully "lose" $50 or $75 to enroll a new member, by spending that much on the required advertising cost per enrollment and the gifts offered as an inducement. The club knows from past experience that *on average* the profit per copy on books sold to the new member will repay the investment in, let's say, nine months. The club also knows that *on average* a new member will stay in the club for perhaps 3.3 years (the "customer lifetime"), and during that time will buy enough books to yield an additional return of, say, $300 (the "lifetime customer value").

The "customer value" way of looking at marketing expenditure may require some readjustment in your thinking as to what is "expensive" and what is "cheap." Compared to the half-cent or so that it may cost you to distribute a cents-off coupon in Sunday newspapers or register an advertising impression on a television viewer, getting into a database-driven relationship may seem prohibitively expensive. It may easily cost you as much as $1 or $2 to set up the individual prospect or customer file and to engage in follow-up communications. But the ability to isolate your best prospects and to maximize their conversion to best customers with high lifetime value has proven to be well worth the effort.

At any rate, the grid provides you with a starting point to help you determine if the results of your prospect involvement can realistically be expected to repay their cost and to provide an acceptable return on investment.

As an aid to understanding how the grid works, let's apply it to a few specific products (Fig. 10). We'll start in the lower right corner and work our way up.

DRAIN CLEANER. We give it a Motivation score of only 1—most people don't spend much time thinking about clogged drains, and they figure that any good drain-cleaning product will work. The Customer Value score is also only 1—one container doesn't cost much, and lasts a long time.

COUGH DROPS. Similar problem. You don't need them very often, although when you do they can be very important to you, so we give it a Motivation score of 4. One box doesn't cost much and lasts a long time, giving it a Customer Value score of less than 1. Not a good candidate.

CHEESE. We put "everyday" cheese in the unpromising zone because the Buyer Motivation is quite low, even though the Customer Value score may be fairly good. Cheese is cheese. But a whole line of expensive gourmet cheeses could be

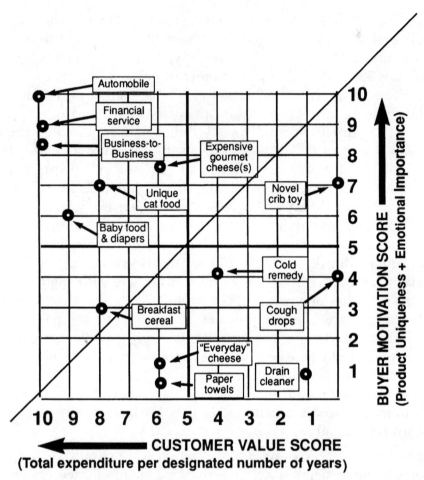

FIGURE 10.   The Prospect/Customer Involvement-Potential Grid Showing How Particular Products Scored.

another matter. It may be a small niche market, but high Motivation and Customer Value scores could make getting involved with heavy users very worthwhile.

BREAKFAST CEREAL.   We put it just above the dividing line—you might figure it differently. Breakfast foods make strong claims for product superiority, but a skeptical public brushes most of them aside. Yet breakfast is an important—some say the *most* important—meal of the day. And breakfast food is one of the few packaged goods that people consume every single day, giving it a good Customer Value score. Breakfast cereal isn't a wildly promising candidate, but we can envision a daring prospect or customer involvement program that could increase its chances greatly.

Let's imagine a new breakfast cereal called Kellogg's Optimum. We don't just sell the product, we sell a new way of life, Optimum Health, by inviting prospects and customers to join our Optimum Health Club. Members get a free Club magazine and discounts on exercise equipment and health publications. The magazine surrounds our breakfast cereal with the aura of a uniquely healthful lifestyle. We bring in other companies to advertise their health products in our magazine and to help defray its publication and distribution costs.

See how it works? See how the grid can stretch your thinking?

CAT FOOD.   We pointed out earlier how ordinary cat food isn't too promising, but a uniquely superior cat food would register high on both the Buyer Motivation and the Customer Value scales. But if the Customer Value alone is high enough, even a product like an "ordinary" cat food may be able to use an interactive program very effectively to flood cat owners with information and service and win their loyalty in return.

Of course if you are a business-to-business marketer, such as Federal Express or Xerox, or an information systems provider, you belong up there in the top-left square of the grid. Yet it is surprising how many companies providing products and services to business fail to build a sturdy follow-up bridge, one that the salesperson can travel safely right to the heart of all those influencers and decision makers in the corporate hierarchy.

That should provide some idea of how the grid works. See if you can puzzle out for yourself why we have positioned other products on the grid in the way that we have. Do you agree or disagree? Where would you place *your* product or service?

"COME HOME TO ANDERSEN": A $1 BILLION THEME SONG

In the field of home remodeling, Andersen Windows has built $1 billion in annual sales through its outstanding use of customer involvement and providing a bridge between the prospect and the sale.

All of the Andersen advertising—whether it is pages and spreads in home magazines with glowing photographs and copy, or television commercials set to the music of the company's familiar refrain, "Come Home to Quality, Come Home to Andersen!"—calls for some form of response. Andersen invites prospects either to check the Yellow Pages for the nearest Andersen dealer or to request more information by calling a toll-free number or mailing a reply form.

Some 300,000 responses a year come pouring in to Andersen's fulfillment supplier.

This information is fed into the prospect database and enables Andersen to determine how seriously interested each prospect is and *where* he or she is in the buying cycle. Respondents then receive:

- An Ideas Brochure, filled with enticing pictures of window treatments and the ways they can be used
- The *Andersen Window and Door Factbook*
- A copy of Andersen's own magazine, *Come Home,* which a company marketing executive calls "the ultimate follow-up to the consumer who has inquired initially about our products." All respondents receive one issue. The most serious prospects receive successive issues.

  Each issue of the magazine contains, among other things, a Project Survey Questionnaire to help determine how seriously interested the prospect is. It also contains offers for three additional guidebooks (which are also available at the dealers), and an invitation to visit the nearest dealer (name, address, and phone number printed right on the magazine's address label) and pick up another guidebook or an accompanying video (or both) for a nominal sum.

Not only does Andersen do a superlative job of building a bridge from the prospect to the dealer, the company also starts at the other end and extends a bridge from the dealer toward the prospect. Andersen sends each of its 15,000 dealers the names and addresses of inquirers located in the dealer's area, along with information as to where that person is in the buying cycle.

It's no wonder that Andersen racks up $1 billion in annual sales! The entire follow-up program is a textbook model of prospect involvement, from beginning to end.

THE INTERNET: THE NEXT DEVELOPMENT IN BRIDGING

The Internet was developed as a way for U.S. Defense Department computers to survive a nuclear attack by linking them in a network that would enable the computers that survived to continue to communicate and exchange data with each other without the help of a "master computer" somewhere.

Soon universities and other institutions eagerly seized on this new technology as a way of exchanging ideas and research data. And hobbyists and enthusiasts began to swap facts and views through "news groups" or special-interest forums.

But from a marketing point of view the most important development was the emergence of the World Wide Web: tens of thousands of pages with instant access scattered through the system, all linked through a cross-referencing system called Hypertext. In the early nineties, programs such as Mosaic and Netscape (generically known as "web browsers") appeared—software that could call up on the screen pages that were not just unadorned text but attractive typography and pictures, even audio and video.

Now an advertiser could establish a "homesite" with a home page and any number of linked additional pages which Internet explorers could access by clicking with the mouse on a key word or phrase that was highlighted, boxed, or underscored.

Before 1995, accessing the Internet and the Web by personal computer could be a little tricky, although perhaps some 20 or 30 million (depending on who was doing the counting) computer users worldwide managed to do it anyway. But then, in that milestone year for interactive marketing, CompuServe, America Online, and Prodigy—the Big Three in U.S. on-line information services—all rushed in to add full access to the Internet as a service for their subscribers. And Microsoft came along with easy Internet access built into its new Windows 95 operating system. In short order the Internet was as close as clicking a mouse to millions of consumers in the United States and throughout the world.

Essentially there are three kinds of advertisers on the Web: those selling a product or catalog of products directly, those seeking to build a brand, and those that combine the two functions (such as an airline, which is both building its brand image and selling tickets).

Despite all the hoopla, "surfing" through the Web can still be very slow and awkward, depending on the speed of your modem—nothing at all like the instant gratification provided by racing through 50 cable television channels with a remote-control device. On the other hand it offers two powerful attractions to advertisers: the fascination of interactivity, and the relatively fixed advertising cost regardless of the size of the audience.

In other media, getting twice as many readers or viewers or listeners usually costs twice as much. But the cost of a home site on the Internet is more like the cost of an outdoor advertising display. A roadside sign just sits there and costs the same no matter how many people look at it. If there is a nearby country fair or other attraction clogging the road with automobile traffic, the sign gets many additional sign-readers for you at no additional cost.

Such is essentially the case when you establish an advertising site on the Web. Up to a point, it costs you the same no matter how many people drop in to visit it. So the cost, spread over a great many visitors, can be very low.

But that leads to a big challenge: fragmentation of the Internet audience. Let's go along with the visionaries and say that by the year 2000, 20 million people will be capable of accessing the Internet from home in the United States alone. The trouble is, if you are an Internet advertiser you will be competing for the attention of all those people with perhaps 20,000 or 30,000 other World Wide Web sites, as well as with thousands of noncommercial newsgroups and other Internet attractions. How will prospects ever find their way to your "door" in this vast metropolis of choices?

Part of the answer is that there are pointers and referrals within the Internet. But a much larger part must come out of a new phenomenon that will be increasingly visible: *advertising of the advertising*. That is, using double-duty advertising in other media which not only conveys its own main message but also flags down Internet surfers and tempts them to visit the advertising at your homesite.

In this way, advertising on the Internet can become a new kind of electronic form of prospect-involvement and bridging. Before very long, when you run advertising in traditional media that invites requests for more information, you may not need to print and mail costly follow-up material. Rather you can store the same information in your Website or on your own on-line bulletin board (BBS) for personal computer users to access. You can also add to it an enjoyable interactive element not possible in a printed follow-up—or even some entertainment or video games to have the prospect linger at your site.

A recent magazine ad for the Lincoln-Mercury Mystique automobile devoted nearly half of the total text to "advertising of the advertising":

MYSTIQUE IS NOW AVAILABLE ONLINE

More information about the new Mystique—including illustrations, specifications, and prices—can now be accessed on Prodigy: jump *Mercury,* on Compuserve: *GO MERCURY,* on Internet: access the Electronic Newsstand in World Wide Web and select the Lincoln-Mercury Electronic Showroom.

Newspaper advertisements for Montgomery mutual funds have routinely displayed their World Wide Web "URL" (address) at the bottom (http://networth.galt.com/montgomery/).

We did visit the Montgomery Website. It was mildly interesting, with pictures of the fund managers and a chance to
hear their consensus on topics such as the significance to
investors of the Clinton financial policy on Mexico. But it did
not really do much to encourage investment in Montgomery
funds. (Since then it has been revised and improved.)

Not too surprisingly (since it's a computer company), but
commendable just the same, Apple Computer's full-page ads
in *The Wall Street Journal,* addressed to a business management audience, devote several sentences to encouraging readers to drop in for a visit at the Apple Website:

> Talk to your information systems people. Ask them how
> Macintosh can fit into your network. Or feel free to visit us
> on the Internet at http://www.apple.com. We'd like to show
> you how Apple computers are working for other companies,
> because we can't imagine a better way to demonstrate the
> power of Macintosh.

Hyperglot, producers of foreign-language-translation software, have done advertising of the advertising in a way that is
growing in popularity. Namely, you can aggressively advertise
your on-line presence in a magazine published especially for
on-line and Internet enthusiasts. Hyperglot's little 4"×5" ad
that we saw in *Netguide* magazine was a model of hardworking
efficiency:

LEARN A NEW LANGUAGE

> Hyperglot, the world leader in foreign-language software, is
> now on the Internet, featuring an on-line interactive catalog
> and downloadable demos of our language-learning software.
> For more information, contact us at [three different kinds of
> Internet addresses listed, followed by more selling copy and
> display of both toll-free number and mail address to contact
> for free catalog].

These are just a few of the early experiments in using
cyberspace to build a bridge between the traditional advertising and the prospect's decision to buy.

Many advertisers may be slow to realize the potential benefits of using the Internet as a bridging medium. After all, they may reason that most families—people who fast-forward past the commercials when they play their home recordings of television programs—aren't likely to gather around the home computer and say, "Hey, let's go look at some advertising tonight!"

But prospects whose appetites have been whetted by your advertising in other media may eagerly seek out your Website for more information or interaction. When they get there, if you offer them artful choices of graphics and information and innovative interactive methods, you may have an entirely new kind of opportunity to strengthen the preference for your product, brand, or service.

FAX ON DEMAND: HERE TODAY AND MORE TOMORROW

Autofax, FaxBack, or Fax on Demand is swiftly gaining ground as a quick-and-easy way to supplement the information in an advertisement.

For example, there is a half-page ad for Daystar, a computer products company, in a computer magazine. The ad copy was devoted mostly to talking about how Daystar products speed up your desktop-publishing work. And prominently displayed beneath the signature logotype: "For more information, call 800-962-2077. Press 4# to order Fastback documents. Press 1# for FaxBack Catalog [of documents]."

When we called, courteous voice mail presented us with a dazzling array of options, and explained that our getting a reply fax would take a few minutes. We requested by touch-tone selection—and soon received—a faxed listing of available FaxBack documents. Using this, we were able to zero in on and punch in the catalog numbers of the description sheets about exactly the particular products we were interested in. They arrived a few minutes later.

This is truly the customized marketing that has so long been predicted. And unlike the comparatively slow and costly follow-up of printed material by mail, once the installation cost and fixed monthly costs have been written off, responding to each additional phone call accessing the FaxBack system costs Daystar nothing more. To the inquirer, the only cost is a few pennies' worth of fax paper.

So through the magic of voice mail and faxback, a half-page ad has been magically turned into additional pages of customized advertising information at very little extra cost. Everybody wins!

HOW LONG MUST A BRIDGE BE?

The obvious answer is: long enough to get to the other side. Unfortunately, when it comes to building a bridge between the advertising and the sale, most bridges fall short.

Have you purchased a car from one of the "Big Three" or one of their import rivals? Perhaps you received a follow-up questionnaire asking about your buying experience, as Lexus executes so well. Or maybe you received a thank-you note from the local dealer. But after that, aside from an occasional "keep 'em warm" message, the construction of the bridge to your next automotive purchase slows down and perhaps even stops entirely.

When even automotive marketers, selling the ultimate high-involvement, big-ticket product, barely begin to construct a solid bridge to the next sale, you can be sure that few marketers even lay a foundation for the *entrance* to the bridge.

YOU'RE NEVER TOO SMALL TO USE BRIDGING

We had a friend who was a struggling young videocassette producer. She wanted to offer her services to advertisers interested in using videocassettes as an advertising medium, but she didn't know whom to contact or how to get through. We suggested that she use two MaxiMarketing principles: (1) fishing for the prospect (see Chapter 3) and (2) building a bridge between the advertising and the sale.

Translating this into action, we recommended that she (1) run a minimum-size regional ad describing her services in *The*

Wall Street Journal, and (2) end the copy with "Write or call for more information." She would then be able to send interested prospects enough information about her services and qualifications to fill a whole page of *The Wall Street Journal*— at a follow-up cost of no more than a dollar or two per prospect. (Today she could reply by fax for virtually nothing.)

She might get only a handful of replies—but they would be truly interested prospects. She would need to convert only *one* of these prospects, by means of her bridge-building follow-up material and personal sales call, to repay the cost of the promotion many times over.

HOW A BRIDGING STRATEGY CAN RESHAPE THE ADVERTISING STRATEGY

Buried in the annals of the *Journal of Advertising Research* are the results of a fascinating study by Dr. Arch G. Woodside, professor of marketing at the University of South Carolina, and William H. Motes, then a candidate for a Ph.D. in marketing at the same university.[3]

What interested us about this study was that it proved something more than they had intended. Although it wasn't their purpose, hidden in their data was a startling revelation of the power of bridging and more: *the power and profitability of designing the up-front advertising to support the bridging follow-up material, rather than the other way around!*

The study's stated purpose was to compare people who responded to image advertising (the invitation to respond was an incidental feature) to people who responded to advertising overtly calling for a response. Woodside and Motes had reviewed the files of an impressive number of trade and business publications going back 15 years, and they found "few published attempts to determine whether or not there are significant differences in the consumer profile of direct-response and image-advertisement inquirers."

They found some very interesting data at their doorstep: the print advertising campaign of the South Carolina Division of Tourism. The promotional program they analyzed in 41 magazines and newspapers was a campaign promoting South Carolina as a wonderful place to vacation.

The image ads were four-color spreads highlighting Charleston and the South Carolina beaches. The action ads were fractional black-and-white units, and although selling the "product" in the headline, they were mostly devoted to the offer of a free South Carolina trip kit and a reply coupon. The four-color image ads mostly talked about the joys of visiting the South Carolina beaches, but also offered the kit and included a reply form.

The researchers found that the advertising cost per inquiry (CPI) from the direct-response-dominated advertising was $3.19; the CPI from the image advertising, with response as an afterthought, was $14.31. They also found, from a random-sample investigation, that the two groups averaged about the same expenditure per party when they visited the state.

The net-net result was that the return on investment produced by each dollar of the direct-response advertising approach was $56.53, whereas the ROI produced by the image-advertising approach was only $11.80! By extrapolation, we estimated that if all the advertising money had been spent on the direct-response advertising, it would have yielded about $28 million in traceable tourist revenue from advertising inquirers instead of about $19 million.

Of course the research doesn't tell us what sales effect the image advertising has on people who see the ads but do *not* respond. Some of them certainly are influenced by the advertising, do travel to South Carolina as a result, and do spend money in the state.

It seems undeniable, however, that the direct-response advertising scooped up most of the best prospects and exposed them to a great deal of *additional* advertising—including the same beautiful color photographs of Charleston and the South Carolina beaches found in the image advertising. From a MaxiMarketing point of view, the ideal ad would have been a double-duty ad approach, one that both projected the desired image *and* developed a convincing left-brain argument for responding to the offer.

What Happened When Alaska Vacation Advertising Faced a Budget Cut?

In 1994, the state of Alaska faced a budget crisis, because the price of oil had dropped considerably and the state's economy was heavily dependent on the oil industry. So the governor's state budget proposed giving the Alaska Tourism Marketing Council (a joint venture between the state and the tourism industry) an advertising appropriation of only $4.5 million rather than its previous $7.5 million.

The director of the Tourism Council, Tina Lindgren, immediately said that they would drop all national television advertising if the budget slash was passed:

> When we looked at the options as a result of a cut adding up to half our budget, *we decided that television would have to go and that we would continue to reprint the state vacation planner and run the print advertising.*[4] [Emphasis added.]

From this, it certainly appears that the Tourism Council considered the vacation planning kit sent out to inquirers to be a more precious and indispensable part of the overall marketing budget than the television advertising—a dramatic vindication by the state of Alaska of the enormous value of advertising material that builds a bridge between the prospect and the sale.

Earthquake Jolts California Tourism Planners

In California, meanwhile, the Los Angeles earthquake of 1994 jolted state tourism officials into adopting a new vacation marketing strategy, one that involves both targeting and bridging.

To encourage visitors to come to California despite the earthquake damage, the state's Division of Tourism ran commercials on network television offering travel information by means of autofax.

Explained Caroline Beteta, director of tourism marketing: "We wanted to get information into their hands as soon as possible, so they could call and get a fax back from us within one minute." Then a follow-up brochure was mailed out immediately.

The response was so good that the marketing planners decided to repeat the strategy the following year—without needing to be prompted by an earthquake. But this time they used a more sophisticated approach.

The universe of prospective visitors was divided into four target audiences, and the Division of Tourism placed customized ad messages for each on different special-appeal cable TV channels: sports channels for sport enthusiasts; the Discovery Channel for nature lovers; Arts & Entertainment and Lifetime for "romantics" or "sophisticates"; and The Family Channel to reach families with children. And of course the autofax direct-response advertising proved to be just the ticket for each target audience.

This new approach, combined with some advertising on network evening news programs, resulted in the generation of 68,000 more inquiries than the previous year.[5]

The challenge facing marketers in today's Information Economy is not simply to integrate their disparate and distinct advertising, promotion, and follow-up programs, but rather to think as MaxiMarketers. In the MaxiMarketing model, there is a single unified flow of interaction with identified individuals, to win and hold customers. In the next chapter we will focus on what you can do to cultivate the relationship once a customer has crossed over the bridge into the castle and tried your advertised product or service.

THE BOTTOM LINE

The new marketing works best when interested prospects receive skillfully prepared follow-up advertising and promotion material. The need for this follow-up varies with the extent to which your product is a unique, high-ticket, high-involvement item, but there is always some possibility of intensifying the relationship with identified prospects no matter what you are selling. And today there is the added opportunity of inviting prospects to visit you at your World Wide Web homesite.

The strategy of bridging requires a unified strategic approach encompassing both the advertising and the follow-up content.

Companies need to delegate responsibility to one person who will oversee the entire process and ensure that all is done professionally. This particular someone must be made responsible for causing the prospect to feel special, and indeed loved. The person(s) in charge of relating to the prospect will pay as much attention to the prospects' attitudes and needs and to gathering information for the prospect database as the best companies now lavish on their best customers.

This bridging strategy will also affect the planning of your up-front advertising. Those who respond to your advertising offers must receive additional selling material of equal quality and greater quantity that not only informs but also engages the prospect in a dialogue. Once you have put a program in place to maximize the value of prospects, you may well want to develop advertising that increases response so as to maximize the number of qualified prospects it generates.

The best advertising out there today doesn't simply hammer away at prospects and nonprospects alike. Rather, it is the first step in a continuum of communication that first selects interested prospects and then begins the MaxiMarketing process of turning them into triers and then into longtime customers.

CHAPTER

NINE

MAXIMIZED CUSTOMER CULTIVATION

USING YOUR DATABASE TO FORGE LASTING, PROFITABLE RELATIONSHIPS

THE BIG PICTURE

Thus far in this book, as you have marched up the steps of the MaxiMarketing model with us, you have followed a logical progression whether you realized it or not. You have proceeded from selecting and finding the target, to choosing from today's overabundance of media, to making sure you will be able to measure your results, to maximizing the impact of your advertising and sales promotion, to building a bridge connecting your advertising with the closing of the sale. Next comes one more critically important but frequently neglected step.

With rare exceptions, making a sale should not be the end of a relationship with a customer but rather the beginning or the continuation of one. (The rare exceptions are those purchases consumers usually make only once in a lifetime, such as a swimming pool or an encyclopedia. Increasingly, however, these exceptions are becoming hard to find, as marketers learn that even these sales can and should be followed up by sales of related merchandise and services, and referrals to other likely prospects.)

Yet until recent years, the thinking of too many marketing strategists tended to focus on making a sale rather than cultivating buyers. Companies allocated little or no time or money to the development of a deepening relationship with customers. Most companies—whether selling products or services, and whether selling them to consumers or to other businesses—failed to calculate and take into account the Lifetime Customer Value (LCV) we have referred to frequently.

But now the Information Age has provided a new kind of corporate asset: the customer relational database, a storehouse of data in the computer about each user that the company can readily draw upon to shape individualized marketing programs. This new asset certainly doesn't replace share-of-mind or brand equity as assets, nor does it minimize their importance. Rather, the customer database takes its place alongside what you already know how to do, as a full-fledged partner in the maximizing of sales and profits. It makes possible a degree of customer cultivation and profitable interaction that until recently was unthinkable and unaffordable.

Marketing has come full-circle: from the person-to-person selling of the village baker and tailor and shoemaker of centuries ago, to the impersonal world of mass media and mass merchandising, and back once again to highly personalized customer accommodation and cultivation—"one customer relationship at a time"—now made possible by new information technology and the new interactive media on a vast scale.

In the early 1980s, service companies such as financial institutions, airlines, car-rental companies, and hotels began to establish frequent-flyer, frequent-traveler, and frequent-buyer programs. They also started to address and relate to each customer separately. And because the Lifetime Customer Value—the aggregated dollar value of total repeat purchases, over the average number of years of a customer relationship— was now being measured, they were able and eager to pour millions of dollars into the development of sophisticated systems for cultivating the relationship with their best customers. There were new models to follow when it came to identifying the 20 percent of the market who were the "heavy users" and provided

80 percent of the revenue, and giving them the special attention they warranted.

Meanwhile, each year manufacturers of packaged goods, soft goods, and hard goods were receiving millions of customer names and addresses—on sweepstakes entries, rebate applications, service contracts, warranty cards, information requests—and throwing them away! The marketing department of these companies seemed to be the last bastion to hold out against the computer revolution, and ultimately to be transformed by it. Manufacturers began to realize that this vast reservoir of customer names constantly spilling over the dam and running out to sea was a source of great power. Companies like Kraft, Nestlé, H. J. Heinz, Samsonite, Le Blatt Brewery, Andersen Windows, Sears, Ford, General Motors, Toyota, and others began to engage in continuing communication and interaction with identified customers, one at a time.

Today almost any company that markets goods or services and wants to survive must adapt itself to this new reality. Unless you are selling a single low-price, low-usage product with very limited LCV, your company can and should make databasing (the use of a database) a vital part of your sales strategy.

The customer database is today's private marketplace, where you can make additional sales, cross-promote, explore new channels of distribution, test new products, begin new ventures, and—most important of all—develop an ongoing personalized relationship with your best customers so as to lock in their loyalty. This chapter shows you how databasing is the steppingstone to those lasting customer relationships that are the pot of gold at the end of the MaxiMarketing rainbow.

Just how far and fast we had come by the mid-nineties, in turning to database-driven strategies in every corner of the marketing world, is illustrated by recent news from H. J. Heinz, famous for its baked beans, ketchup, soups, and other long-standing favorites.

In the United Kingdom, Heinz announced in 1994 a dramatic shift to dealing one-on-one with prospects and customers, proclaiming that it would take the entire $8 million customarily spent on television brand advertising for their separate products and start to spend it on database-targeted direct mail to individually selected customers. According to a Heinz spokesperson, television would now be used only for an umbrella corporate campaign to support their database-driven brand strategy.

Why did this announcement, from a leading fast-moving consumer-goods marketer, provoke bold headlines in just about every business publication in the United Kingdom? After all, using direct mail to promote the sales of a packaged-goods brand is nothing new to Kraft or Nestlé on either side of the Atlantic.

THE DATABASE CHANGES THE RULES OF THE MARKETING GAME

What was new this time was the public acknowledgment at the very highest corporate level for a major change in strategic direction (from bombarding the marketplace on television to going direct) rather than just a tactical move for one or more of their brands. In effect, H. J. Heinz decided to play by a new set of rules. A Heinz spokesperson in the United Kingdom, interviewed by *Precision Marketing* magazine, had this to say:

> With [a] baby food campaign, we addressed the fact that only a certain segment of the market is interested in baby food. We now recognize that the same principle applies to other categories. We want to build a relationship with individual consumers.

And why is a relationship so important? Because in the United Kingdom, private-label brands now represent fully one-third of supermarket sales (compared with about 18 percent in the United States); the plight of the mass-advertised brands has become increasingly desperate. The retailer armed with point-of-sale electronic data and customer reward programs knows who is buying what in real time, and can use this knowledge to help build the store's own private-label brands. On the other hand, the manufacturers of advertised brands, dependent as they are on mass-media advertising and after-the-fact research, are comparatively out of touch with the marketplace. Noting the retailer's advantage in terms of closeness to the consumer, Heinz is determined to close the gap by building its own direct one-to-one relationships.

AN IRISH CHAIN MAKES ITS OWN LUCK

Retailers keep getting better at playing the one-to-one database marketing game. The Superquinn chain of supermarkets in Dublin builds customer ties through its Superclub, the brainchild of Fergal Quinn, the chain's chief executive officer. Quinn wasn't satisfied to see his supermarket shoppers arriving and leaving without his knowing who they were or what they were buying, or without giving them a good reason to return. So he launched what quickly became perhaps the number-one database-driven loyalty program instituted by a supermarket anywhere in the world: the Superclub reward program.

Customers signed up to earn merchandise prizes, and every purchase was credited to the individual. But Quinn soon realized that it would take too long for members to get the prize of their dreams just by shopping at the supermarket. The answer lay in an aggressive partnering strategy. Superclub signed up with Irish Ferries; UCI Cinemas; Texaco; Ireland's largest insurance broker; a home-improvement chain; and others, so that the whole family could be involved in collecting the points to be exchanged for prizes.

When Quinn noticed that many of his customers were forgetting to bring to the store the membership cards they use to record their points, he invented a bar-coded key-ring card. You never leave home without your key ring, and in Ireland you never leave home without your Superclub key-ring card. Next came a "snap-off key tab" that allows other family members to carry the bar-code identification on their key rings, too.

In less than a year Superquinn had signed up some 200,000 club members in a country with a population of 3.5 million, which is equivalent to 14 million members in the United States. Membership continued to climb and Quinn went on to sign up two-thirds of all the households in Dublin.

Now Quinn knows who his best customers are, how much they spend with him, and lots more. He can multiply the effectiveness of every promotion by tailoring the offer to the prospect, and he can charge the producers of the products he sells for the privilege of selecting whom they choose to target.

The catalog or prizes redeemed for points earned by purchases is only part of this remarkable program. It is all the other "soft" benefits and innovative policies that make the Superclub truly unique in the world.

One of the most unusual innovations is the "Goof Scheme." When it began, customers coming in were handed a little card listing 15 different "goofs" to look for—violations of Superquinn's quality standards. The "goofs" or mistakes on the list might be:

- a supermarket cart with a wobbly wheel
- a decorated birthday cake that is ready 15 minutes later than promised
- a grocery bag that is packed wrong, with the soft items on the bottom where they can get squashed by hard, heavy items on top
- a thermometer reading showing that the meat refrigerator was not cold enough

Each time a customer reported one of these faults, he or she was awarded 200 points in the customer club rewards program.

Now Quinn has abolished the list and replaced it with an even stronger policy: a customer wins points for finding anything unsatisfactory in the store, even when it comes to matters of personal opinion, like the tenderness of meat.

"We have turned our customers into 'quality control inspectors,'" the director of the Superclub, Frank Murphy, told us.

While Murphy admitted that this new policy opens the door to exploitation of the satisfaction pledge by shoppers merely for the sake of acquiring points, he says Superquinn feels that the additional customer loyalty it engenders is worth the extra expense.

Here are some of the other ways Quinn pampers the people who shop at his supermarket:

- *Customers greeted by name.* Every cash register location has two display units. One shows the customer the amount of the purchase and the number of points earned. The other, not visible to the customer, shows the checkout clerk the customer's name. This makes it possible for the clerk to smile and address the customer by name.

  On some days, the customers are invited to wear name tags. Customers love it—and there's a better chance that all store personnel will be able to greet them by name the next time.

- *Free birthday cake.* If the computer reveals that it is the member's birthday when he or she checks out, a signal flashes on the display screen. The word goes out to put the customer's name on a birthday cake and present it to the customer at the door when he or she leaves!

- *Candy-free checkout lines.* Candy products near the cash register are ordinarily considered a great source of extra revenue for grocers. But Quinn feels that the parent's peace of mind in not having to argue with children demanding sweets is more important.

- *The store's own private lottery.* Customers can buy a lottery card for what amounts to a handful of coins. Everyone wins at least 40 points and has a chance to win up to 1 million points. Proceeds from ticket sales go to the Rehab Foundation, which offers shelter, training, and rehabilitation for people with disabilities. This is something all shoppers feel good about while gaining an instant reward.

- *On-site playhouse for children.* This has meant employing a special staff, buying equipment, and setting aside valuable floor space. Says Quinn, "The benefits are impossible to quantify in hard figures, but I have no doubt at all that in terms of building customer loyalty, the benefits have greatly outweighed the cost."

- *Support for charity.* All fresh-baked and prepared foods not sold by the end of the day are given to charity.

- *Special recognition for special customers.* If a customer spends a good amount every week for 25 or 30 weeks, the manager will approach her and say, "Mrs. O'Connor, you are a very good customer, so in the future, when you want to cash a check, don't bother to use your check card. We'll be happy to cash a check up to [a specified limit] for you. Think of us as your bank."

The entire Superquinn program is a model of the MaxiMarketing approach to customer cultivation, in which formation of a customer rewards club is not the end of the customer-bonding strategy but just the beginning.

Of course, as soon as every store in town starts its own customer club, the competitive advantage of exchanging points for rewards may be neutralized. But by seeking promotional partners, and by continuing to pile one brilliant customer benefit on top of another until the appeal is irresistible, a retailer can take the lead over the competition and maintain that lead indefinitely.

WORKING ASSETS: THE ALL-TIME CHAMPION COMMUNAL MARKETER

In San Francisco, Working Assets buys long-distance telephone service at wholesale prices from a major carrier, then sells phone service at retail to subscribers. It comprises more than 100 long-distance phone-service providers in the United States, yet has only a minuscule share of market when compared to AT&T, MCI, and Sprint. President Peter Barnes wanted to do something more creative than simply have his customers pay their phone bills each month. He wanted to forge a relationship built on something more than cheap talk, so he turned Working Assets into "a socially responsible telephone company." The goal was to carve out a niche populated by like-minded customers.

Each month, when Working Assets resells telephone time to subscribers, the company donates 1 percent of each bill payment to progressive nonprofit organizations working for the environment, for economic justice, for human rights, and for peace. In the company brochure, Barnes tells his customers that

> In 1994 alone we donated $1.4 million to organizations as wide-ranging as Greenpeace, the Children's Defense Fund, Amnesty International, Planned Parenthood, and Oxfam America. Every year, you vote for the organizations we'll support. Your calls generate the money; your voice determines how it's spent.

The company's monthly phone bill mailing package reports on current political issues, and provides a special number to call when you want some action. Working Assets subscribers made themselves heard more than 350,000 times last year by calling their elected representatives with the help of their long-distance phone company. Barnes also makes customers feel good when paying their phone bills: They can round off their monthly charges to an even amount, to add a bit more to the total donated.

Working Assets claims that its rates are as low as those of AT&T, MCI, and Sprint. But what has led to this niche marketer's rapid growth is not price or service, but the consumer's excitement at belonging to a tight-knit affinity group. The success secret behind its remarkable performance is the army of customer-advocates spreading the word about Working Assets to their friends, family members, and colleagues. Free word-of-mouth advertising, and the joy of working together with other subscribers, cultivates a relationship that even big-spending AT&T and MCI can't dent. Working Assets spends very little on media advertising. When you've got rock-solid customer relationships and self-generated new-business development, who needs boring (or even clever) advertising?

BROCK USES ITS OWN PRODUCT TO CULTIVATE BUSINESS CUSTOMERS

Cultivating customers is as important in business-to-business marketing as it is when targeting consumers. By creating an ongoing, involving, rewarding relationship with your known best prospects and customers, you can maximize the development of the company's overall sales and profits.

Brock Control Systems in Atlanta is a business that is growing rapidly by providing the infrastructure for database-driven marketing. Unlike the cobbler with his barefoot children, Brock also uses its own product to build relationships with prospects and customers. Founded in 1984, Brock describes itself as a "software solutions provider" and now has over 1000 business customers and 30,000 users worldwide. Revenues have risen from $13 million in 1991 to over $30 million 3 years later.

Brock sells customer interactive software that companies—and Brock itself—can use to establish and maintain long-term, profitable relationships with customers. The *relationship* is key.

But what does the software actually *do?* "TakeControl Marketing" is a centralized relational database designed to manage database marketing, marketing campaigns, inbound and outbound calling, and response-tracking. It provides an on-line library of references and background information on products, competition, the handling of objections, and other sorts of intelligence that the user organization defines as helping the telephone representatives to deal with prospects. Before conducting a telemarketing campaign, a company can boost the overall marketing effort's productivity by automatically merging and cleaning lists, tracking leads, maintaining mailing lists, and coordinating fulfillment with the calling process.

"TakeControl Field Sales" provides reps with the information they need to convert a lead into a sale. This software contains a description of the opportunities to close, a list of all parties that can influence or facilitate the deal, and action plans.

Here's an example of how it can work. The 200-plus field salespeople for Intergraph Corp., a major supplier of computer graphics, were accustomed to making their rounds with three-ring binders, frantically referring to outdated specification sheets and frequently missing out on orders because prices and products seemed to change overnight.

Brock's customized software was integrated with Intergraph's existing hardware and software to ensure that the salespeople got a daily update on pricing and configuration changes. This not only sped up order processing and reduced errors to near zero (customers love it when their orders are handled correctly), but opened the door to more comprehensive applications.

Today, Intergraph sales representatives, outfitted with laptops, keep detailed accounts of every contact they make. They generate forecasts and recommend steps that the company can take with each account to improve the relationship and reach the designated targets. Management is able to send qualified leads to the field and to track results as the salespeople follow up using the information in the database.

Brock's software product as used by their customers and Brock's own database-driven customer-service policies demonstrate the vast infrastructure now in place to support the customer cultivation process. Providing this type of capability is one of the fastest-growing segments of the Information Economy.

THE SEVEN "SELLS" OF THE CUSTOMER-CULTIVATION PROCESS

Whether you are a consumer marketer or a business-to-business marketer, an ongoing database-driven relationship with customers can maximize your overall sales and profits in any of seven important ways:

1. *Re-sell:* Maximizing repeat sales
2. *Up-sell:* Maximizing the revenue per sale and per customer

3. *Keep-sell:*   Maximizing customer loyalty
4. *Cross-sell:*   Maximizing cross-promotion
5. *Add-sell:*   Maximizing line extension
6. *New-sell:*   Maximizing new-venture success
7. *Friend-sell:*   Maximizing advocacy and referrals

Let's examine these one at a time, and see how various companies are benefiting from relationship marketing—the final stage in the MaxiMarketing process.

1.   RE-SELL: MAXIMIZING REPEAT SALES

If the television advertising for Total breakfast cereal keeps hammering away at the idea that it gives you all of your daily vitamins and minerals, you as a consumer may become convinced to try their brand. But if the makers of Total capture your name and address and store them in a customer database, they are in a position to turn that contact into a deeper brand loyalty by means of direct interaction with you.

We see three basic ways of accomplishing this (some overlap is possible, for a program might use two or three at the same time):

A. Establish an ongoing rewards program.
B. Give preferred treatment to your best customers.
C. Direct customized offers to targeted segments of the database.

A. ESTABLISH AN ONGOING REWARDS PROGRAM.   "The more you buy from us, the more rewards you get" is the basic principle involved here. The airlines' frequent-flyer miles, and the Betty Crocker catalog with household products, redeemable in part by proofs of purchase, are two examples we have already cited. Both promotions illustrate the kind of continuity program that can be established with the aid of a customer database.

But there are limitations inherent in this approach for low-priced products. If an average user buys a $1 or $2 tube of toothpaste once or twice a month, the manufacturer cannot afford to provide handsome rewards for repeat purchases. And even if a minimal reward were tied to each purchase, it would take customers 20 years to accumulate enough points to earn a toaster.

One way to overcome this limitation is with an umbrella promotion covering many products, just as Betty Crocker accepts proofs-of-purchase from over 200 General Mills products. Companies that don't have that many products to sell may be able to forge alliances with other advertisers in a cooperative program.

Still another solution is to offer impressive rewards that don't cost you much to provide, perhaps through a partnership arrangement. Thus you may be able to negotiate a deal with a hotel chain that will permit you to offer a free one-night stay in a room that otherwise would have stood empty. You gain a valuable premium at no cost, and the hotel operator gains at little cost the chance that the customer may stay and pay for a second or third night.

But it is in the service field, such as travel, retailing, and credit card promotion, that we have seen the most dramatic development of ongoing rewards programs. There the potential annual expenditure per customer is much higher, and therefore the dollars available for promotion are that much greater.

However, when service companies stimulate repeat sales, the sale usually involves not only an ongoing rewards program but also the principle of preferential treatment for good customers.

B. GIVE PREFERRED TREATMENT TO YOUR BEST CUSTOMERS. There are two magic numbers in customer-database marketing. One is "80," and the other "20." These are the numbers forever being quoted in the time-honored business truism that you get 80 percent of your business from 20 percent of your customers.

The 20 percent are the customers known in packaged-goods marketing as the *heavy users*. If you can somehow steal—or keep from losing—more of this kind of customer, you should come out ahead of the game. And if that is the case, the theory goes, why not concentrate most of your care and your marketing expenditure on this most productive portion of your market—and make it even *more* productive?

There is even a catch phrase out there that is all about pursuing the heavy user: *selective database marketing.* Let's look at how airlines and hotels are rewarding frequent buyers, and keep in mind as we do so that how well your company retains and attracts heavy users now may well be the cornerstone on which it builds its future. Somewhere in these case histories there may be that spark of an idea that will ignite a new sales concept for one of your operations.

THE FREQUENT-FLYER PROGRAMS.   It is worth examining the frequent-flyer programs that are now a worldwide staple of the airline industry, because this was really the "granddaddy" of databased customer-cultivation programs.

Airlines were hard-hit in the late 1970s by skyrocketing fuel costs and by government deregulation, which removed what was in essence a system of price-fixing and guaranteed income. With deregulation, the airlines began to look for new ways to squeeze out a profit.

So they developed the programs that every business traveler in the world knows so well by now, the frequent-flyer programs that woo and reward the heavy users with mileage credits redeemable for free flights.

American was first, with its AAdvantage program in 1981. United Airlines followed 4 months later and soon the other major carriers in the United States jumped in with their own programs.

By mid-1994, however, American, United, USAir, and Continental were forced by the number of miles being accumulated to increase the number of miles needed to earn a free domestic coach ticket. This announcement led skeptics to declare once again that frequent-flyer programs must eventually sink under their own weight. They may have been a brilliant marketing ploy in the 1980s, said these scoffers, but they have become a costly burden in the 1990s. Right?

Wrong. Much of what passes for gospel concerning frequent-user loyalty programs just isn't so. To understand the twists and turns in the airlines' marketing strategy, you must understand several things about the programs. First, there *is* a cost to the airline when it awards an unsold seat. Most marketers like to think that the success of frequent-flyer and frequent-traveler programs is based on the ability to give away a perishable commodity, an unsold seat or room that would not have generated revenue anyway.

In fact, the cost of a meal, additional fuel, servicing the award, and other factors could add up to more than $50 for a transcontinental round-trip ticket. Of course, that still is not much compared to the high *perceived* value in the customer's mind.

Second, the airlines *want* people to think that they rue the day American Airlines launched the first program, because that only serves to increase the perceived value of the reward. However, as Jeff Blyskal pointed out in *Worth* magazine:

> These programs are not giveaways. The airlines may have started these programs purely as marketing devices, but they are now often lucrative profit centers. All those award miles put dollars in the airlines' pockets and passengers in their seats.[1]

How do they do it? The factor at the heart of their success: the power of "partnering." Industry insiders estimate that as much as one-half of the mileage redeemed by frequent flyers is now awarded by a promotional partner and not by the airlines. All those banks, rental-car companies, hotels, and long-distance phone companies are paying the airlines up to 2.5 cents a mile for the air-travel awards they hand out to their own frequent users. And now that American and United are selling the miles to any size business for its own awards program, travelers are able to accumulate mileage from the butcher, the baker, and the candlestick maker.

If the award for a domestic flight is 25,000 miles and the airline receives, on average, even as little as 1 cent a mile from participating partners for half of the miles redeemed, the airline pockets $125 for the "free" ticket. At an incremental cost to the airline of between $30 and $50, it almost beats selling real tickets! Every seat given away in a frequent-flyer award is a seat that would have gone unsold and generated no income at all before 1981.

But aren't these programs just the latest version of the S&H Green Stamps craze of the 1950s and 1960s? When people tire of the game and market saturation destroys any competitive advantage, won't they fade away just as trading stamps did? They may. But then again, they may not. For something new has been added to the old equation.

That something is the consumer database, generated as a by-product of today's reward-for-loyalty programs. The information acquired, stored, and used to increase customer value is critical to the program's payout. How well the smartest airline transforms this data into special treatment for its best customers is what provides it with a competitive edge. Thus the "learning curve" built into the interaction process could keep these programs going indefinitely.

For example, in all the years each of us has belonged to the American, United, Delta, and TWA frequent-flyer programs, we have never received a letter asking us why we stopped flying to Europe, to Asia, or to wherever with them. Not so for KLM. One of us received a letter from KLM that began:

> We've missed you. Each one of our passengers is very important to us, but we haven't seen you aboard KLM for quite a while. Won't you tell us why? We've enclosed a brief survey and comment card....

> Who could resist? But there was more.

> If you *are* planning a trip abroad, we hope you'll join us on KLM, because we have a very special gift reserved for you.

Buy a Business Class or Royal Class ticket now, and KLM will send a complimentary Coach Class Companion Certificate for a future trip to Amsterdam, Paris, London, Rome, Vienna, or Barcelona. This is another example of what we call "datamotion": using information in the database to move the market to action.

Keep in mind that a 5 percent increase in customer retention generally produces a 25 to 75 percent increase in profits. Now think how valuable a frequency marketing program can be when it resells and keeps customers and also becomes a profit center. It's a magical outcome not only found in the air-line industry. Zellers, the leading mass-market retailer in Canada, and Edgar's, an upscale department store in South Africa, also have transformed relationship programs into inde-pendent profit centers.

Marriott Leads the Way for the Hotel Industry.   **In January 1984,** Marriott launched its Honored Guest Awards program, which obviously seeks to increase the lifetime value (LTV) of their business travelers. The program has adopted a point system similar to those used by the airlines. Members receive points for staying at Marriott Hotels, for flying with its three participating airlines partners, and for renting a Hertz car. Marriott awards 100 points for each night's stay, plus 10 extra points for every additional dollar the guest spends on hotel services such as the restaurants and bars.

Marriott tempts you mightily not to rush off to a restau-rant somewhere else in town for your lunch or dinner engage-ment, but rather to stay in the hotel and invite your guests to join you in the hotel bar or dining room. Run up a $150 tab and you are awarded *1500 points*, compared to the measly 100 points you earned from your night's stay.

When you have chalked up 17,500 points—no problem for a frequent business traveler on a generous entertainment account—you are entitled to a weekend anywhere in the world at a Marriott facility. At 150,000 points you get 12 days and 11 nights at any Marriott hotel in the world, two round-trip tickets to any destination serviced by the three participating airlines, and a full-size Hertz car for a week.

The program was launched via precisely targeted direct mail. Several million mailings went out over a six-month peri-od to frequent Marriott guests and to the frequent-traveler lists of the participating airlines.

Marriott has been able to single out its own best customers because it maintains them in a database called MARSHA (Marriott Automated Reservation System for Hotel Accommodations). This system enables a hotel manager to write to a guest who has stayed at that hotel more than five times a year: "I know you've been here many times. You're one of my best customers. Next time you stay here, please stop in and say hello. If you ever need anything, just let me know." The *very* best customers get a letter from Bill Marriott himself.[2]

Recently asked whether the 5-million-member program is worth the cost, Ralph Giannola, vice president of consumer marketing, said:

> It's definitely been worth the investment. Every study we've done of the behavior of people who've joined Honored Guest—their percentage of stays with Marriott now, compared with before they joined the program—indicates the revenue gain far exceeds the costs of the program.

In another interview, Giannola said:

> A frequent-guest program may be an expensive method of retaining customers—but it's still more cost-effective than the intense marketing necessary to build significant new clientele.

And he added a key point:

> We have an advantage: We have the longest-running program. We jumped in and scooped up the best prospects, and none of our competitors has been able to come up with a program compelling enough to pull them out of our program. The people last into the game tend to suffer the most. For them, it becomes a defensive program. They're just trying to keep their share from shrinking; they have a lot of costs and not a lot of revenue benefit.[3]

HOW SHISEIDO IN JAPAN KEEPS CUSTOMERS LOYAL.   Japan's economic slowdown hasn't slowed Shiseido, which grew at a rate of 10 percent a year in the late 1980s and early 1990s. It is bigger than Japan's number-two and number-three cosmetics firms combined. Shiseido does it with great products, great distribution, great advertising—and an unswerving commitment to re-selling the customer with a comprehensive-relationship marketing program.

Back in the 1980s, Shiseido began to forge a one-to-one relationship with the consumer by launching the Shiseido Club and enrolling 10 million Japanese women. Members are invited to apply for a Shiseido co-branded Visa card entitling them to special membership discounts from participating retailers, hotels, and theaters. Shiseido was one of the first companies in the world to realize the value of having its name on the plastic in a woman's wallet, and at one point the Shiseido card accounted for one-third of all the Visa cards in Japan.

Each month the Shiseido cardholder receives a mini-magazine in the envelope with her Visa card statement. It's chock full of celebrity interviews, club talk, travel ideas, fun things to do, products to buy, and of course, educational information about Shiseido cosmetics. There is lots of "telling" and very little "selling." The club includes a continuity purchase rewards program, with members earning points when they buy designated Shiseido products. From time to time Shiseido mails members a questionnaire asking about buying behavior and attitudes.

Shiseido also publishes a full-size magazine with a circulation of 400,000 that rivals *Vogue* and *Harper's Bazaar* in quality and impact. Shoppers pick up their free copies at leading department stores and at the Shiseido beauty shops located throughout Japan.

There are 10,000 Shiseido beauty counselors and 25,000 beauty shops. There are Shiseido restaurants everywhere. There is a Shiseido Boutique in the Ginza (Tokyo's most popular shopping district), and there are Shiseido consumer specialty catalogs selling European knits, fine jewelry, and other merchandise by direct mail.

Shiseido does it all—and the results show up on the bottom line.

How Sears Improved Customer Retention by 11 Percent. Among retailers, Sears has provided an outstanding example of giving the best treatment to the best customers. The Sears relationship marketing program is restricted to "best customer" only.

Sears Best Customers (SBC) qualify when they spend more than $1000 annually, shop in four or more merchandise categories, and come into the store more than six times a year. Store clerks recognize SBC members by a Best Customer sticker on their charge card. As soon as an SBC member is identified, the department manager is alerted and, whenever possible, the customer receives special recognition. The department manager will personally thank the customer for visiting Sears, and, at times, call attention to private offers for "best customers" alone or offer other exclusive services.

Other member benefits include priority installation and repair service on home appliances, special zero-percent-financing offers, free specialty catalogs, private sales events, and money-saving certificates. According to Al Malony, former senior marketing manager at Sears Merchandise Group, "Many millions of dollars in net profit can be attributed to the fact that Sears improved retention by over 11 percent with SBC."

ANY MARKETER OF ANY SIZE CAN BENEFIT.   Don't make the mistake of concluding from these examples that selective database marketing doesn't fit your company—that it is applicable only to businesses like airlines and hotels selling a perishable commodity or to retailers that have face-to-face contact with customers. The basic principle of establishing an ongoing rewards program and providing preferred treatment for preferred customers can profitably be applied to almost any kind of business.

If you own a small inn or restaurant, for example, you may be able to join a partnering program that gives you, along with other participating establishments, promotional exposure to a vast customer database you could never reach on your own.

One such partnership program is the Transmedia Card, which began in 1987 and by 1993 had signed up 2700 restaurants and more than 250,000 cardholders. Transmedia has structured an arrangement through which, it seems, everybody comes out a winner. It buys meals in advance at a 50 percent discount from participating restaurants, advancing them anywhere from $1000 to $300,000. Thus for each $200 worth of meals at the menu price, the restaurant receives $100 (much more than its actual cost for the food and drink it must provide in exchange).

The end user of the service, the restaurant's customer, is attracted by a 25 percent discount offer. When a customer charges meals worth, let's say, $200, and presents the Transmedia card, the restaurant owner sends the charge slip to Transmedia. Transmedia whacks off $50 representing the customer's guaranteed 25 percent discount, bills the customer's Visa, MasterCard, or American Express for $150, and applies $100 of that to the money previously advanced to the restaurant.

Transmedia's gross margin is the remaining $50. The restaurant's big gain is its listing in the little pocket-sized directory of Transmedia establishments that is mailed periodically to every cardholder.

Merchants in the same neighborhood or shopping mall can also create their own partnering, by banding together and forming a local discount-club cooperative. If 20 merchants pool their customer listings to form a master database, it costs each of them only one-twentieth as much, per thousand mailings sent to that database, to solicit club members as it would to send out the same number of solo mailings to their own customers.

C. Direct Customized Offers to Targeted Segments of the Database. Just as there are many solar systems within our Milky Way, so too there are many different kinds of customers within a customer database.

"The Old Way Is No Longer Effective." For example, the Women's Specialty Retailing Group (WSRG) has developed a highly targeted approach to customer retention. WSRG, which operates approximately 1350 stores under the names of Casual Corner, Petite Sophisticate, Caren Charles, August Max Woman, Ups 'n Downs/Capezio, and Career Image Company Stores, accounts for about half of the net sales of the parent company, U.S. Shoe. "The old way of doing business—simply placing a good storefront in a good mall position and carrying quality merchandise—is no longer effective," said Greg

Lechner, WSRG marketing director. "Women shop less frequently at fewer stores, giving more of their purchasing dollars to a select group of stores. The highest return on advertising investment comes from dollars spent targeting existing customers rather than trying to lure new ones."[4]

WSRG does that by maximizing its databasing, to build relationships and sales. After a failed attempt to obtain information by recruiting customers for a mailing list, individual stores began to collect customer phone numbers. They found that about 85 percent of the customers will furnish their numbers (most of the rest will give an address). WSRG then merges these numbers with a public data source, such as Infobase in Conway, Arkansas, so as to compile detailed customer information, which includes income, education, family size, the amount of money spent, the types of purchases made, the purchase cycle, merchandise class, size, color, vendor, coupon usage, and method of payment.

After having refined its targeted approach for four years, WSRG is still coming up with ways to treat its customers more like individuals by varying the number, content, and format of its mailings. For example, Petite Sophisticate recently sent a pantyhose new-product announcement to customers who had bought suits and dresses rather than to those who bought shorts and T-shirts.

The database, which has over 5 million names, allows WSRG to develop personalized incentive mailings. For example, a customer who buys a suit has the potential of being a much bigger customer over the long term than one who stops in for a T-shirt, says Lechner. "Consequently, even though these two customers may have spent the same amount of money at Casual Corner over the last six months, the potential for bringing that suit customer up to another plateau is much greater, so we invest more dollars in communicating with the suit customer."

WSRG uses database information to increase sales by inviting the biggest spenders to seasonal fashion shows and special events. Customer communications include thank-you notes after the initial purchase; catalogs; updates on the newest fashions; sales announcements to the more promotion-responsive customers; and product-specific announcements for people who have shown an interest in a particular product type.

Keeping the customer coming back for more with "data-motion" that resells and resells is one of the driving forces of the MaxiMarketing process. You can do it (if you haven't already started) by establishing an ongoing rewards program, giving preferred treatment to your best customers, and sending special offers to targeted segments of your database.

2. Up-sell: Maximizing the Revenue per Sale and per Customer

The direct marketers have always known the power of the up-sell. Selling a set of the world's greatest books directly by mail? Just add a checkbox at the bottom of the reply form for the gold-embossed, leather-bound edition at an additional $100 and, like clockwork, 10 percent of the respondents will upgrade to the more profitable deluxe edition.

Now both product and service companies using main-stream channels of distribution have also discovered the magic of the up-sell offer. American Express showed the way by promoting its more expensive Gold Card to Green Card Members, and the $250-annual-fee Platinum Card to Gold Card members. Each step up the ladder selects out those cardholders willing to pay more to reap additional benefits.

Automotive marketers, with their newly sophisticated database capability, are in a great position to up-sell individual new-car buyers from the model owned to a higher-priced, higher-profit model. Retailers across the United States and the world can learn from the up-sell experience of Neiman-Marcus. In 1991, the Dallas retailer improved on a good thing by introducing NM Plus, which provided a stepping-stone to the up-sell status of InCircle best-customer membership.

3. Keep-sell: Maximizing Customer Loyalty

Scripps-Howard, the Cincinnati, Ohio—based publisher of 21 newspapers, has watched industry circulation and advertising figures head south over the past 10 years. Household penetration has dropped from around 1.3 papers a day in 1945 to less than 0.5 today. In the past 20 years, the newspaper category's share of all advertising has dropped from almost 30 percent to less than 25 percent.

"Historically, we have spent millions of dollars a year taking price points off the cover price just to maintain our home-delivery circulation," says Jeff Hively, director of corporate development at Scripps Howard. "We were looking for a better way."

In May 1993, working with Frequency Marketing, Inc., America's prime resource for developing and executing continuity programs, Scripps-Howard found a better way when its *Rocky Mountain News* (Denver, Colorado) launched the *NewsCard* program. This single effort was designed to increase circulation, reduce turnover (called "churn"), and enhance communication with its best customers—both subscribers and advertisers. The goal was to retain long-term subscribers by establishing an ongoing relationship with them that would reduce the need for discounting (which had run as high as 50 percent) and upgrade short-term subscribers to becoming more profitable long-term customers. A secondary goal was to build a marketing database that would help circulation efforts as well as offer advertisers a more exact picture of readers.

Subscribers obtain the card by buying a 6- or 12-month subscription. The card expires with the subscription, but in the meantime it is good for discounts of 15 percent or more at participating merchants: 18 retailers representing over 300 outlets in the Denver area. These include dry cleaners, video stores, tape and CD stores, shoe stores, hair salons, restaurants, florists, and others.

The merchants get extensive free exposure through an integrated campaign of newspaper, direct-mail, outdoor, and radio advertising. They also get access to a new customer database and the opportunity to turn new customers into repeat customers. Hively:

> We use frequency marketing to build loyalty. It's not a program for acquiring trial subscriptions. It's for renewing and

retaining customers long-term. We hope subscribers will consider it a value-added benefit for receiving newspaper home-delivery service. Those who pay for subscriptions three, six, or twelve months in advance are typically our most loyal—with the highest propensity to be long-term readers.[5]

The paper's goal was to obtain 80,000 subscribers by December of 1993; by October of that year it had obtained 90,000. After four months, approximately one-quarter of the paper's subscribers had paid for 6- and 12-month subscriptions. This was a major shift from before, when few customers paid in advance and most of those paid a discounted price.

Alan Brown, executive vice president of client services at Frequency Marketing, told the Direct Marketing Association's annual conference that the *NewsCard* program cost is significantly less than other marketing methods. After four months in the program, "our retention rate is tracking at about 75 percent, and improving month to month," he said.

4.   CROSS-SELL: MAXIMIZING CROSS-PROMOTION

Any company that has a number of different products, services, or divisions under its roof can use its combined customer database to introduce customers who have purchased one type of product or service to its other opportunities.

Of course a "combined customer database" isn't always as simple as it sounds. We know of one large bank that is attempting to combine all of its accounts into one accessible, cross-promotable master list, and it estimates it will take several years to do this. But of course once it has been done, the unified relational database becomes a priceless asset.

First Commerce Corp., a New Orleans–based bank, for example, ran a cross-selling test designed to sign up checking accounts from existing customers who did not have them. The program began with a customer appreciation note, signed by a personal banker. The bank followed with one of three offers: a year of free checking, a year of free overdraft protection (Ready Reserve), or an order of free checks. Single-service customers (those with just a mortgage or just a savings account, for example) received the strongest offer (a year of free checking), while those with four or five accounts received the weakest (first order of checks free) on the assumption that they were the easiest to sell.

Interestingly, prospects responded best to the offer that cost the bank the least: the year of Ready Reserve. As a result, First Commerce used that offer for the rollout campaign to all those prospects its model had identified as the best checking-account prospects.[6]

As long as you have several products or services, and the names and addresses of customers, you can contact a customer who has bought one item from you and promote the others. (This may sound obvious, but if it *is* obvious, why do companies so often neglect doing it?)

THE HEWLETT-PACKARD REVOLUTION.   Hewlett-Packard began building a centralized database for direct marketing in 1988; previously, virtually every business unit stored its own customer information. By the end of 1994, the company's Direct Marketing Organization in Santa Clara, California, had compiled a unified relational database with around 4.5 million records, and was expecting 2 million more shortly.

In November 1993, H-P launched *Revolution,* a magazine for their customers. With a circulation of 700,000 and still growing, the publication covers the firm's products, "keeping customers up on technological developments and how different companies use H-P products and systems," says Theresa Streit, manager of computer product client services, adding that it is the best thing that has happened at H-P to reach targeted customers, to cross-sell them, and to build ongoing relationships.

H-P uses the database to create product-specific mailings, targeted by means of such data as what kind of equipment customers own and how they use it.

With that knowledge, H-P knows when prospects may be ready to upgrade a system or buy cross-sold products. The database also supports a technical center, where a representative can bring a customer's history on-screen during an inquiry phone call.[7]

BLOCKBUSTER IDEAS.   As a hint of just how much maximized databasing may mean in the future, consider the "Take 10" program that Blockbuster Video has been testing. Video stores are plagued with the problem of customers who walk out because they can't find a title they want to rent. But most video stores use membership cards that capture a great deal of information about their customers. So Blockbuster's program uses this resource to deal with the problem.

Customers who can't immediately find something to rent can swipe their membership card through a Take 10 reader in a kiosk in the store. A computer analyzes the customer's rental history, recognizes trends, and promptly prints out a personalized list of ten related movies that the customer has never rented and that are currently available. Besides listing the films, the printout contains targeted coupons for future rentals and purchases. Some consumers may also receive cross-sell offers for other Blockbuster-owned businesses. Says David Minter, corporate director of research and database marketing, "If your household rents children's movies, you may get a coupon or the address of a nearby Discovery Zone," the indoor-playground company in which Blockbuster owns a majority stake. People who rent concert videos may receive offers for one of Blockbuster's 270 music stores.[8]

THE UNIVERSITY OF CALIFORNIA MARKETS EDUCATION.   The University of California, Irvine, is a marketer of continuing education programs, courses, and seminars, and as such, sells to consumers and businesses. Its database contains both students and prospects, with the file segmented by course of enrollment, time enrolled, and more. "Unlike other direct marketers, we cannot increase the use of our product or expect repeat business in the traditional sense," says David Simons, a direct-marketing specialist at the university. "Once someone has taken one of the courses or enrolled in a series to receive a certificate, there is no repeat business in this area."

The school's real opportunity is to cross-sell related or other academic programs, says Simons.

A student taking courses in the information technologies program may be a prospect for a personal interest course in cooking, music, or art. On the other hand, a certificate recipient in hazardous-materials management will find the university's annual Regulatory Update course most valuable.

Simons points out that the database offers the university other strategic capabilities. By profiling students, the faculty can design courses that reflect student interests, and the university can buy media that match student demographics. Simons:

> Using modeling techniques, the university can choose the most responsive names for its mailings, thus maintaining response rates while minimizing expense. And through questionnaires and surveys, the university can sample attitudes about its products and services in order to provide superior customer service.[9]

5.   ADD-SELL: MAXIMIZING LINE EXTENSION

A popular marketing ploy of the 1990s is to put your famous brand-name on a new product and get it successfully launched without having to fight for shelf space in your usual retail outlets.

Today, establishing a new packaged-goods product in the U.S. retail market can cost up to $50 million. Massive TV advertising expenditure often is required to make a dent in public consciousness and to convince retailers that the new product deserves shelf space. But if you have an extensive customer database as Kraft Foods in the United States and H. J. Heinz in the United Kingdom do, you can go directly to consumers who already know and trust you. You may be able to extend your line with new products without the risk and cost of going the traditional route.

Broderbund Software, for example, uses its database to stay in touch with buyers of upgrades and add-ons. The company has obtained most of its 1.25 million names through software registration cards, and through space ads offering a demonstration disk. With the database it can repeatedly get additional revenue from previous buyers. It recently offered

"Print Shop Deluxe Companion"—to 150,000 users of DOS and Windows. Mason Woodbury, director of direct marketing at Broderbund, says that response to such efforts varies with the product, but can go as high as 70 percent.[10]

The House of Seagram uses its database of customers (and prospects) to target the right prospects for new products, something that is particularly valuable in a low-incidence category such as premium distilled spirits, says Mary Ellen Griffin, director of direct marketing:

> In a recent new-product introduction in which direct marketing was the only advertising medium, a significant number of all trial purchases were driven by database-minded consumers who had received the direct-marketing communication.[11]

6.   NEW-SELL: MAXIMIZING NEW-VENTURE SUCCESS

One of the most important uses of the customer database is as a launchpad for building new profit centers. If it is a huge database, it may provide all the prospects you need. If it is smaller, it can still help you to launch a new venture by providing you with a hard core of especially profitable customers right off the bat, while the slow process of building business from outside sources gets under way.

A GENUINELY "PLEASANT" STORY OF DATABASED SPINOFFS. Pleasant T. Rowland founded Pleasant Company in 1986 to develop and market The American Girls collection of dolls. She started the company after she went looking for dolls for her nieces and found nothing but Barbie dolls and Cabbage Patch babies.

An author of primary-school reading books, Rowland believes that girls in her target market—ages 7 to 12—love to read and still enjoy playing with dolls, although the U.S. toy industry believes that girls abandon dolls after the age of six.

Initially, Rowland's dolls for The American Girls Collection represented different periods in American history. Two of the characters are Addy, from the Civil War era, and Samantha, "a bright Victorian beauty."

To bring the stories to life, Rowland simultaneously developed a book for each character and historically accurate clothes and accessories. A young girl can act out the stories and learn how everyday objects such as school-lunch buckets, Christmas dolls, china, and furniture have changed over time.

A slipcased set of the six books goes for $75; the dolls are $85 each; purchase of accessories can quickly add up to several hundred dollars. Yet clearly, to the amazement of the Barbie-fixated doll industry, Rowland has found a market. Sales in 1993 were over $100 million; by 1994 they had grown to $150 million, and they are expected to pass the $200 million mark in 1995.

While the books are available from bookstores and museum gift shops, and through Pleasant Company catalogs, the dolls have sold almost exclusively through the catalogs from the company's very beginning. "We did not have the muscle to compete in getting shelf space," says Rowland. "Our product was subtle. There was a lot of depth that would not be immediately recognizable in a retail environment." By 1995, they were mailing over 36 million catalogs!

With the brand established, Pleasant Company has used its database in launching several new businesses. They entered publishing with *American Girl,* a bimonthly magazine for girls aged eight and up. This advertising-free publication includes historical and contemporary fiction and nonfiction. Among the stories are those about Addy, Samantha, and the other American Girls characters. A subscription goes for $20 a year; the magazine is available in bookstores and on newsstands, and through the Pleasant Company catalog. Since its launch, *American Girl's* circulation has grown to more than 450,000, making it among the top ten children's magazines in the United States.

Another new business introduced recently was American Girls Pastimes, a collection of 20 activity books. Each includes a cookbook, craft book, paper doll, and theater kit for each of the American Girls characters, and each is appropriate for a different period in American history. According to the company, more than 15 million American Girls books have been sold since the line was introduced.

Yet another profit center is the manufacture of clothes for 7- to 12-year-old girls that match the garments created for the American Girls Collection dolls. This line is successfully, and very profitably, distributed in retail outlets.

GENERAL MOTORS UNLEASHES THE POWER OF DATABASING. When General Motors introduced its co-branded credit card, a totally new business venture from America's leading automotive manufacturer, the GM car owner database was a prime target. Now, with 15 million members, the credit card member database has become fertile ground for promoting Chevrolet, Oldsmobile, Buick, Pontiac, and Cadillac automobiles. At the same time, the database of the automotive divisions continues to be a happy hunting ground for signing up new card members.

The successful entry of GM into the overcrowded credit card category is an outstanding example of the synergistic power of database-driven marketing.

7. FRIEND-SELL: MAXIMIZING ADVOCACY AND REFERRAL

As any advertising executive will tell you, the best advertising, hands-down, is word-of-mouth: one satisfied customer telling a friend. The trick is not so much to get the satisfied customer talking as it is to plant the information with the *friend* in such a way that the word-of-mouth referral results in a sale.

Which is why MaxiMarketers formalize their advocacy or referral efforts every chance they get. As we mentioned in the last chapter, Upjohn's Rogaine literature had a back flap that included both a business-reply card that the recipient could pass on to a friend, and two referral cards: "Please pass along to a friend who's concerned about hair loss. For more information call, toll-free..." Since Upjohn was already sending out the information, why not include something to be passed along at no extra cost?

MCI'S MONUMENTAL FRIEND-SELL COUP. From the moment Gerald Taylor, MCI's president of consumer marketing, launched this brilliantly conceived program in the spring of 1990, it was much more than a discount promotion. By inviting subscribers to form a "calling circle" of first 12 and later

20 friends and family members—all of whom were entitled to a discount *if they too became MCI customers*—the No. 2 long-distance company gave its subscribers a stake in getting millions of AT&T customers to switch.

And switch they did. In the next three years, MCI's share rose from 13 to 20 percent. In fact, the Friends & Family membership plan inaugurated a whole new era in high-tech database marketing. Each month, MCI listed on the phone bill the names and numbers of the "nominees" in the "calling circle" not yet converted to MCI. And each month MCI urged members: "To save 20 percent (later increased to 50 percent) on calls to each of the nominees, help us encourage them to join MCI and your circle." The computer technology required to track the program boggles the mind.

By the end of 1993, MCI had won over millions of AT&T callers. AT&T responded by running full-page newspaper ads proclaiming "We want you back," and by bombarding MCI converts with checks worth up to $100 if they returned to the fold. But half-a-billion dollars of mass-media advertising didn't stop the downward spiral in AT&T's market share until AT&T later fought back with its own True Savings program.

In 1994, Joe Nacchio took over as president of AT&T's consumer long-distance, and AT&T launched a series of brilliant counterattacks. MCI responded with counter-counterattacks, and as this is written (October 1995) the Great Phone War still rages. But no matter what the final outcome, MCI did write an unforgettable chapter on the art and profitability of the friend-sell when they launched Friends & Family.

AMERICA ONLINE'S FRIEND-SELL DISK.   Not long ago, America Online sent a novel free upgrade disk to subscribers. The package had two parts: the disk with installation instructions, plus a separate kit with a disk that the member could mail to a friend. The offer from America Online outlined the double benefit: "You'll earn 10 free hours of on-line time when your friend joins. Your friend also gets 10 hours free time to try America Online." All the member had to do was add an address and stamp; America Online had already printed the member's name as a return address—so the package was coming not from

America Online but from a friend. It was one of the most impressive examples of maximizing referrals we've seen.

This completes our "Seven Sells" of the customer-cultivation process. It is an overview of just some of the possible payoffs awaiting you in the wonderful world of database-driven customer promotion. As you move up the learning curve, getting smarter with each new round of interaction with your customers, you can become one of the next wave of Maxi-Marketing winners finding ever new and better ways of applying the MaxiMarketing process.

SOME TESTED AND PROVEN RELATIONSHIP MODELS

Of all the ways a database can be built and utilized to maximize sales, the most productive is establishment of a continuity program or a club that asks the customer or selected prospect to commit in some way to an ongoing relationship.

With only a few modifications, the continuing-relationship models we identified in the first edition of *MaxiMarketing* have held up well over the intervening years. What has changed is the number of examples (many of them cited in earlier chapters) now available to illustrate each of the strategies and the ingenuity of pacesetting marketers in putting the techniques into practice.

Here is a recap of what we see as the four most frequently followed pathways to bonding with the customer in a relationship that goes beyond simply selling a product or a service.

1. *The Reward Model.* The all-time champion method for holding your best customers is a continuity program that rewards desired behavior.

The reward model is as old in the packaged-goods field as the Betty Crocker catalog launched by General Mills generations ago. What makes it an extraordinarily powerful marketing tool today is the ability to track identified member behavior each time a sale is made and to use the database-recorded information for customized promotional follow-up.

Reward programs range all the way from the long-established airline frequent-flyer programs that give away free trips to the success of retailers in awarding points convertible to cash-back (Waldens Preferred Reader Program) or merchandise rewards (Zellers Club Z in Canada) linked to frequency of purchase.

We have gone into the workings of frequent-flyer clubs earlier in this chapter. But we haven't mentioned a most unusual example that recently came to our attention. It's the "Frequent Burial Club."

Yes, you heard us right! Here is what it is all about.

An important niche market for the airlines is the funeral director. Any time there is a death far from home, the body of the deceased must be shipped by air to that person's hometown. USAir doesn't call it the "Frequent Burial Club," but they do offer funeral directors "One Free for Every Ten Shipped Via USAir."

The latest converts to the customer loyalty reward model are automotive manufacturers issuing co-branded credit cards with 5 percent of charge card purchases going toward a rebate on the cardholder's next car purchase. The GM and Ford co-branded cards in the United States can earn credits adding up to thousands of dollars off the price of a car. Toyota is now doing the same in Japan.

What the car manufacturer gets is the opportunity each month in the credit card statement to promote the features of the latest models to millions of hot prospects. And month after month the database is enriched by the answers to such questions as: "When do you expect to buy your next car?"; "What do you want in your next car?"; "How many miles do you drive each year?"; "Does the family own a second car?"; and so on.

2. *The Contractual Model.* The single most important characteristic of this continuing-relationship model is that all or part of the cost of the program is totally or partially covered by a paid subscription or an enrollment fee. The customer funds the program.

For example, there is the way Nintendo bonds with its most frequent buyers. Nintendo publishes a paid-subscription magazine for video-game players. It's a monthly, slick-paper, 115-page, full-color extravaganza crammed full of hot Nintendo video-game tips subscribers can use to get the better of non-subscribers. The annual subscription price is $18. With more than 2 million subscribers to its paid-subscription magazine, Nintendo has its best customers paying an aggregate of $36 million a year to help keep their relationship with Nintendo going strong.

Nintendo is not the only company following the Contractual Model. Harley-Davidson charges $35 for continued membership in the Harley Owners Group after giving away the first year of membership free. Edgar's department store in South Africa adds an automatic charge of $2 to the customer's monthly statement for membership in The Club. There are 1.4 million members who willingly pay to gain automatic entry in the monthly sweepstakes giveaway and to enjoy the many other benefits of club membership.

3. *The Value-Added Model.* The benefits offered by companies that follow the value-added model can stand alone or can be combined with the "hard" benefits (discounts and prize awards) of the Reward Model.

A paragon of the value-added approach is The LEGO Company, the modular toy that has literally conquered the world of toys by capturing and holding a unique position in the marketplace. LEGO building blocks are sold in nearly 670,000 shops in some 125 countries. Over 300 million children around the world have played with these little objects. In an industry driven by short-lived fads, this manufacturer has had close to a quarter century of consecutive years of growth.

LEGO goes far beyond the actual product to add value to the brand name. There are the LEGO Theme Parks for all to visit and enjoy with the limitless possibilities of LEGO brick construction demonstrated to fire the imagination of both children and adults.

The LEGO Shop-at-Home Catalog offers direct sale of 200 products generally not available in stores. It's a valued service to LEGO builders and a source of useful database information for the LEGO Company.

The database-driven LEGO Builders Club is growing rapidly. Club members get a newsletter, contests, private offers, and even a special mailing of Happy Birthday greetings.

There is the special excitement of the LEGO Imagination Center at the Bloomington, Minnesota, Mall of America, where millions of visitors marvel at giant models of dinosaurs and spaceships. The dramatic four-story courtyard has a play area where children can build their own LEGO models. You can begin to see how The LEGO Company's total involvement with the family has led to a 70 percent penetration of American households for a simple little toy.

Turning to a very different type of toy (this one for grown-ups), we'll take a brief look at how the Value-Added Model contributes to Harley-Davidson's success in marketing heavy-weight motorcycles. From near-bankruptcy in 1981, Harley has become the undisputed king of the road today.

Here is a brief rundown of the benefits and activities listed in the Harley Owners Group membership handbook.

- An awards program honoring frequent use of your Harley.

- An emergency pick-up service that reimburses members who are at least 50 miles from home and require towing service.

- The Fly and Ride service that enables members to rent a Harley at 10 popular touring centers in the United States plus locations in Canada, Australia, and Germany.

- An insurance program that offers reasonably priced coverage of your Harley and accessories.

- A Mileage Merit Program that awards pins, patches, and engraved plaques at different levels of mileage recorded within a specified time frame.

- Up to $50 tuition reimbursement provided for an accredited motorcycle safety course.

- Members get *The Enthusiast* magazine, published three times a year, and *Hog Tales,* the official publication of the Harley Owners Group, published six times a year.

- Local HOG chapters sponsored by Harley-Davidson dealers offer great ways to meet new friends and participate in chapter activities.
- And much more.

In fact, there are so many value-added activities and benefits that most of the new Harley owners elect to continue as members in the club after the first year and pay the second-year $35 ongoing membership fee (the Contractual Model).

4. *The Educational Model.* In the Educational Model, the company provides prospects or customers in the database with useful information periodically. The Andersen Windows program we discussed in the previous chapter is an outstanding example.

As we have said and demonstrated earlier in the chapter on bridging, many companies need to do a much better job of providing the information needed by prospects and customers. Andersen Windows is the exception, doing that job exceedingly well.

Another excellent example of the power of the Educational Model is provided by Earth's Best Baby Food, a relative newcomer in the baby foods market in the United States. This entrepreneurial company has risen from nowhere to challenge the giant traditional brands—Gerber, Beech-Nut, and Heinz.

Parents who enroll in the Earth's Best Family Program receive three issues of *Family Times,* a newsletter crammed with informative articles about the danger of pesticides in baby foods and the Earth's Best method of achieving product purity. Emotional bonding between the product and parents is promoted by means of expert tips on baby feeding, day-care alternatives, sibling rivalry, administering medicines, and a question-and-answer column by pediatrician Dr. Jay Gordon.

To provide an additional source of revenue for Earth's Best and partially amortize the cost of the newsletter, non-food products are sold to enrollees. These have included a personalized Birthday Keepsake scroll, a T-shirt, a decorated baby bib, and a water mat filled with colorful floating objects. These products in turn serve as free advertising for the Earth's Best brand by displaying the brand logotype on each item offered.

Thanks to the solid foundation Earth's Best has made in applying the Educational Model to build solid relationships with customers and all the other aspects of their interactive, database-driven marketing program, it seems likely that the company will continue to thrive and to gain on the competition.

THE BOTTOM LINE

If your business facilities burned to the ground, and all your physical equipment, fixtures, and inventory were destroyed, but you possessed a product or company name that the public trusted, you would still own a substantial business asset.

And if you also had stored in a fireproof vault a computerized list of the names and addresses of a great many of your good customers, plus data about their demographics and behavior, you would be the owner of another substantial asset of perhaps equal value: the customer database.

The fusion of your brand or company image with what you can do with a well-constructed customer database unleashes a new source of corporate wealth and energy. It permits you to take better care of your present customers and that helps you to win more new customers in countless ways.

The right customer-care and customer-reward programs help you to retain the loyalty of your present customers despite the best efforts of your competitors to steal them away. It helps you to sell a new product to those who have purchased from you before. It helps you in cross-selling, launching line extensions, and starting entirely new ventures.

As we have seen, it doesn't matter whether you are a manufacturer, a retailer, a business-to-business marketer, or a direct-order marketer—you can utilize this information core that is at the heart of marketing strategy in the Information Age.

And it doesn't matter how small or new your business is; you can substitute inventiveness for clout. In this marvelous era of

*the desktop computer, a few thousand dollars invested in
personal computer hardware and software can start you down
the road to satisfying the individual tastes and requirements of
each of your customers. And you can generate superb computer-
personalized communications with customized offers or
reminders.*

*Never forget what business you and your company really are
in: the business of "customer acquisition and care." Put someone
in charge of identifying, locating, and bringing in the best new
customers, and someone else in charge of loving the customers
you already have, and you are ready to move down the New
MaxiMarketing road to business success!*

THE MAXIMARKETING OF TODAY AND TOMORROW

There is a lot of wonderfully humorous material floating around out there in Cyberspace, passed from hand to hand by means of forwarding it from one e-mail address to another. It is the electronic equivalent of the newspaper clippings we used to carry in our pockets, when we had read something so choice we just had to share it with our friends.

Here are some amusing predictions from the past that floated into our e-mail box recently.

1876. A Western Union company internal memo. "This 'telephone' has too many shortcomings to be seriously considered as a means of communication. The device is inherently of no value to us."

The head of the British Post Office chimed in: "The telephone may be of some use to Americans, but Britain has no need for it. We have plenty of messenger boys."

1895. Lord Kelvin, president of the Royal Society: "Heavier-than-air flying machines are impossible."

1899. Charles H. Duell, Commissioner, U.S. Office of Patents: "Everything that can be invented has been invented."

1927. Harry M. Warner of the famous Warner Brothers movie studio, when asked if silent movies were not on their way out: "Who the hell wants to hear actors talk?"

1929. Irving Fisher, Professor of Economics, Yale University: "Stocks have reached what looks like a permanently high plateau."

1946. Dr. Vannevar Bush, presidential science advisor: "Now there's been a lot of talk about a 4000-mile rocket. I can say, right now, such a thing will not be possible for a long time. I think we can safely leave it out of our thinking."

1962. Decca Recording Company, rejecting the idea of a recording contract for some musical group of British kids with a really weird name, The Beatles: "We don't like their sound, and guitar music is on the way out."

It would seem that attempting to read the clouded crystal ball is always a risky affair, and never more so than today. We live in a time when the accelerating rate of change makes us all feel as if we're riding the giant roller coaster in an amusement park—without a seatbelt.

Who would have predicted, in 1975, that the awesome power and capacity of a giant $8 million Cray mainframe computer, taking up the space of six refrigerators, would be equaled 20 years later by a $2000 laptop smaller than a briefcase?

Who would have predicted, in 1990, that a vast new advertising medium, the World Wide Web of the Internet, would be girdling the globe by 1995?

Nonetheless, it certainly *is* possible to note which way the wind seems to be blowing, and how fast it is gathering speed. And there *are* lessons from the past that can help us as we peer into the future.

SORRY, NO LIGHTNING BOLTS

One of the things we have noted, as combatants on the front lines of marketing warfare and observers of business practice over the last two decades, is that the future reveals itself one day at a time, and with each minor or major change, yesterday's assumptions are no longer entirely valid. Today is tomorrow's yesterday.

One consequence of this is that no single bolt of lightning suddenly can ever create a lasting new reality in which you can gain a permanent advantage. Constant change is the overwhelming reality of our times.

American Airlines may have thought otherwise when they introduced the first frequent-flyer program in 1981—but that was before every other airline in the world jumped in to neutralize their advantage.

MCI may have thought so when it unleashed its historic Friends & Family reward program and enrolled 11 million long-distance telephone subscribers—but that was before AT&T counterattacked with a simpler and more appealing True Savings program.

This doesn't mean that these innovative first steps weren't eminently worthwhile and profitable. It simply means that today's pacesetters can't afford to rest on their laurels for very long.

In the same way, no one trendy marketing approach is ever going to be your pathway to a permanent competitive advantage in the Information Age. First it was "database marketing" and "customer-focused marketing." Then it was "integrated marketing" and "relationship marketing" and "one-to-one marketing." Now we are hearing about "mass customization" and "multimedia."

These are all valid and valuable perspectives. Indeed, we were among the first voices to predict the shift from mass marketing to one-to-one individualized marketing in our first book *MaxiMarketing,* and to define it in our second book *The Great Marketing Turnaround,* published in 1990.

We have argued for marketing integration in all of our books. Not for a merely cosmetic integration, which coordinates consistent positioning, logotype treatments, and typography, but a genuine synthesis of advertising and sales promotion and database-driven customer cultivation into a single unified strategy.

We have been proponents for more than a decade of the importance and the techniques of building a relationship with customers in order to maximize lifetime value.

We agree that marketers must explore and evaluate the new electronic media, as we have pointed out many times in the past.

But as important as each of these windows into the new marketing of the new Information Economy may be, not one of them, when taken alone, can provide you with a reliable view of what is needed today.

A BROAD TENT FOR THE NEW MARKETING

MaxiMarketing, as you have seen in this book, is all of the above, and much more. The problem with a single-minded view of how to achieve marketing success is that it inevitably leads to an attempt to obliterate what has gone before and to force every possible situation into the mold of the latest buzz-word. If you embrace the mystique of "positioning," "product branding," or "value pricing" as the sure road to a competitive advantage, or a "one-to-one future" as the new nirvana, you will wake up sooner or later to a sobering reality.

What is different about MaxiMarketing as a resource for today's hard-pressed managers is our insistence that there is no single panacea. Our journey has brought us to a fundamental realization of the wholeness of the marketing process and its many interwoven systems.

For example, in order to produce the most effective targeting of your best prospects, you must start with a clear understanding of the relationship you expect to have with them later in the conversion process and as customers. If you are going to go "fishing" for prospects, you will want to apply the principles of whole-brain advertising and double-duty functionality. And, when you choose to follow one of the four targeting strategies, you must also think through the "bridging" strategy that goes with it.

Nothing stands alone in the MaxiMarketing paradigm. It is a holistic and flexible system that incorporates the seven steps in the present model while remaining open to whatever new considerations the future will bring. The antithesis of MaxiMarketing is the Industrial Age compartmentalization that saw advertising, promotion, research, media buying, and direct marketing as distinct and separate entities handled by fenced-in departments.

Marketing grows ever more complex. It is an ever-evolving discipline. It builds on past experience while taking advantage of new opportunities. Each new challenge demands a firm grasp of what has gone before, a clear picture of the present situation, and an understanding of the most attractive new options at the moment.

The seven stages of the MaxiMarketing process provide a multifaceted frame of reference, anchored in what still works well from the past—including, when called for, mass-media brand-building advertising—and what shows promise of working well in the future.

In our 10-year MaxiMarketing odyssey, we have operated with a basic assumption: There is no such thing as a one-size-fits-all instant marketing fix for everyone in every category across the business spectrum. Our goal is to provide an overall point of view within which MaxiMarketing insights can enable you to fashion your own unique, multifaceted winning strategy.

For example, we have emphasized that although relationship-building is important for most products and services it is not appropriate for all, as we demonstrated in the Prospect/Customer Involvement-Potential Grid (Fig. 10) on p. 234. We recognize that there are low-cost, infrequently purchased convenience products for which individually maintained end-user databases would be neither advisable nor profitable. In many cases, there is still no substitute for a powerhouse campaign of stunning 15- or 30-second television commercials or for obtaining a critical advantage through the way in which the product is distributed or competitively priced.

The MaxiMarketing approach includes the value in certain cases of bringing customers together—both with each other, and with company personnel. The Harley Owners Group weekend rides, the Saturn automobile "family reunion" gathering of 40,000 customers, the Nestlé baby-food rest stops along the highways of France, and the Nike cyberbabble on the Internet are certainly not the old mass-media advertising of the past, but neither could they have been predicted and explained by the "database marketing revolution."

Still another important difference that sets MaxiMarketing apart from a single-minded focus on "one-to-one" marketing is to be found in our brief for giving far more importance to building a bridge between the advertising and the sale. This may involve marketing to a database of prospects, but often it precedes it. In other words you may follow up an inquiry with a letter, a free sample, a brochure, an audio- or videocassette, or a CD-ROM to good effect without enshrining the inquirer's name, address, and other personal data in a fully implemented prospect database.

THE DANGER OF A NEW COMPARTMENTALIZATION

Embracing any one school of thought—the quick fix of the moment—risks replacing one form of restrictive marketing compartmentalization with another.

We have argued against the folly of the old compartmentalization, in which the advertising manager is solely in charge of advertising, the sales promotion manager is restricted to coming up with promotions, the database manager is in charge of customer contact, and all of these programs are separate and poorly coordinated.

The real integration of marketing must take place inside the brain of a powerful executive in the top echelon of the company—either the CEO or a marketing VP with unlimited power over all contact and communication with prospects and customers. Only such a key figure has the power to lead the way and demand that all of the components of the MaxiMarketing process be examined and made to work together as a whole in close harmony.

Following a MaxiMarketing seminar we presented in Chile, one of us was interviewed by a Santiago-based marketing communications consultant. He is Mark M. Klugman, who served in the White House as a speechwriter for President Ronald Reagan before moving on to marketing. His write-up of the interview showed a keen understanding of the New MaxiMarketing, with its holistic approach to acquiring and keeping customers. Here is part of what he wrote:

> In general, the center of attention in marketing is shifting away from the instruments and toward the information. Though many companies have been sold, correctly, on the marketing instruments—telemarketing, personalized direct mail, infomercials, co-branding, affinity groups, etc.—they see that new instruments do little good without a new strategy that grows out of the technology.
>
> It is because database marketing derives from direct marketing, and direct marketing grew out of mail order, that some of the methods and instruments are the same. But the paradigm has changed.
>
> The new focus is on the creation of personalized customer relationships.
>
> A new accounting calculates the lifetime value of a customer and invests accordingly.
>
> A new advertising—even while building brand image—always seeks measurable customer responses and the names of potential customers.
>
> A new competitiveness seeks to identify the customers of competing brands and to capture them.
>
> A new loyalty works to satisfy and retain customers, because it is cheaper to keep, grow, cross-sell, and up-sell an existing customer than to find a new one.
>
> A new arithmetic ranks marketing activities by measuring the cost per response or per sale.
>
> A new marketing research compares alternative advertisements and media on the basis of empirical results.
>
> A new science uses predictive modeling to target those consumers most similar to existing customers.
>
> And a new pragmatism lets database marketing learn from and be applied to areas that mail-order marketers never dreamed of.

THE MORNING AFTER THE REVOLUTION

Recently, Jacques Altover of CERN, the French particle-physics laboratory, described development of the World Wide Web as "potentially one of the biggest revolutions in the history of communication, including the invention of printing and the telephone."

There's that word again. *Revolution* has been the favored way to describe radical change ever since the days of the French Revolution's guillotine. Every time you turn around, there is another story proclaiming a cyber-*revolution,* or a media *revolution,* or a marketing *revolution.*

The revolutionary fundamentals of the communications and information technology of the Information Age are in place. The new landscape, predicted in the preface to *Maxi-Marketing* a decade ago, is now a reality. It is time to wake up to the realization that this is the morning *after* the revolution.

The revolutionary turnaround, to a computer-driven, more interactive and personalized marketing, is behind us. Now comes the *evolution!* Rather than sweeping away everything that has gone before, the new marketing is evolving out of what still works in the tried-and-true way of doing things and the new possibilities. More often than not this means adding or adapting to what has gone before, rather than coming up with a totally new idea. If you possess an evolutionary view of the new marketing, you are more likely to be among the "fittest" marketers, those who survive and prosper in today's information economy.

Some visionaries predict that there may be as many as a billion people worldwide on the Internet by the year 2000. Perhaps. But we have a safer prediction.

In the year 2000, we believe, there still will be printed advertisements in magazines. There still will be commercials on radio programs. There still will be television networks. There still will be direct mail. And there will be advertisers who still are not making the most effective use of the evolving traditional media, still are failing to take full advantage of the steps in the MaxiMarketing process.

Anyone who believes that the mass media belong on the trash heap of the Industrial Age hasn't been looking at the recent numbers. America's "Big Three" TV networks, after sliding from a peak of 91 percent down to 61 percent, have seen their viewing audience pick up again. Mass marketers still come up with more than $75 million just to buy a TV commercial during the Superbowl game each year, and love every 30 seconds of it. Possession of a trusted, advertising-supported brand name remains a tremendous corporate asset, perhaps even more so as media and product proliferation make it ever more expensive to build a brand name.

What we see happening more and more is the evolution of mass marketing into a paradoxical-sounding new force: *direct mass marketing*. We see direct-response advertising in mass media and specialized media used to locate and identify best prospects for intensified one-to-one cultivation by phone, mail, and interaction via computer terminal.

In addition there are a number of other evolutionary marketing changes we see taking place today, changes that will have a profound impact on strategic planning in the remaining years of this century.

1. PRODUCT BRANDING IS EVOLVING INTO RELATIONSHIP BRANDING

In the past, branding a product—whether it was Nike, H. J. Heinz, AT&T, or Federal Express—had to do almost entirely with the quality of the product or service itself and how it was perceived in the mind of the consumer as a direct result of the company's image-building advertising.

But with the ability to identify prospects and customers by name and address, learn more about them, and interact with them in an ongoing relationship, a new form of branding is evolving: "relationship branding." You no longer simply brand and promote what you sell. You brand and promote the *relationship* as well.

There is no longer simply the MCI brand of long-distance phone service, there is also the MCI Friends & Family relationship. In the mind of the consumer the relationship brand is the perception not just of the quality of the phone service, but of how he or she and the phone company interact to create added value.

Federal Express doesn't simply advertise "absolutely, positively on time." It introduces a service that puts computer hardware and software on the desktop of customers to track packages, it's a branded POWERSHIP relationship.

In South Africa, as you leave the airport, there is billboard after billboard emblazoned with the single word "Voyager"— the relationship brand of South African Airways.

One of the oldest examples of the impact of a relationship brand on the sale of a product is the National Geographic magazine subscription promotion strategy. You don't just subscribe to the magazine, you become a member of the National Geographic Society.

National Geographic has tested direct mail with colorful graphics and photos on the outside envelope versus a plain white envelope with the Society logotype. The latter always wins. "They're looking for the brand," says the magazine's creative director.[1]

Five common denominators of a branded relationship program are that it

1. Has a name.
2. Has its own logotype.
3. Usually offers membership.
4. Is advertised.
5. Includes a continuing involvement.

You can see how the old is transformed into the new by observing the power of mass-media advertising in the establishment of many of today's most powerful "relationship" brands, from the GM co-branded credit card to AT&T's True Savings and True Rewards and the Federal Express Powership program.

2. PROMOTIONAL PARTNERING IS EVOLVING INTO DATABASE PARTNERING

Sharing the cost of a premium promotion or a co-op mailing or a sponsored entertainment event or celebrity appearance is as old as promotion itself. But the partnering that is evolving today, as more and more companies maintain sizable consumer databases, goes far beyond yesterday's one-time events. With the new database partnering the impact on your bottom line can be enormous, and the benefits continue year after year after year.

For example there is the Citibank AAdvantage credit card program, which permits cardholders to earn American Airlines frequent-flyer miles with their card purchases. American Airlines gains continuing exposure to more than 30 million Citibank cardholders for its AAdvantage program. Meanwhile Citibank gets the opportunity to promote its credit card to 28 million AAdvantage members in the American Airline mailings to their frequent-flyer club members.

Zellers' Club Z in Canada, as pointed out earlier, makes Club Z points available at Midas, Esso, Gino's Pizza, and dozens of other outlets. The consumer speedily accumulates points for prizes, and Zellers turns relationship marketing into a profit center by selling the points to their partners.

An example of how "database partnering" can benefit smaller companies is the dramatic success of the Air Miles program in Canada. Launched by Loyalty Management Group (LMG) nearly three years ago, it has done everything right while the Air Miles venture in the U.S. market did almost everything wrong and failed.

The program in Canada appeals mainly to consumers who do not travel a great deal and who are not the heavy business travelers courted by the usual airline frequent-flyer program. By banding together a large number of participating sponsors, Air Miles in Canada makes it easy for participants to accumulate the points needed for a free flight.

At the heart of the Air Miles program in Canada is the company's trademarked Coalition Database Marketing concept. By sharing the costs of promotion, small businesses offering air-mile credits can target their best prospects at very little cost.

Mailing costs in Canada put effective use of database marketing out of the reach of most smaller businesses. But LMG makes sophisticated targeting affordable for its many promotional partners by enabling them to share the costs of running the database, conducting the market analyses, and sending direct-mail offers to collectors.

LMG performs predictive modeling and other high-tech database marketing services for sponsors, often manipulating as many as 70 pieces of information in order to identify consumers likely to respond to an offer. While the cost of building a huge database and determining optimum segmentations would be prohibitive for a local clothing or grocery store, LMG's innovative management and "database partnering" make it possible.

3. CUSTOMER LOYALTY IS EVOLVING INTO COMMUNAL BONDING

Marketers have always sought to keep customers coming back for more. But what is emerging now is something more than the individual recognition or rewards of a loyalty program. What we are seeing now in the most effective programs is what we call *communal marketing.* Customer loyalty is raised to a higher level by expanding the bond between the seller and the buyer to include a bond among the buyers themselves in a community of like-minded individuals.

Harley-Davidson has made the joy of owning one of their heavyweight motorcycles as dependent on the sense of community with other Harley owners as on the superior performance of the bike itself. When 60,000 Harley Owners Group members showed up at the club's 10th Anniversary Reunion in Milwaukee, we saw just how tight that bond can be.

Communal marketing as practiced by Harley-Davidson has many dimensions. The company works hard to include their own personnel in the "bonding circle." To Harley owners, the company's management is not some distant impersonal entity, but real people who meet and talk and ride with their customers. Says Mike Keefe, the marketing manager:

> When there is a gathering of thousands of cyclists, we don't hire a promotion firm to stand at the literature table, answer

questions, and show off the new models, as the Japanese manufacturers do. Harley-Davidson executives hop on their "Hogs," ride to the rally, and personally represent the company there.

LEGO plastic building bricks for kids build a sense of community in a number of different ways. Kids and their parents come together to admire fantastic LEGO creations and to try to build their own at the LEGOLAND Park in Billund, Denmark. LEGOLAND has welcomed 20 million visitors since it opened in 1968. There is also the shared experience of visiting at America's premiere shopping center, The Mall of America in Bloomington, Minnesota, the LEGO Imagination Center, a dramatic four-story courtyard composed of giant LEGO beams, columns, and arches and displaying amazing LEGO constructions.

4. PASSIVE RECEPTION OF ADVERTISING IS EVOLVING INTO ACTIVE SEEKING

Until very recently, almost all advertising in all of the media has been passively received rather than actively sought after. For the most part you as a consumer don't go looking for the advertising, it comes looking for you. You are there in your easy chair, and message after message comes knocking on the door of your mind. Whether it happens when you are turning the pages of a magazine or newspaper, listening to the radio, or watching TV, it is unsolicited. You are the passive recipient of an endless stream of pitches competing for your attention, and all you do is decide which ones to consider and which to ignore.

But much of tomorrow's advertising will be entirely different. One of its purposes, sometimes its only purpose, will be to serve as a signpost directing interested members of the audience to *additional* advertising that you as a consumer will actively seek out.

One striking example of this activity is the television campaign for Rogaine, cited in Chapter 8. The ad doesn't attempt to convince you that Rogaine can prevent hair loss, but rather to persuade you to send for Rogaine's brochure and video-tape—which, hopefully, *will* convince you.

Another example is the magazine advertising for Alaskan tourism. The purpose of their advertisement with the headline "100 Pages of Free Advice for Anyone Wishing to Experience the Vacation of a Lifetime" is not to sell you immediately on taking an Alaskan vacation. It is to sell you on actively seeking information about Alaskan vacations. It is advertising that directs the audience to more advertising.

Follow-up advertising is no longer an adequate phrase to describe what is happening. We prefer to call it *voluntary advertising*—meaning, advertising that asks the consumer to raise her hand and volunteer for *more* advertising. It stands in sharp contrast to "broadcast" advertising impressions, which are sprayed via radio, television, magazines, newspapers, and direct mail onto passersby whether they like it or not.

This new phenomenon presents important challenges to the advertiser's creative team.

The first part, "advertising the advertising," must not be treated as a casual, unimportant afterthought, as is so often the case. Instead the signpost within the advertising pointing to the additional advertising must be strong, clear, and inviting, as in the case of the Alaska ad's headline.

The second part of the challenge is that neither must the additional advertising be treated as a routine job. This may seem obvious, but too often we have answered ads and sent for more information, only to receive something bland and disappointing rather than powerful and compelling.

Now we are entering a new era, one in which the voluntary advertising function that was once grossly underfunded is destined to receive its full due. The new factor in the equation is the World Wide Web. There is every indication that the Internet will become a vibrant new medium for the delivery of "additional information."

Just between the middle of 1994 and the middle of 1995, the number of "servers" on the World Wide Web leaped from 700 to 22,000—and many of these contained hand-holding information from many different companies. By the end of this century there may be as many as a half-a-million advertisers worldwide hanging out their signs on the Web and inviting Net-surfers to drop in.

It is not only an opportunity, it could also become a headache for tomorrow's advertiser. "What if we build a Website—and nobody comes?" is the way the question was posed by Rob Auster, director of new-media marketing for Marriott Ownership Resorts.[2] One answer is being provided by Internet Traffic, a new kind of agency. Internet arranges partnerships between Web advertisers: "You provide a link to my home page on yours, and I'll provide a link to your home page on mine." Another part of the answer will surely be for the Website advertiser to provide intriguing signposts in the traditional advertising media, directing the prospect to make the right turnoff to its Website on the information superhighway.

Then when the visitor *does* arrive, perhaps having come there out of little more than curiosity, the advertiser's job has barely begun. If the purpose is brand-building, the site must be so useful or enjoyable that visitors will want to return again and again. This can be accomplished by means of constantly updated, vitally needed information, dialogue (including the dialogues that customers hold with one another), interactive games and puzzles, entertainment, and so on.

ADVENTUROUS BRAND-BUILDING AT THE ZIMA WEBSITE

Zima Clearmalt liquor, a recently introduced product of Coors Brewing Company, faces a special challenge because not only is it a new brand, but it stands all alone in a new liquor category. Its best prospects are members of the young, post-baby-boomer Generation X, and one of the best places to find the more affluent and wired-in members of that new consumer generation is on the Internet. So Zima has established an amusing, irreverent homesite on the Web, where a browser can easily while away an hour or so.

The mind can hardly encompass the vast distance between the staid, insipid liquor advertisements of half a century ago (e.g., a gentleman doffing his tall silk hat alongside a bottle of

I.W. Harper Bourbon, under the headline "It's Always a Pleasure") and the New Age whimsy of the Zima Website. The latter is almost like an onscreen Zima street fair, with any number of booths and tents to be explored.

There is an Answer Man Booth ("Where did the name Zima come from?"), some computer games to download, a message booth where you can exchange messages with "the Zima," a membership booth where you can fill out an application to join Tribe Z (providing personal and liquor-usage data for the database) and get things like Zima T-shirts and caps, a booth for giving and getting tips on favorite Web locations, and so on. It's all done in a flip, cool, conversational style that seems well tuned to the new generation (undoubtedly because members of that same new generation created it). It is so varied and entertaining that it isn't difficult to imagine a visitor wanting to come back again and again.

But that's *still* not all! As a member of Tribe Z, you get to decide how the clubhouse will be decorated. And eventually you'll be able to add your own home pages to this site. In other words, there's a good chance you'll be camping out with Zima in cyberspace.

The Zima Website provides a glimpse into how the consumers of the future will actively seek out rather than passively endure contact with advertising. (If you'd like to see for yourself, log onto the Internet and use your Web browser to go to the URL address http://www.zima.com). What you will see is the holistic expression of the New MaxiMarketing in action. Brand-building advertising, database-building, relationship-building, "bridging," direct marketing—all going on at once.

In France, where over 6 million households have for many years possessed a Minitel videotex terminal rather than a phone book, a Minitel symbol in television commercials alerts viewers that they can find additional information on their Minitels. A similar symbol indicating a Website may soon become common in television commercials in every country.

The Internet is destined to become the ultimate bridge between the advertising and the sale. The evolution from passive reception of advertising to active seeking took a giant leap forward with the ability to roam the World Wide Web with such graphic browsers as Mosaic and Netscape. It costs so much less to establish a site on the Web than to print up ar.d mail out expensive advertising and promotional material. It can be as easily interactive as clicking a mouse button. It can offer the option of downloading information loaded with colorful graphics. It's a new "bridging" medium with unlimited potential for initiating or extending a prospect or customer relationship.

Another attribute that makes the Internet such a close fit to the MaxiMarketing model constructed 10 years ago is the accountability provided to marketers. Bruce Judson, general manager of Time Inc., writes in the Summer 1995 issue of *The Advertiser:* "The Internet is a highly accountable environment. Marketers can track the number of visits their sites receive—and where in the site consumers spend their time. A marketer might determine that there is great interest in one aspect of an established site and relatively little interest in a second one." And the monitoring process by the advertiser can go on in real time.

The creative dynamos behind the Websites of Music Boulevard and PrePRESS Solutions understand what is fundamentally different about this new form of advertising. *It is information- and interaction-driven.* To reach the cyberspace market effectively requires the MaxiMarketing way of thinking about what is effective advertising and how to make it happen.

Within a year, there may be literally hundreds of thousands of business and personal sites on the Web. In this cyberspace wilderness, how will your prospects find their way to your door? One way is to make a deal with a media link placement service that can arrange for multiple listings (in the form of links) with up to 500 selected Websites. The result could be a marked increase in traffic by visitors. Another would be advertising your Website location and attractions in the traditional media.

Creating your first homesite on the Internet may be an intimidating experience. But, it is getting easier all the time. And like it or not, you are going to have to be there sooner or later. So why not join the race into cyberspace now? You can build your own site with available software or hire an expert to design it for you. Or you can do as many smaller merchants are doing, simply rent space in somebody else's Web mall.

There is no escaping the lure of the fastest-growing form of mass media in history. Go for it.

5. SINGLE-FUNCTION ADVERTISING AND PROMOTION IS EVOLVING INTO MULTIFUNCTIONAL INTERACTIVE MARKETING ACTIVITIES

There is a way to maximize the value of your marketing strategies without adding a cent to your budget. The secret lies in the extra benefit that can be extracted by arranging for a single effort to accomplish two, three, or more different objectives.

Single-duty advertising and promotion may go entirely out of style, because doing only one thing at a time is the most costly way to use a portion of the marketing budget today. The most cost-effective strategy calls for going beyond merely conveying a brand image, or presenting a sales argument, or announcing a discount promotion. At its best it can mean combining two, three, or four functions in a single advertising or promotional effort to accomplish multiple objectives.

The beauty of multiduty advertising or promotion is that the additional functions often come along for a free ride.

One of the most striking examples of using a promotional event to make an advertising campaign do quadruple-duty was the famous British Airways advertising campaign right after the Gulf War. We told the story in Chapter 7 about how the fear of terrorism at the time had reduced the number of seats occupied on most flights to just 30 percent.

Full-page ads and double-page spreads in newspapers in 67 countries announced "Everybody Flies Free on April 23," and said that the lucky travelers would win their free tickets in a drawing.

Just think in how many ways the campaign paid off for British Airways:

1. *Image*—the offer further embellished BA's image as "The World's Favorite Airline."
2. *Promotion*—the sweepstakes drawing attracted millions of entries.
3. *Public relations*—tens of millions of dollars of newspaper and TV coverage was free.
4. *Database*—entry-form questions generated vital information about how often and where each person entering the drawing would be traveling by air in the next six months.

Advertising, promotion, public relations, and database-building—with a single budget expenditure. Within three months of the campaign, British Airways bookings were up to prewar levels.

Another multifunctional way of stretching an advertising budget that is gaining in popularity is to share the cost of advertising with another advertiser, or to provide an incentive for another advertiser to promote your brand.

In November of 1994, American Airlines announced the AAdvantage Incentive Miles program, a daring extension of its partnership awards program. Michael W. Gunn, American's senior vice president of marketing, said that it was "the first program that lets companies of all sizes customize promotions that offer travel as an incentive for customers or employees." Incentive Miles allows even the smallest company to partner with the number-one frequent-flyer program in the world. Local companies can offer AAdvantage mileage vouchers in denominations of 500, 1000, or 5000 miles, as an incentive to their customers or employees. At the time the program was announced, small businesses could participate in the program for as little as $1200 (for 60,000 miles). Recipients redeem their vouchers through American Airlines, which credits the miles to the customer's or employee's AAdvantage account.

The advertising of participating companies does two jobs at the same time: It promotes its own product or service through the promise of frequent-flyer miles as a reward with purchase, and it also promotes the AAdvantage frequent-flyer program, to the benefit of both American Airlines and the advertiser.

Building a Database while You Build Your Brand

The millions your company may be spending on advertising to build a brand image for your product or service can serve an additional purpose at little additional cost. When your double-duty advertising invites and encourages response from interested prospects, and captures useful information about your customers, you can build not one but two important company assets: (1) your consumer brand franchise and (2) your in-house database.

The most important double-duty use of advertising today is to gather information while delivering the brand message. Since we first advocated this MaxiMarketing activity, it has become quite common in the United States and Europe. (The rest of the world still lags behind.) Automotive advertising in America now routinely includes a postpaid reply card asking all the right questions for building a prospect database:

- Name, address, and age
- The vehicle you currently drive
- Have you ever purchased/leased a new vehicle from us?
- Have you ever owned a luxury vehicle?
- When do you plan to acquire your next car?
- How do you plan to pay?
- Which car brands do you plan to consider?
- How would you classify your occupation? [And so on.]

THE AWESOME POWER OF A "CARING AND DARING" STRATEGY

The companies that become our MaxiMarketing winners of tomorrow will practice the principles set forth in this book—plus something more. They will exhibit the two defining characteristics described in our previous book, *Beyond Maxi-Marketing: Success Secrets of the MaxiMarketing Winners*.

The "caring" we saw in action goes far beyond what most companies call "customer satisfaction programs." What we found was a passionate commitment to taking care of customers in ways that make a real difference in the enjoyment and enrichment of each individual's life experience. We saw that the companies doing extraordinarily well often care enough to put the customer's best interest first—even when it means temporarily putting the corporate bottom-line second.

We place equal emphasis on "daring," because despite our call for maximized accountability in advertising and marketing, some of the biggest and best ideas can't be tested in advance and require a leap of faith by the marketer. Innovation is the one ingredient in the marketing mix that will never go out of style, and it becomes even more important in the chaotic environment of the modern-day marketplace.

When a college student named Fred Smith wrote a paper proposing an overnight delivery service, with all packages to be flown to and from a central hub in the United States, his professor gave him a C grade because the idea was so impractical. There was no way Smith could convince his professor, or almost anyone else, that his daring idea would work. The only way he could prove that he was right was to go out, years later, and raise enough money to launch Federal Express.

About five years ago Peter Brabeck, chief marketing strategist for the giant worldwide Nestlé Corporation, decided to buy the Casa Buitoni, the Italian villa of the Buitoni family, originators of the product over 150 years earlier. He then remodeled it to make it the brand's world headquarters, with offices and test kitchens and guest accommodations, and incorporated a picture of the villa into the trademark that appears on every Buitoni product.

There was no way Brabeck could have adequately tested the brand value of the Casa, or his vision of launching a Casa Buitoni Club that would inaugurate a "relationship-branding" strategy by a mass-market food manufacturer. It was a leap of faith, part of a daring move based on his profound belief that "advertising is out—credible communication with the consumer is in."

Another MaxiMarketing Winner that stands ready to pioneer each new trailblazing idea with a leap of faith is the Amil Group, a health plan that has become one of the fastest-growing companies in Brazil for the past decade.

The CEO, Dr. Jorge Ferreira, became convinced that having the ability to offer a 50 percent discount on pharmaceutical prescriptions would give Amil a tremendous competitive edge over other health plans. But there was no way to negotiate that big a discount with pharmaceutical companies for his customers.

So just as he had earlier invested millions in purchasing helicopters before launching the Amil Rescue Plan, he took another "leap of faith" and set about creating a chain of pharmacies—under the FarmaLife brand name—that could be positioned in the future to offer Amil health-plan members half-price prescriptions.

Two years after opening the first FarmaLife shop in Rio de Janeiro, the Amil Medicine Plan, with 50 percent savings on prescriptions, was launched with a saturation, prime-time TV campaign. The stunned competition complained that "it wasn't fair," and the Amil customers could hardly believe their good fortune. The anticipated move by thousands of Brazilians to switch to Amil from other plans followed.

Amil's march toward becoming a billion-dollar company is a prime example of MaxiMarketing success, one that could not have happened without Dr. Ferreira's willingness to take a "leap of faith" to gain yet another competitive advantage.

"WE DID IT! WE DARED TO FAIL!"

Recently a television documentary appeared that can serve as an inspiration to gutsy marketers. It told the story of Norman Vaughn, who while still a college student joined Admiral Richard E. Byrd's historic expedition in 1927 to the South Pole. Byrd was so appreciative of the young man's services that he named an Antarctic mountain after him.

All his life thereafter, Vaughn, who became an expert Arctic adventurer in his own right, dreamed of returning some day to the Antarctic to climb his own peak, Vaughn's Mountain.

Finally, at the age of 87, he got pledges of a million dollars to finance a scientific expedition to go up the mountain—even though he had never climbed a mountain in his life!

But when a good part of the money failed to come through, the expedition stalled, leaving Vaughn and his crew waiting for months at the lower tip of South America. Finally, the climb had to be abandoned.

The following year, with severely reduced financing, just four people—the 88-year-old Vaughn, his younger wife, and two experienced guides—took a commercial flight to Argentina, then another commercial flight, intended for sight-seers, to a landing field near the base of the mountain.

From there it took him eight days, struggling in the cruel cold, to make a climb that an experienced climber could have made in one.

When he finally realized his lifelong dream and tottered out onto the little field of snow at the very top, he danced for joy and exclaimed, "We did it! We did it! *We dared to fail!*"

How touching, and how inspiring. While this octogenarian was bursting with pride that he had climbed "his" mountain at last, he was even prouder of the fact that he had been willing to risk failure in his quest.

There you have a sobering but at the same time exhilarating truth about marketing success. To climb to the heights, you must be willing to risk failure.

And there is something else to be inspired by in Norman Vaughn's story: *He never gave up!*

The New MaxiMarketing cannot guarantee you success. But it certainly can make your climb far less hazardous. For 10 years now, we have seen how MaxiMarketing insights increase the chances of going all the way to the pinnacle of business success. We wish you a rewarding and triumphant journey!

NOTES

CHAPTER ONE

1. Alvin Toffler, *The Third Wave*, William Morrow and Company, New York, 1980, p. 248.
2. Alvin Toffler, *PowerShift*, Bantam Books, New York, 1990, p. 25.
3. Ted Kumpe and Piet T. Bolwijn, "Manufacturing: The New Case for Vertical Integration," *Harvard Business Review*, March–April 1988; "Kicking Down the Debt," *Time*, November 7, 1988; "Customized Goods Aim at Mass Market," *Japan Economic Journal*, October 1, 1988.
4. "'Old' Coke Coming Back after Outcry by Faithful," *The New York Times*, July 11, 1985, p. D4.
5. Patrick Oster, "The Eurosion of Brand Loyalty," *Business Week*, July 19, 1993, p. 22.
6. "Brand Scoreboard," *Advertising Age*, August 23, 1993, p. 12.
7. Bob Ortega and Gabriella Stern, "Retailers' Private Labels Strain Old Ties," *The Wall Street Journal*, September 9, 1993, p. B1.
8. Russell Mitchell, "Sorry, We Don't Take Cash," *Business Week*, December 12, 1994, p. 42.
9. Mark Robichaux, Jeffrey A. Trachtenberg, and Gautam Naik, "Interactive Home-Shopping Channel Salted by US West, Nordstrom, Penney," *The Wall Street Journal*, May 18, 1994, p. A4.
10. Michael Shrage, "The Message Is the Message," *Adweek*, April 1985, p. 2.
11. Lorraine C. Scarpa, "Fast, Flexible, Computerized, That's Today's Analytic World," *Brandweek*, November 15, 1993, p. 25.
12. Toffler, *PowerShift*, p. 17.

13. Eben Shapiro, "Consumers Leaving New Twists on Old Products on the Shelves," *The Wall Street Journal*, February 1, 1994, p. B1.
14. Stuart Elliott, "Advertising," *The New York Times*, December 30, 1993, p. D16.
15. "Food Marketer: Slow the 'Frenetic' Pace of New Product Introductions," *Marketing News*, March 1988, p. 17.

Chapter Two

1. Theodore Levitt, *The Marketing Imagination*, The Free Press, New York, 1983, p. 115.

Chapter Three

1. Jeffery D. Zbar, "Blockbuster's Database to Fuel Future Expansion," *Advertising Age*, July 16, 1994, p. 26.

Chapter Four

1. Brian Lowry, "Julia Child Serves Advice," *Advertising Age*, July 8, 1985, p. 53.
2. Keith J. Kelly, "Flops Fail to Derail Place-Based," *Advertising Age*, August 8, 1994, p. 12.
3. *Facts About Newspapers*, Newspaper Association of America, 1994.
4. Christy Fisher, "'USA Today' Links Rates to Results for Advertisers," *Advertising Age*, March 5, 1993.
5. Christy Fisher, "Papers Jostle for Space on the Info Superhighway," *Advertising Age*, April 25, 1994, p. 35.
6. "Five-Minute Commercials to Become Standard?" *MediaWeek*, August 22, 1994, p. 23.
7. Elizabeth Jensen, "Still Kicking," *The Wall Street Journal*, September 9, 1994, p. R3.
8. Richard Brunelli, "Pearle Vision Assigns DMB&B AOR for Network and Cable," *MediaWeek*, August 24, 1992, p. 3.
9. Joe Mandese, "This Fall, The Peacock Starts Talking Back," *Advertising Age*, July 25, 1994, p. 22.

10. Diane Joy Moca, "San Jose TV Station Hooks Up Advertisers to Interactive Phone," *Advertising Age*, December 6, 1993, p. 33.
11. "The Power of Spot TV," Television Bureau of Advertising, 1993, p. 28.
12. Bill Carter, "As Cable Makes Inroads, Networks Cast a Wider Net," *The New York Times*, March 21, 1993, p. D1.
13. Liza Schoenfein, "Ad-Directed Channels a Reality," *Advertising Age*, April 4, 1994, p. S-6.
14. Elaine Underwood, "Why I'm a Home Shopper," *Brandweek*, April 19, 1993, p. 24.
15. QVC Inc. Annual Report, 1993, p. 16.
16. Underwood, "Why I'm a Home Shopper," p. 28.
17. Sharon Edelson, "Burdine's Home Shopping Spot to Air in Lieu of Spring Catalog," *WWD*, February 8, 1995, p. 20.
18. Andrea Adelson, "Advertising," December 28, 1993, p. 19.
19. Joshua Mills, "A Surge in Advertising Across the Radio Dial," *The New York Times*, July 25, 1994, p. D3.
20. Rebecca Pirto, "Why Radio Thrives," *American Demographics*, May 1994, p. 42.
21. Ibid, p. 46.
22. Patricia Strand, "New Cars Make Magazines Tempting for Detroit," *Advertising Age*, October 19, 1992, pp. S-2, S-17.
23. Patricia Hamilton, "Farm Journal Feels Its Oats," *D&B Reports*, July–August 1988, p. 22.
24. "Chevy Blazer Print Launch Uses Database Marketing," *Inside Media*, August 1, 1994, p. 9.
25. Raymond Serafin, "Chrysler's Cirrus Takes on Japanese," *Advertising Age*, August 15, 1994, p. 45.
26. Laura Bird, "'Custom' Magazines Stir Credibility Issues," *The Wall Street Journal*, February 14, 1994, p. B6.
27. Gary Strauss, "Show-and-Tell Format Called 'New, Fresh,'" *USA Today*, February 23, 1993, p. 1.
28. Jo McIntyre, "Apple Performa Infomercial Bags 100,000 Calls," *Advertising Age*, January 30, 1995, p. 6.
29. Leah Rickard, "Buick Goes Golfing with Car Shoppers," *Advertising Age*, December 6, 1993, p. 18.
30. Emily DeNitto, "SmithKline Goes Interactive to Link Pet Owners to Vets," *Advertising Age*, March 14, 1994, p. 21.
31. "Europe Goes Interactive," *Time*, March 13, 1995, p. 33.

CHAPTER FIVE

1. Mark Landler, "What Happened to Advertising?" *Business Week*, September 23, 1991, p. 67.
2. Stuart Elliott, "Consumer Product Companies Seek Better Methods to Gauge the Effect of Marketing on Their Sales," *The New York Times*, October 19, 1993, p. D8.
3. "U.S. Mail Order Sales for '93 Up 7% over Previous Year," *Friday Report*, June 10, 1994, p. 1.
4. Edward M. Tauber, "Editorial: The Never-Ending Question," *Journal of Advertising Research*, December 1984/January 1985, p. 9.
5. Stephen Fox, *The Mirror Makers*, William Morrow and Company, New York, 1984, p. 188.
6. Justin Martin, "Ignore Your Customer," *Fortune*, May 1, 1995.
7. Kevin Clancy and Robert Shulman, *The Marketing Revolution*, HarperBusiness, New York, 1991, p. 165.
8. "Copy Testing Still a Nebulous Area," *Advertising Age*, December 1, 1975, p. 54.
9. Alvin A. Achenbaum, "Impediments to Marketing Productivity," a paper delivered to the New York chapter of the American Marketing Association, February 7, 1985.
10. Laura Bird, "Loved the Ad. May (or May Not) Buy the Product," *The Wall Street Journal*, April 7, 1994, p. B1.
11. John Caples, *Testing Advertising Methods*, Fourth Edition, Prentice-Hall Inc., Englewood Cliffs, New Jersey, 1974, p. 3.
12. David Ogilvy, *Confessions of an Advertising Man*, Atheneum, New York, 1963, pp. 94–95.
13. Harold J. Rudolph, *Four Million Inquiries from Magazine Advertising*, Columbia University Press, New York, 1936.

CHAPTER SIX

1. Stephen Fox, *The Mirror Makers*, William Morrow and Company, New York, 1984, p. 26.
2. Ibid, p. 183.
3. Ibid, p. 50.
4. Ibid, p. 70.
5. Ibid, p. 50.

6. Ibid, p. 70.

7. Claude Hopkins, *My Life in Advertising/Scientific Advertising*, Crain Books, Chicago, 1966, p. 124.

8. Fox, op. cit., p. 71.

9. Ibid, p. 185.

10. Ibid, p. 73.

11. Rosser Reeves, *Reality in Advertising*, Alfred A. Knopf, New York, 1961, p. 153.

12. Fox, op. cit., p. 183, and Pierre Martineau, *Motivation in Advertising*, McGraw-Hill Book Company, New York, 1957.

13. David Ogilvy, *Confessions of an Advertising Man*, Atheneum, New York, 1963, pp. 111–112.

14. Fox, op. cit., p. 179.

15. Advertisement by *The Wall Street Journal* in *Advertising Age*, May 14, 1984, pp. 18–19.

16. Laurie Freeman, "Lou Centlivre Has One Thing in Mind: F-U-N," *Advertising Age*, July 25, 1985, p. 3.

17. "Advertising," *The New York Times*, October 10, 1995, p. D11.

18. Fox, op. cit., p. 253.

19. Ibid, p. 48.

20. Alvin Achenbaum, "Impediments to Marketing Productivity," a talk before the New York chapter of the American Marketing Association, February 7, 1985.

21. *Art Direction/The Magazine of Visual Communication*, May 1983, p. 45.

22. Martineau, op. cit., quoted in Reeves, op. cit., p. 78.

23. Herbert D. Maneloveg, "Public Wants More Product Info," *Adweek*, October 7, 1985, p. 40.

24. David Ogilvy, *Ogilvy on Advertising*, Crown Publishers, New York, 1983, p. 205.

CHAPTER SEVEN

1. Mark Landler, "What Happened to Advertising?" *Business Week*, September 23, 1991, p. 68.

2. Magid M. Abraham and Leonard M. Lodish, "Getting the Most Out of Advertising and Promotion," *Harvard Business Review*, May–June 1990, p. 51.

3. Don E. Shultz and William A. Robinson, *Sales Promotion Management*, Crain Books, Chicago, 1982, pp. 71, 125.

4. Ibid.
5. Ibid, p. 415.
6. Louis J. Haugh, "Questioning the Spread of Coupons," *Advertising Age*, August 22, 1983, p. M-31.
7. Mary McCabe English, "Like It or Not, Coupons Are Here to Stay," *Advertising Age*, August 22, 1983, pp. M-26, M-28.
8. Nancy Giges, "Coupon Loss Put at $500 Million," *Advertising Age*, March 4, 1985, p. 75.
9. Irene Park, "The Min/max Approach to Couponing," *Marketing Communications*, March 1985, p. 32.
10. Fara Warner, "Hold the Comics, Sports, and Give Me That FSI," *Brandweek*, March 21, 1994, p. 40.
11. Park, op. cit., p. 33.
12. Haugh, op. cit., p. M-32.
13. "Head of Waldenbooks Steps Down," *The New York Times*, March 12, 1991, p. B1; John Mutter, "Walden's Preferred Reader Used as Marketing Tool," *Publisher's Weekly*, August 31, 1992, p. 30.
14. Copyright United Feature Syndicate. Reprinted in *Advertising Age*, August 22, 1983, p. M-26.
15. Alvin Achenbaum, "Impediments to Marketing Productivity," a talk before the New York chapter of the American Marketing Association, February 7, 1995.

CHAPTER EIGHT

1. Charlene Watler, "Like the Dress Pictured in This Ad? That's Too Bad, You Can't Have It," *The Wall Street Journal*, May 10, 1985, p. 37.
2. *Boardroom Reports*, September 15, 1985, p. 15.
3. Arch G. Woodside and William H. Motes, "Image versus Direct-Response Advertising," *Journal of Advertising Research*, August 1980, pp. 31–37.
4. "Industry Mulls Fund Options," *Travel Weekly*, March 7, 1994, p. 39.
5. "A Positive Spin," *Travel Weekly*, November 7, 1994, p. S4.

CHAPTER NINE

1. Jeff Blyskal, "The Frequent Flyer Fallacy," *Worth*, May 1994, p. 60.

2. "Marriott Tests Direct Response Waters for Honored Guest Awards Program," *ZIP Target Marketing*, March 1985, p. 13.

3. Heather Schroeder, "Marketing Update," *Business Travel News*, March 30, 1992, p. 9.

4. "Building 'Share-of-Customer' Becomes a Priority at U.S. Shoe's Women's Specialty Retailing Group," *Colloquy*, vol. 4, issue 1, p. 8.

5. "Frequent-Reader Program Is Good News to Loyal Customers," *Colloquy*, vol. 4, issue 2, p. 8.

6. Anita S. Brown, "The Art of the Cross-Sell," *Direct*, April 1994, p. S9.

7. Len Egol, "Market Leaders," *Direct*, October 1994, p. 51.

8. Jeffrey M. O'Brien, "Market Leaders," *Direct*, October 1994, p. 45.

9. Gary Ostrager, "Leading Players Tell What DMB Has Done for Them," *DM News*, July 25, 1994, p. 26.

10. Larry Jaffee, "Broderbund Software Uses Database to Build Good After-Market Business," *DM News*, April 10, 1994, p. 23.

11. Ostrager, op. cit., p. 26.

Chapter Ten

1. *DM News*, May 15, 1995, p. 8.

2. *Advertising Age*, May 15, 1995.

A note from the authors:

An invitation to be updated every month about MaxiMarketing developments around the world

IN our travels to other parts of the world to fulfill speaking engagements, we find increasing evidence that the MaxiMarketing approach to getting and keeping customers is being widely adopted by a new generation of marketing strategists on six continents.

We see it in a pace-setting pizza chain in Spain. An extraordinary supermarket in Ireland. A world-leader customer loyalty program in Canada. A cat-food seller in Europe. A health-care provider in Brazil. An award-winning Guinness Stout promotion in Malaysia. An innovative department store in South Africa.

And we continue to note remarkable developments in the U.S. that we did not have the space to cover in this book or have come to our attention since it was completed.

There are important lessons to be gained from studying each of these new MaxiMarketing breakthroughs. Furthermore, everywhere in the world we have found great eagerness to learn more about what other marketers are doing in other countries and what can be learned from them.

So we have begun publication of the world's first truly international marketing newsletter, *MaxiMarketing Insights.* It is being distributed in 25 countries at the time of this writing, with more soon to be added.

In it we report and analyze important developments both in the U.S. and abroad in applying the new marketing of the information economy, and provide a forum where our far-flung readers can exchange news and ideas with us and each other.

Because we look upon our subscribers as marketing colleagues, each new subscriber is given a certificate naming him or her as an Associate of The MaxiMarketing Center.

For information about subscription availability in your country and a free sample copy (English-language edition only*), just fill out and mail the reply form. Or fax it to (212) 779-1856.

— Stan Rapp and Tom Collins

Note: **MaxiMarketing Insights** *is published in English, but in many countries a translated edition is available by subscription.*

- -

The MaxiMarketing Center
333 East 30th St., Dept. 2-A
New York, NY 10016

I am interested in learning more about your global newsletter, *MaxiMarketing Insights.* Please send me a free sample copy and information on subscription availability.

Name...

Title..Company...

Address...

....

Phone No. .... Fax No. .... E-mail Addr. ....

INDEX

ABOUT THE AUTHORS

STAN RAPP and THOMAS L. COLLINS cofounded and for 23 years guided Rapp Collins Worldwide, an advertising agency network that now has capitalized billings of over $1 billion annually in 28 international offices. In recent years, one or the other of the authors has been a valuable resource to Mobil Oil, Beneficial Finance, Samsonite Luggage, IBM-Japan, the Coin Retail Group in Italy, the Amil Health Plan Group in Latin America, and other top companies in the United States, South America, and Europe.

David Ogilvy, at the time the first edition of *MaxiMarketing* was published in 1986, said, "The authors of this book are competitors of mine, but this does not blind me to its value. Everyone who works in advertising *must* read it." Each of their books published since then, chronicling the sweeping changes in marketing, has been met with enthusiastic praise by the business press worldwide and by managers at top corporate performers on six continents.

Stan Rapp is publisher and Tom Collins is executive editor of *MaxiMarketing Insights*, an internationally oriented newsletter with subscribers in more than 25 countries. Stan Rapp is one of a select group of pioneering industry leaders elected to the Hall of Fame of the Direct Marketing Association in America, and Tom Collins has won numerous awards as a preeminent copywriter and creative director.